The Study of Liturgy and Worship

Founded in 1897, the Alcuin Club seeks to promote the study of Christian liturgy and worship in general with special reference to worship in the Anglican Communion. The Club has published a series of annual Collections, including *A Companion to Common Worship*, volumes 1 and 2, edited by Paul F. Bradshaw, a new edition of the classic text *Christian Prayer through the Centuries*, by Joseph Jungmann (SPCK, 2007); *The Origins of Feasts, Fasts and Seasons in Early Christianity* by Paul F. Bradshaw and Maxwell E. Johnson (SPCK, 2011); by the same authors, *The Eucharistic Liturgies: Their Evolution and Interpretation* (SPCK, 2012); and most recently *The Cross and Creation in Christian Liturgy and Art* by Christopher Irvine (SPCK, 2013). The Alcuin Liturgy Guide series aims to address the theology and practice of worship, and includes *The Use of Symbols in Worship*, edited by Christopher Irvine, and two volumes covering the celebration of the Christian Year: *Celebrating Christ's Appearing: Advent to Christmas* and *Celebrating Christ's Victory: Ash Wednesday to Trinity*, both by Benjamin Gordon-Taylor and Simon Jones. The Club works in partnership with GROW in the publication of the Joint Liturgical Studies series, with two studies being published each year.

Members of the Club receive publications of the current year free and others at a reduced rate. The President of the Club is the Rt Revd Michael Perham, its Chairman is the Revd Canon Dr Donald Gray CBE, and the Secretary is the Revd Dr Gordon Jeanes. For details of membership and the annual subscription, contact The Alcuin Club, 5 Saffron Street, Royston SG8 9TR, or email: alcuinclub@gmail.com

Visit the Alcuin Club website at: **www.alcuinclub.org.uk**

The Study of Liturgy and Worship

An Alcuin Guide

Edited by Juliette Day
and Benjamin Gordon-Taylor

First published in Great Britain in 2013

Society for Promoting Christian Knowledge
36 Causton Street
London SW1P 4ST
www.spckpublishing.co.uk

British Library Cataloguing-in-Publication Data
A catalogue record for this book is available from the British Library

ISBN 978–0–281–06909–5
eBook ISBN 978–0–281–06910–1

Typeset by Caroline Waldron, Wirral, Cheshire
First printed in Great Britain by Ashford Colour Press

eBook by Graphicraft Limited, Hong Kong

Produced on paper from sustainable forests

Contents

Contributors

Myra N. Blyth is Fellow and Tutor in Worship and Pastoral Studies at Regent's Park College in the University of Oxford. She is a Baptist minister and represents the Baptist Union of Great Britain in the Conference of European Churches Dialogue Commission.

Paul F. Bradshaw is Professor of Liturgy at the University of Notre Dame, USA, a priest-vicar of Westminster Abbey, and a consultant to the Church of England Liturgical Commission. He was formerly Editor of the international journal *Studia Liturgica*.

Rosalind Brown is Canon Librarian and Nave Canon at Durham Cathedral. She is a published hymn writer and has written books on ministry and preaching.

Juliette Day is a university lecturer and Docent (Adjunct Professor) in Church History at the University of Helsinki, and Senior Research Fellow in Early Liturgy at Blackfriars Hall, University of Oxford. She is a consultant to the Church of England's Liturgical Commission and a trustee of the Alcuin Club.

Siobhán Garrigan is Associate Professor (Reader) of Theology at the University of Exeter, where she is also Director of EXCEPT – The Exeter Centre for Ecumenical and Practical Theology.

Benjamin Gordon-Taylor is a lecturer in liturgy and Dean of Chapel at the College of the Resurrection, Mirfield, and Director of the Mirfield Liturgical Institute. He is a trustee and Editorial Secretary of the Alcuin Club, and has co-authored or contributed to a number of Alcuin Club publications.

George Guiver CR is Superior of the Community of the Resurrection, an Anglican religious community in Mirfield, UK.

Katharine E. Harmon is a lecturer in Liturgical Studies at the Catholic University of America, Washington, DC. She received her doctorate in theology from the University of Notre Dame and is a member of the North American Academy of Liturgy.

Christopher Irvine is Canon Librarian at Canterbury Cathedral and an honorary senior research fellow in the School of History, University of Kent. He is a member of the Church of England Liturgical Commission and the Cathedrals Fabric Commission for England.

Gordon Jeanes is Vicar of St Anne with St Faith, Wandsworth, in the Anglican Diocese of Southwark and is the secretary of the Alcuin Club. He was formerly the Geoffrey Cuming Fellow in Liturgy in the University of Durham.

Maxwell E. Johnson is Professor of Liturgy at the University of Notre Dame, and is a pastor in the Evangelical Lutheran Church in America. He is currently Vice-President of the North American Academy of Liturgy, and a member of Societas Liturgica, and the Society of Oriental Liturgy.

David J. Kennedy is a part-time lecturer in Liturgy at Durham University and Cranmer Hall and Wesley Studies Centre, Durham, and Vice-Dean and Canon Precentor of Durham Cathedral. He was formerly a member of the Church of England Liturgical Commission and chair of Praxis.

Lizette Larson-Miller holds the Kaehr Chair in Liturgy at Church Divinity School of the Pacific, and is Professor of Liturgical Studies at the Graduate Theological Union in Berkeley, California. She is a priest of the US Episcopal Church and co-editor of the North American Academy of Liturgy's Proceedings.

Trevor Lloyd is the former Archdeacon of Barnstaple. As a member of the Church of England Liturgical Commission from 1981 to 2002, he chaired the group that drafted the marriage services, and also the General Synod Steering Committee that saw them through the Synod process. He is Vice-Chair of the Group for the Renewal of Worship and a member of the Alcuin/GROW editorial board.

Ruth A. Meyers is Hodges-Haynes Professor of Liturgics and Dean of Academic Affairs at Church Divinity School of the Pacific (a seminary of the Episcopal Church), Berkeley, California, USA. She is Chair of the Episcopal Church's Standing Commission on Liturgy and Music.

Bridget Nichols is Lay Chaplain to the Bishop of Ely. She is a member of the Church of England Liturgical Committee and a visiting scholar at Sarum College,

Salisbury, UK. She is Chair of the Society for Liturgical Study and reviews editor of the journal, *Anaphora*.

Thomas O'Loughlin is Professor of Historical Theology in the University of Nottingham. A Roman Catholic presbyter, he has written on how knowledge of the earliest communities can be used as a critique of our own liturgy.

James Steven is Director of Liturgy and Worship at Sarum College in Salisbury, UK. He is also a visiting lecturer in liturgy at King's College London.

Phillip Tovey is Deputy Warden of Readers and Postgraduate Officer for Curates in the Diocese of Oxford (Church of England), and a liturgy lecturer at Ripon College, Cuddesdon, Oxford. For the past 20 years he has been a participant in International Anglican Liturgical Conferences.

Liam Tracey OSM is an ordained presbyter of the Roman Catholic Order of Friar Servants of Mary (OSM). He is Professor of Liturgy at St Patrick's College, Maynooth, Ireland, where he is also Director of Postgraduate Studies in Theology.

Louis Weil is the Hodges-Haynes Professor Emeritus of Liturgics at Church Divinity School of the Pacific, Berkeley, California, USA. In 2012 he received the Berakah Award from the North American Academy of Liturgy for his contribution to the field of liturgical studies.

Thomas R. Whelan is Associate Professor of Theology at the Milltown Institute, Dublin, where he currently serves as Dean of the Faculty of Theology and Spirituality. A Roman Catholic, he holds degrees in music and theology, and lectures in liturgical and sacramental theology.

Abbreviations

ARCIC	Anglican–Roman Catholic International Commission
BCP	*Book of Common Prayer* of the US Episcopal Church
CW	*Common Worship*
CWCI	*Common Worship: Christian Initiation*
CWPS	*Common Worship: Pastoral Services*
ECUSA	Episcopal Church of the USA
EOW	*Enriching Our Worship*
IALC	International Anglican Liturgical Consultation
ICEL	International Committee on English in the Liturgy
LWF	Lutheran World Federation
NPW	*New Patterns for Worship*
PCOTS	*Pastoral Care of the Sick*
TMWB	*The Methodist Worship Book*
WCC	World Council of Churches

Introduction

The study of liturgy and worship has gone through many transformations over the centuries which have broadly followed, rather than led, the intellectual currents of the day. In the medieval period, the focus was on sacramental theology and canon law; in the Reformation era, forms of scriptural interpretation made distinctive alterations to the content and leadership of worship; in the nineteenth century, the emergence of the scientific method coupled with the discovery and study of new sources from the early Church brought early and Eastern Church traditions to the attention of the Western Church. Also in this century, the challenges faced by industrialization, urbanization and fears of secularism placed the participation of the people in worship and the provision of appropriate liturgies to the fore; this bore fruit in the twentieth century through the Liturgical Movement and the reforms of Vatican II, which were mirrored in most other Western churches. Despite the social impetus for liturgical change, the study of worship, especially in the training of ministers, continued to be based upon the historical origins and development of the liturgical texts; there is nothing wrong with this approach and much useful and interesting work continues to be done on liturgical history, but naturally it excludes a whole range of topics, many of which are present in this volume. New scholarly methodologies in the social sciences, in anthropology, in philosophy and linguistics have been adopted by liturgists to add to the already well-developed textual and historical methods. This has refreshed research and teaching, which more often than not will start with exploring the experience of worshippers and different elements of the liturgical rite. The second distinctive transformation in this field has been the growth of ecumenical dialogue and exchange, particularly over the last 60 years. No longer is liturgical study seen as a means to assert and distinguish the particular identity and apostolicity of Christian denominations; in research, teaching and liturgical reform it is now a truly ecumenical exercise.

These two key transformations in the approach to the study of worship and liturgy explain the rationale for this book. At the outset, the Alcuin Club, in keeping with its founding aims, wished to provide a one-volume, introductory book to support students beginning their studies in this field which would also be accessible to the informed and interested general reader. The choice of topics reflects the most important and interesting directions in contemporary research, areas which we consider essential for a proper understanding of contemporary worship, especially for those training for a liturgical ministry. The contributors stand at the forefront of teaching and research in their subjects and thus can make available to readers the latest methods, sources and results of their research in an accessible manner, which it is hoped will challenge and inspire. It is noticeable, too, that this volume represents an ecumenical and international collaboration. Some writers present their topic clearly within their own church tradition, be it Catholic, Anglican, Lutheran or Baptist, but all are aware of the wider implications of their area for the study of worship traditions in other churches; many chapters bring together sources and insights from different denominations to highlight theological and contextual convergence (and divergence). The contributors are exclusively anglophone, hailing from the UK, USA and Ireland, although very many of them bring to their writing their own direct experience of world cultures and worship traditions.

Accordingly, this book is arranged thematically and comprises four parts: Foundations, Elements, Event and Dimensions. Thus, we begin with general considerations of the nature of worship, move to explore the different components of worship, and only then present introductions to particular liturgical events; lastly, the implications of worship for the life of the Church in the world are drawn out. Each of these sections is further divided into appropriate topics in a manner that will enable the student to read a concise, free-standing introduction to the subject. The chapters are designed to encourage additional exploration, and to this end each is accompanied by some suggested further reading. References within the text of each chapter can be identified in the full Bibliography.

This project is the fruit of a long period of gestation, and we would like to record our sincere thanks to the scholars who have contributed chapters, and to those whose support, encouragement and assistance have brought it to completion, among them the Trustees of the Alcuin Club and Ruth McCurry of SPCK. We were to have been joined as co-editors by the Revd Dr Cody Unterseher, a young scholar of great promise, who tragically died just as our collaboration was to begin. We dedicate this book to his memory.

Juliette Day and Benjamin Gordon-Taylor

Foundations

Chapter 1

Worship

Louis Weil

The word 'worship' has embraced a wide range of meanings and associations in its evolution in English usage. Current use has limited that rich diversity to a narrowly religious frame of reference, which was not the case in earlier use. The word, which is peculiar to the English language, is found as early as the ninth century when it appears in the form *weoröscipe* with the meaning 'deserving of or being held in high esteem'. Inherent in this definition is its root meaning as 'the ascription of worth or value'. This meaning was common down to the sixteenth century, and was generally applied to persons of distinction or renown.

Although this application to persons of rank or honour seems to have been the predominant sense of the word, by the fourteenth century there emerged its use as reverence paid to a being regarded as divine, and thus to God. This transfer into the religious sphere was a quite natural one in which honour shown to a person of dignity and importance might be appropriately applied, all the more as it were, to the One who is most worthy of such honour. Linked to this development we find, from the fifteenth century onward, the use of the word in reference to 'places of worship', that is, to church buildings in which the people gathered each Sunday to honour the Holy One who is most worthy of worship, there to do 'acts of worship'.

In common use today, the early non-religious sense of 'worship' as 'respect shown in honour of a person' has virtually disappeared, and the word is used almost exclusively within a religious frame of reference, generally applied to ritual actions performed when the people gather for worship, most particularly on Sunday as the principal day of Christian religious observance. This narrowing is reflected in the use of a term which is commonly heard, at least in the USA: 'worship service'. One problem with this term is that it is tautological, since 'service' in this context is inherently an act of worship. A yet more critical problem is that it associates the word 'worship' with what is little more than a form or list of items which make up a particular liturgical celebration. This reflects an impoverished understanding of the profound meaning of the concept of worship, even when limited to a religious context. In this chapter, our goal is to explore this larger sense of the word, which continues to carry an abundance of associations that extend far beyond the mere contents of some form of liturgical rite.

SOME PRELIMINARY OBSERVATIONS

J. D. Crichton has characterized worship as a human religious phenomenon, and certainly that is the context with which the word is most generally associated (Crichton, 1992, p. 7). In that regard, it is not restricted to any one religious tradition, be it Jewish, Christian or Muslim. As we explore the term, however, we find that the word has often been used in ways which stretch beyond the more specifically defined contexts of religious identity. Worship takes place in a striking variety of ways, often quite apart from the usual categories of any one religious tradition. In other words, 'worship' is larger in scope than, for example, liturgy or ritual. It involves a reaching out towards a transcendent reality in which one senses a Presence that lies beyond the day-to-day patterns of human experience. Although this is a profoundly human experience, it is often understood as a response to that which is beyond the ordinary context of daily life.

In a specifically religious context, on the other hand, worship is understood as some form of response to the One who is called God. This response may be made with words or music, gesture or dance, or in silent awe. In liturgical rites, particularly since the invention of printing and the consequent standardization of liturgical texts, words have been the dominant mode of that response. But the phenomenon of a response at least akin to worship in human experience long pre-dates such a primary role played by language. We can imagine primitive men and women, for example, suddenly faced with some extraordinary event in nature, looking on in wonder as the event – such as a dramatic electric storm – unfolded before their eyes. They were reduced to stunned silence, or perhaps to stammering or gesturing, as the power of the event filled them with fear, a fear tinged with awe. And they wondered at the source of such an event and sensed the presence of a power far beyond the limits of the human. This awe became a constituent aspect of what eventually developed as an act of worship.

Such an experience was not always private or individual; it would often have been a shared experience that elicited a shared response. As primitive as we may judge such a response to have been, we see in this the root of what becomes in later human development an ordered pattern of common worship of this Presence of the totally Other who has come to be identified as God. The events and occasions in which this Presence has been recognized become the triggers of what develops as shared acts of worship. At the heart of such acts, there is a 'remembering' of the past event as a shared story which is retold in the context of the repeated act. This retelling of the story serves to reinforce its important place in the common memory of the community. This retelling also offers occasions when new participants might be invited into this dimension of the community's life, to hear the story and thus to become integrated into the ongoing retelling of the past event on those repeated occasions when at least some aspect of the story is retold and thus remembered.

These occasions of worship employ words and objects as carriers of the Presence. In the common memory they are bound up with events and experiences to which the worshippers ascribe ultimate meaning and value – and, thus, 'worthship', which is the root meaning of the word. In the act of worship, the past events, being remembered, become the reference point of the present occasion. In that remembrance, the Divine Presence is engaged and through this the worshippers are sanctified and their unity as a people strengthened.

In addition to the roles played by words and objects, common practices emerge on these occasions in which the physical body of each worshipper performs gestures and actions: these might typically include bowing or kneeling, standing or prostration, and also processions in which all of the worshippers are involved in a common action at the same time. We may note that such bodily gestures are found, often with only slight variations, in very different religious traditions.

WORSHIP AND THE NUMINOUS

Although reason plays an essential role in making religious belief possible, the rational aspect of religious faith does not offer us the full picture of how human beings experience the reality of the Divine Presence, the Other whom we call God. We see this particularly with regard to the subject of this chapter, 'worship'. Although it is probably accurate to claim that the rational element in religious faith has come to occupy the foreground in human experience, the non-rational – which is *not* to say the irrational – fulfils a significant role in much religious experience.

With regard to this question, there appeared in 1917 a work which played a seminal role in the exploration of this other dimension of religious faith and practice, *The Idea of the Holy* by Rudolf Otto. In this work, Otto's central claim is that 'religion is not exclusively contained and exhaustively comprised in any series of "rational" assertions' (Otto, 1923, p. 4). What Otto then sets out to do is to bring the various aspects of religious faith and experience into relation with one another so that the complementarity between the rational and the non-rational aspects of religious experience may be made clear.

Otto moves directly to the heart of his argument with a discussion of 'the holy', which, he says, has come in ordinary usage to carry only a part of its full significance. He suggests that 'the holy' is often used to mean nothing more than that which is 'completely good'. But this is inadequate for its authentic sense, which involves what Otto calls 'an overplus of meaning'. He goes so far as to say that it is this overplus of meaning which was the earliest sense of the term. Thus, the use of the term as 'that which is completely good' reflects a later stage in its development as it gathered other derived meanings and associations. The recovery of the original sense of the word for which Otto appeals is 'the **numinous**'. This is the term he uses for that which is above and beyond mere goodness. Otto speaks of the human encounter with the numinous as a unique mental state which is not so much to be defined or analysed as to be experienced. It thus becomes known not as a process of the mind but rather as an experience of the whole person. It cannot be taught; it can only be evoked or awakened.

Otto invites his readers to reflect on their own religious experience, more specifically on *deeply felt* religious experience. Such experience is akin to the experience of great beauty, as in nature or the arts, or of being enraptured as when one falls passionately in love. In such a context, one feels 'ravished' by this encounter. The numinous experience in religion is not reducible to a formula or a definition. It is, Otto suggests, something akin to a 'creature feeling', a sense of human limitation in the presence of the Holy, a sense of being quite literally overwhelmed by the Other, a feeling of total dependence. This feeling may be found in a wide range of contexts, as, for example, 'in the fixed and ordered solemnities of rites and liturgies, and again in the atmosphere that clings to old religious monuments and buildings, to temples and to churches' (Otto, 1923, p. 12). To name such an experience, Otto says, there is only one appropriate expression: *mysterium tremendum* – an awesome mystery.

Many years ago, while engaged in research in the library of the University of Cambridge, I decided to visit nearby Ely Cathedral. I had been to the cathedral many times in the past and greatly admired its architecture. I had heard that the diocese of Ely was celebrating the nine-hundredth anniversary of the present structure. I chose to go on a weekday afternoon when, I hoped, there would not be many other visitors and, as it turned out, I was the only person in the building, so I was able to set my own pace as I walked through this great church, admiring its beauty. At one point, I found myself in a side aisle off from the altar area, in the ambulatory. When I looked towards the high altar, I saw that a new marble memorial had been placed in the floor before it, and I walked over to see what it said. There I read the simple claim that, for over 1,600 years, Christians had gathered to worship in that place.

As I stood there, this realization swept over me so powerfully that I trembled. I felt a sudden awareness of generation after generation of Christians who had worshipped there, and of the celebrations of baptism and matrimony and burial which had marked those occasions in the lives of the people of that community. Above all, I sensed the countless celebrations of the Eucharist for which, Sunday after Sunday for well more than a millennium, Christians had gathered there to fulfil this commitment of their faith. Suddenly all those people were with me, gathered from all the preceding centuries, and I sensed the awesome unity of our life in Christ.

My experience that day embodied what Otto called 'the numinous'. It was essentially a non-rational experience in which my whole being was caught up into an overwhelming sense of the Divine Presence. And although I stood alone in that sacred place, I had a profound sense of my membership in the community of faith which stretched both backward and forward in human history, the body of the incarnate Lord. It was an experience of profound awe in the presence of the One who was both totally Other and at the same time wondrously immanent. It was, I felt, an experience of authentic worship, not in the familiar context of liturgical prayer and yet overflowing with the substance of such prayer.

For Otto, this experience of awe is fundamental to a sense of the numinous. It is an experience which could be known by primitive men and women, but which we also find at a far later stage in human development, even in our own time, when a sense of the presence of the Holy breaks into the ordinary pattern of our lives. It is an experience of an overpowering Presence before whom we sense that we are nothing more than dust and ashes. Otto speaks of this experience as '"the feeling of our creaturehood" . . . that is, the consciousness of the littleness of every creature in face of that which is above all creatures' (Otto, 1923, p. 22).

Although this experience is not generated through participation in public worship, many Christians witness to having had such an experience in the context of a liturgical celebration. The purpose of liturgical rites is not the manipulation of the emotions of the worshippers. Yet, within the ordinary pattern of Sunday worship, perhaps at the singing of a favourite hymn, or the hearing of a beautiful anthem sung by the choir, or at a particular phrase in the words of the preacher, one may feel suddenly touched at a very profound level and find one's faith confirmed and strengthened anew through the impact of this experience. William James tells of an experience reported by a clergyman which was 'like a great orchestra when all the separate notes have melted into one swelling harmony that leaves the listener conscious of nothing save that his soul is being wafted upwards and almost bursting with its own emotion' (James, 1902, p. 66). Although James does not note the non-rational aspect of this description, it is nonetheless evident that his words confirm Otto's insight.

Music also has a particular power, at least for many hearers, to produce an aesthetic response which is remarkably akin to the religious feelings we have discussed. In our increasingly secularized society, one probably finds this more often in the concert hall than in our churches. It is interesting to note that in California, where only a very small percentage of people attend church with any regularity, performances of the major religious compositions in the musical repertory – including not only cantatas and oratorios, but even settings of the Ordinary of the Mass – draw large and enthusiastic audiences of people, many of whom would not darken the door of a church. One cannot help but see in the 'devout' way that such works are generally received that the hearing of such great works is an authentic experience of the numinous, of the Divine Presence whom they would never think to name.

THE NUMINOUS IN THE LITURGY

It must be admitted at the outset that the fruit of the liturgical renewal of recent decades has often produced pedestrian models of corporate prayer in our churches. Some commentators have seen this as the result of the goals of the Liturgical Movement in general. Their judgement is that the quest for greater comprehension has produced rites which embody little sense of the sacred. Although the shrillest expressions of such views have emerged as criticism of the Roman liturgy subsequent to the Second Vatican Council, this critique is not limited to the Roman Church, and it is relevant to the subject of this chapter. (Examples of Roman Catholic critiques of the revised Roman rites include Mosebach, 2006; Nichols, 1996; Torevell, 2000; Woods, 2008.) In general, the idea of the numinous has not been seen as a value during these decades of liturgical renewal. On the whole, this is perhaps best explained as a mistaken identification of the numinous with the obscure, yet it is evident in Otto's analysis of the numinous that this is not an inevitable linkage. As Otto has shown, the numinous operates at the non-rational level, whereas the obscure generally operates at the rational level where it simply means 'that which is not understood'. It was certainly a goal of the reform efforts in the various liturgical traditions that obscurity in this sense should be eliminated; but the elimination of the numinous is of an entirely different order.

Let us consider how a sense of the numinous came to play a role in the early history of the liturgy. This question was raised by Edmund Bishop in an article, 'Fear and Awe Attaching to the Eucharistic Service', published in 1909, some eight years before Otto's work. Bishop does not, therefore, use the term 'numinous', later to be coined by Otto, but he was addressing the same issue. Bishop's concern in this essay was historical, that is, when and where this issue first arose. Briefly then, Bishop found the first trace of this concept in the fifth *Mystagogical Lecture* attributed to St Cyril of Jerusalem, and so he dated the development to the mid-fourth century (Bishop, 1909, pp. 92–7). More recent scholarship suggests that the *Lectures* were written by John of Jerusalem, Cyril's successor, and thus they would date from some four decades later.

Theological developments in the fourth century contributed to an emerging attitude of fear and awe particularly towards the eucharistic elements. The most significant of these included the reaction against Arianism. Orthodox Christianity insisted on the deity of Christ and rejected the view of Arius that Christ was a creature, subordinate to the Father, contrary to the teaching of the Nicene Creed.

For St John Chrysostom, this claim of the full deity of Christ directly affected the understanding of the Eucharistic Prayer. The ministers were to fulfil their duty 'with fear and trembling' (*On the Incomprehensible Nature of God*). In a substantial Appendix to *The Idea of the Holy*, Otto discusses the influence of St John Chrysostom on the incomprehensibility of God. Otto points to Chrysostom's use of such terms as 'amazement', 'fear', 'anguish', 'vertigo', 'trembling' and 'awe'. With such terms, Chrysostom emphasized the utter transcendence of God, yet experienced in the Eucharist as a living presence.

A second development was a growing emphasis upon the Real Presence of Christ in the Eucharist. Chrysostom speaks of the role of the priest in the *epiclesis* of the Eucharistic Prayer, and asks, 'When [the priest] invokes the Holy Spirit and offers that awful sacrifice, and keeps on touching the common master of all, tell me, where shall we rank him? What purity and what piety shall we demand of him?' (*The Treatise on the Priesthood*, 6.4). Whereas in the earlier centuries it had been common to speak of the consecrated bread and wine as 'figures' or 'symbols', in the fourth century a more realistic and materialistic theology of the Real Presence began to emerge. In this context, a new vocabulary was employed by such writers as Chrysostom and Cyril in which change in the elements was emphasized so that the bread and wine were seen to be 'converted' into the body and blood of Christ. Although this was understood as a spiritual conversion, it nevertheless contributed to what we may call a numinous aspect to the consecrated elements, with the result that the celebration of the Eucharist became an occasion of fear and awe (see Davies, 1971/2, pp. 216–23).

WORSHIP AND SILENCE

We close this discussion of worship with what might seem a tangential matter: the role of silence. At a time when many liturgical celebrations move along with almost relentless activity and noise, the role of silence in public worship as an expression of a contemplative understanding of corporate prayer may appear to be a lost dimension of the liturgy. In general, we often associate it more with the contemplative patterns of monastic prayer; but has it a place in the context of a parish community?

Otto speaks of two ways in which the numinous is expressed in Western art: those means are through **darkness** and **silence**. Regarding the first, he singles out Gothic architecture as particularly conducive to an encounter with the Holy. Semi-darkness, he suggests, speaks with particular power to the soul. One must acknowledge immediately that this is not an appropriate context for the celebration of the liturgy by an assembly of people on a Sunday morning. Such a celebration, with its interplay of proclamation, song and movement, requires light and sound.

Yet this does not exclude the possibility that silence may have a very positive relation to the liturgy of the assembly, in a kind of counterpoint to the ritual action, for example as an act of preparation for the corporate worship that will follow. On several recent occasions I have attended the principal celebration of the Eucharist at the Church of St Gervais in Paris, which is a centre for the Community of Jerusalem. The first time I attended, I had been advised to be at the church a full hour before the liturgy would begin at 11 a.m. I arrived early to find the church in semi-darkness and utter silence. From the moment I arrived, I realized that there was a profound sense of contemplation among the people who had already gathered, some seated, some kneeling, some prostrate. The silence was palpable, and it continued even as other people came in, silently took a place and entered into the corporate prayer which they found already under way.

The silence was broken only at 11 a.m., when a bell sounded and the congregation stood as the sacred ministers entered the sanctuary. As we began to sing the music for the entrance, I realized that, as our corporate prayer had now become verbal, it rested, as it were, on a cushion of silent prayer. I have never felt more ready to enter into the liturgical action than I was that day, and I was reminded of an early rabbinic saying that, if one is going to pray for an hour at the liturgy, one should precede that prayer with an hour of silence.

Yet even within our more typical patterns of Sunday morning, there are opportunities for the use of silence, even on a modest scale, which could deepen the experience. There are, in fact, traditional places of silence within the ritual structure which, because of inadequate liturgical catechesis, have not been integrated into normative practice. The salutation prior to the collect of the day invites the people to pray, but often the 'Let us pray' flows directly into the collect itself rather than, as the invitation implies, offering the people a time for silent prayer.

In a similar way, in the Liturgy of the Word, when the congregation often hears three readings from Scripture in a row, an opportunity to reflect in silence upon a reading when it is completed is often lost, as we are moved along too quickly to the singing of a gradual psalm or hymn, or to the Alleluia prior to the gospel. Even if such silences are rather brief, experience shows that they can offer what is needed to assimilate the word proclaimed. Yet again, in the Prayers of the People, the invitation to pray for the intention just offered all too often moves immediately to a versicle and response rather than offering the people an opportunity for silent prayer.

These are practical ways to implement silence in the normative patterns of Sunday worship. Once learned, the people realize that their worship is more than a series of items listed in the Sunday bulletin – as is suggested by the phrase 'worship service' – and that it is actually corporate prayer in which they fulfil one of the primary expressions of their faith as the People of God.

In the fifth-century Orthodox Liturgy of St James, the 'Cherubic Hymn' is sung to accompany the presentation of the gifts of bread and wine which are to be consecrated. This great hymn, sung at one of the most dramatic moments of the rite, reminds us of the silence which is the ultimate response to this sacred action – the response of awe. The text offers us a fitting conclusion to our discussion of worship.

> Let all mortal flesh keep silence,
> 　　　and with fear and trembling stand;
> ponder nothing earthly-minded,
> 　　　for with blessing in his hand
> Christ our God to earth descendeth,
> 　　　Our full homage to demand.
>
> At his feet the six-winged seraph;
> 　　　Cherubim with sleepless eye
> Veil their faces to the Presence,
> 　　　as with ceaseless voice they cry,
> 'Alleluia, alleluia!
> 　　　Alleluia, Lord Most High!'

Further reading

Bishop, E. (1909), 'Fear and Awe Attaching to the Eucharistic Service', in *The Liturgical Homilies of Narsai*, tr. R. H. Connolly (Cambridge: Cambridge University Press).

Chrysostom, J. (1982), *On the Incomprehensible Nature of God*, tr. P. W. Harkins (Washington, DC: Catholic University of America Press).

Chrysostom, J. (1999), *The Treatise on the Priesthood*, tr. and notes W. R. W. Stephens (Peabody, MA: Hendrickson Publishers), pp. 27–86.

Crichton, J. D. (rev. edn, 1992), 'The Theology of Worship', in C. Jones, G. Wainwright, E. Yarnold and P. Bradshaw (eds), *The Study of Liturgy* (London: SPCK/New York: Oxford University Press).

Davies, J. G. (1971/2), 'The Introduction of the Numinous into the Liturgy: An Historical Note', *Studia Liturgica* 8.4.

Nichols, A. (1996), *Looking at the Liturgy: A Critical View of Its Contemporary Form* (San Francisco, CA: Ignatius Press).

Otto, R. (1923), *The Idea of the Holy: An Inquiry into the Non-Rational Factor in the Idea of the Divine and Its Relation to the Rational*, tr. J. W. Harvey (London: Oxford University Press).

Chapter 2

Liturgy

Benjamin Gordon-Taylor

DEFINITIONS AND DISTINCTIONS

The nature and definition of liturgy has been extensively studied, yet, while many discussions of definition can be found, no single definition can do justice to its many aspects. This can be interpreted positively, as by the liturgical theologian Anscar Chupungco: 'liturgy is a rich complex – I should say a happy confluence – of theology, history, spiritual insight, and pastoral care' (Chupungco, 2010, p. 51). The Catholic liturgical historian and theologian Josef Jungmann believed that 'no complete agreement has been reached about the definition of the liturgy . . . because different elements may be stressed in the group of ecclesiastical institutions which are generally classed as liturgical' (Jungmann, 1975, p. 851). While many discussions of definition may reflect to a greater or lesser degree the confessional standpoint of their authors, there has also been much ecumenical convergence in the field of liturgical studies which has had a beneficial effect on how liturgy is defined and which has created the conditions for a much greater sense of shared endeavour in study and practice. The significance of this was perceived and to some degree predicted at the ecumenical World Conference on Faith and Order in 1963, saying of liturgy:

> It is of crucial importance that we should investigate its forms and structures, its language and spirit, in the expectation that this process may throw new light upon various theological positions and affirmations, perhaps even lending new meaning to them, and thus open new possibilities in ecumenical dialogue.
>
> (Rodger and Vischer, 1964, p. 70)

Subsequent history has borne out this hope. Indeed the whole of this book is intended to assist the student to understand and define the meaning of 'liturgy' in the context of a number of themes and across the several traditions, and so the present chapter, as a general introduction to the scope of the term, is intended to be for the reader in part a signpost to the fuller treatments of specific dimensions and topics on which more detail will be found in subsequent chapters. Nevertheless, an overview is needed to give some indications as to the components a definition would need to include, on the basis of which the student is therefore advised to read further a range of material which deals with the definition of liturgy, in order to get a sense of the relative influence of these factors and in order to relate them to his or her own tradition, as well as to obtain a comprehensive impression of the various aspects. Yet it must be remembered that the liturgical worship of the Church is primarily celebration, an action of praise by and with the Church, something that is primarily done before it is studied.

The pioneer of the Liturgical Movement of the early twentieth century, Lambert Beauduin, defined liturgy succinctly as 'the worship offered to God by the Church itself' (Jungmann, 1975, p. 851). This basic understanding of liturgy as the action of the Christian assembly is indicated by the derivation of the English word 'liturgy' from the Greek *leitourgia*, literally 'the work of the people', which in ancient usage has a secular sense of what would now be called public work for the benefit of the community, or the self-giving act of an individual in response to the needs of others. The New Testament uses the term both in this and in the specifically religious sense of officiating as a minister (see, for example, Romans 15.27; 2 Corinthians 9.12; and Acts 13.2). This theme of service was also identified at the World Conference on Faith and Order in 1963, which spoke of the 'twofold service to God and to the world which is expressed in the biblical term *leitourgia*' (Rodger and Vischer, 1964, p. 69), a reminder that liturgy and Christian service of neighbour are inseparable aspects of the baptismal life.

Broadening still further in scope, as well as the action of the Church in worship, 'liturgy' has come to denote the structured body of text and ritual by which the Church as a corporate body offers worship to God. This is sometimes referred to as *ordo* – literally 'order' – and it is usually authorized by the official processes of the ecclesial bodies in which and by whom it is employed, yet in some traditions it may be mandatory, in others an alternative or indicative guide to freer forms of worship. The latter may nevertheless have some sort of structure, however loose, and for that reason might still be described as 'liturgical' in nature, even if more dependent on extempore prayer, song and action. After all, it was the usual practice in the early Church for the Eucharistic Prayer to be improvised according to certain norms or guidelines; only later did what was originally only spoken become also written, as relatively fixed liturgical texts came into being.

Liturgy or worship?

There has been an ongoing debate about the relative meaning of the terms 'liturgy' and 'worship'. The assumption that they are synonymous has led rather unhelpfully to an association of 'worship' with Reformed traditions and 'liturgy' with Catholic and Orthodox. In Anglicanism, both have featured as indicators of these ecclesiological strands within that tradition. However, the assumption that they are synonymous is not sufficient to do justice to either, and so this book deliberately separates them and seeks to make a significant distinction not based on ecclesial tradition. Mark Earey has sought to bring them together in the term 'liturgical worship' (Earey, 2002), yet this is also a clue to the nature of the distinction. As Louis Weil shows in the previous chapter, *worship* is the prerequisite for *liturgy*. As Christopher Irvine and Anders Bergquist have written, worship is 'the more fundamental reality, the response of the whole person towards God in praise, adoration, and thanksgiving. The liturgy is a structured set of words and movements that enables worship to happen' (Irvine and Bergquist, 2011, p. 45).

To put the distinction at its simplest, *liturgy* is the means whereby *worship* is offered to God by the Church. Liturgy is consequent on the offering of worship and serves its needs. In this sense it can truly be understood as 'the work of the people', in that it is a humanly composed yet prayerfully inspired and historically shaped and influenced matrix of text and action which finds its corporate expression in ritual, symbol, speech and song, each divisible into associated aspects such as the use of space and the place of the visual arts, and the use of language, but all functioning as a unity in the outpouring of praise. While the relative proportions of these elements may vary across and between traditions, all are present to some degree and are interdependent as means of expressing the worship of the Church of Christ. It is therefore appropriate to speak not only of liturgi*cal* worship but also liturgy *as* worship.

Ecclesiology

In the historic churches of East and West, and in many Reformed traditions, the forms and orders of liturgy are expressive of the nature of the Church and its beliefs, most particularly as a place of the presence of Christ in his Church and a context for encounter and transformation in the proclamation of the word and the celebration of the sacraments, whatever relative emphasis these may receive.

For example, in the Roman Catholic tradition the hugely influential Constitution on the Sacred Liturgy which emerged from the Second Vatican Council in 1963 (the same year that the Faith and Order Conference was held in Montreal) defines liturgy as a 'an exercise of the priestly office of Jesus Christ', in which 'public worship is performed by the Mystical Body of Jesus Christ, that is, by the Head and his members' (*Sacrosanctum Concilium*, 1996, §7). Significantly for ecumenical dialogue and for liturgical renewal and revision, the presence of Christ in the liturgy of the Church was to be identified not just in the eucharistic elements but in other dimensions of the liturgical celebration: 'He is present in his word since it is he who speaks when the holy scriptures are read . . . he is present when the Church prays and sings' (*Sacrosanctum Concilium*, 1996, §7).

In the Anglican tradition, also affirming the celebration of the liturgy as the place of Christ's presence in his Church, the official liturgies of the churches of the Anglican Communion are explicitly expressive of the doctrine of those churches, a principle which derives from the place of the Book of Common Prayer in the Church of England as *in particular* containing the doctrine of that church, along with the Thirty-Nine Articles of Religion and the Ordinal (see Canon A5 of the Canons of the Church of England). In the Anglican tradition, therefore, liturgy, theology and ecclesiology are inseparable one from another, but it is in the liturgy itself that this relationship is most typically to be seen.

STRUCTURES

Liturgy implies and entails a structured, active expression of worship, and historically this has evolved to incorporate, in the case of the Eucharist, ritually performed and interrelated dimensions of word and sacrament, or, in the case of forms of daily liturgical prayer, structured proclamation of the word, almost exclusively in speech and song, accompanied by prayerful response and intercession. Within liturgical structures, different genres of text in addition to readings from Scripture are combined and performatively spoken and sung, for example, in the Eucharist the collect or opening prayer, prayers of intercession, and the Eucharistic Prayer. Alongside these there have evolved architectural settings and furnishings which form the physical structured context for liturgy, although the corporate worship of the Church can be and historically has been offered in a variety of settings according to need and circumstance.

The structured content of liturgy is undergirded by the structured nature of liturgical time, expressed in the calendar of the Church in its division of the year, months and days as a means of encountering and reflecting on the mystery of God in Christ. As well as a particular theological understanding of time itself, the structured reading of Scripture in the liturgical worship of the Church, the lectionary, plays an important role in the Christian reckoning of time, although these aspects receive differing emphasis across the traditions. The observing of the calendar also has a very visual aspect in some traditions, for example, in the use of liturgical colours to denote seasons and festivals, on all of which more will be found in the chapter 'Time' in this book.

A particular example of attention to the structure or shape of the liturgy is the classic work of the Anglican Benedictine Gregory Dix in *The Shape of the Liturgy* (Dix, 2005 (1945)), especially in respect of the Eucharist and its evolution. Dix's argument, put simply, was that the structure of the Eucharist in all its emerging liturgical forms could be reduced to a four-action 'shape', namely 'Take', 'Bless', 'Break', 'Give'. This is often taken at face value today, yet Dix's proposal has been subject to much challenge and revision in the years since its first publication in 1945, and in this respect the student must read Dix in conjunction with Simon

Jones's introduction to the most recent edition (Dix, 2005). Nevertheless the work of Dix taken as a whole does underline the importance of structure as a defining characteristic of the nature of liturgy.

CONNECTIONS

The relationship between forms of liturgical prayer and doctrine, and the relative influence of the one upon the other, has always had a central place in the convictions and deliberations of the churches of East and West.

Liturgical theology

Liturgical theology encompasses both the nature of liturgy *as* theology and the properties of liturgy as *a source for* theology. Liturgical theology has emerged as a distinct field within liturgical studies since the early 1960s, particularly though not exclusively in North America, although before that there were significant steps towards this, for example, Romano Guardini's brief but influential *The Spirit of the Liturgy*, written in 1930, in which the author describes liturgy as 'the treasure-house of the thought of Revelation' (Guardini, 1937, p. 10). The relationship between liturgy and theology in its several aspects has been the subject of a great deal of work in the last 50 years. For the student, a comprehensive impression of this is very conveniently given in the compendium *Primary Sources of Liturgical Theology: A Reader* (Vogel, 2000), which contains extracts from most of the main writers, with linking commentary; in addition, Kevin Irwin provides a very succinct introduction in his *Liturgical Theology: A Primer* (Irwin, 1991).

Discussion has centred on a number of important themes, and key explorations of these have become significant texts in liturgical studies. The pioneer of the modern discipline of liturgical theology was the Orthodox scholar Alexander Schmemann, whose book *Introduction to Liturgical Theology* (1966) and the article 'Liturgy and Theology' (1972) can still serve as classic introductions to ideas since further expounded and examined. Schmemann drew attention to the significance of *ordo*, literally 'order', in relation to the theological nature of liturgy, thus making a significant claim for the place of structure. Though he was an important shaper of liturgical theology as a discipline, paradoxically Schmemann argued against the need for something called 'liturgical theology', since he believed that Christian theology is in any case properly liturgical in nature, having 'its ultimate term of reference in the faith of the Church, as manifested and communicated in the liturgy' (Schmemann, 1972, p. 95). This relates to the notion of liturgy as 'primary theology', later developed by Kavanagh and others (see below).

LEX ORANDI, LEX CREDENDI

A typical starting point for the discussion of the relationship between liturgy and theology has been the phrase *Lex orandi, lex credendi*, 'the law of praying is the law of believing', with a particular focus on the question of which has more greatly influenced the other: has belief been shaped by the evolving shape and content of the liturgy, or vice versa? However, a third question must also be asked: is it, in fact, a relationship of interdependence? The phrase, which originates in Prosper of Aquitaine's early fifth-century writings, as it has been received is both an abbreviation of Prosper's words in their original context and sometimes a distortion of his actual meaning and context, so eager have liturgical theologians often been to adopt the adage as a principle; this has led to what Maxwell Johnson has called a 'lack of consensus in liturgical theology today' (Johnson, 1993, p. 203). Nevertheless, to take one example among many seeking to address the questions posed by the phrase, Kevin Irwin both sums up the issues and provides a typical and succinct assessment which takes into account the problems of origin and interpretation and their implications for method in liturgical theology, concluding that, despite these, 'liturgical theology of whatever methodological shape is crucial for the vitality of the Church in any and every age' (Irwin, 2002, p. 67).

Liturgy as 'primary theology'

For many liturgical theologians the key principle of liturgical theology is the proposition that liturgy is 'primary theology': that the study of theology in the academy is consequent upon the worship of the Church, and properly inseparable from it. Significant writers on this principle include the American Benedictine Aidan Kavanagh, especially in his influential work *On Liturgical Theology*, who sets out the issue in this way: 'the theology we most readily recognize and practice is . . . neither primary nor seminal but secondary and derivative' (Kavanagh, 1992, p. 75) whereas primary theology is that enacted by the celebration of the liturgy in the assembly and in the transformation thereby of the assembly: indeed, following Schmemann, the celebration of the liturgy is theology itself. Gordon Lathrop picks up on this in asserting that 'the meaning of the liturgy resides first of all in the liturgy itself', and that '*Primary liturgical theology* is the communal meaning of the liturgy expressed by the gathering itself' (Lathrop, 1998, p. 5). For him, actual participation *in* the liturgy is the only means of truly coming to understand what is written *about* liturgy. Thus David Fagerberg acknowledges a debt to Schmemann and Kavanagh in understanding liturgical theology as 'the theological work of the assembly, not the work done by an academic upon liturgical material'. Liturgical theology is that primary theology which 'is found in the structure of the rite . . . Liturgical theology is the faith of the Church in ritual motion', the final statement borrowed from Kavanagh (Fagerberg, 2004, p. ix).

Nevertheless studies have been made of the nature of liturgy and of liturgical text as *sources of* theology, while not intending to undermine the principle of the celebration of the liturgy as 'primary theology'. They include Mark Searle's example, which takes the liturgy of initiation as a case study, concentrating on the theology contained in the prayer over the water (Searle, 1991). It might be said that the emergence of revised and reformed rites in the late twentieth and early twenty-first centuries has suggested that there is a great deal of work to be done by way of theological commentary on them as they become familiar and embedded in the life of the churches, and there is every reason for students of liturgy to have this in mind from the outset as they study the rites of their own and other traditions.

Liturgy and mystery

Another important but sometimes neglected theme in liturgical theology is mystery, in its theological sense of a characteristic of God and of divine initiative which points to what has been called the 'moreness' of God, and which is related to that strand of thought known as *theologia negativa* or 'negative theology'. The pioneer in this area was the German Benedictine Odo Casel, whose work in translation, *The Mystery of Christian Worship* (Casel, 1962), has become a classic text. Casel is a figure whose ideas have been much evaluated, criticized and revived. His central theory of the 'mystery-presence' of the saving events of Christ (Incarnation, Passion, resurrection, and so on) in the liturgy, based on an interpretation of the patristic evidence for an emerging sacramental theology in the fourth century and after, has been strongly influential, to the extent of forming a key theological building block in the reform of the liturgy and the renewed ecclesiology which flowed from the Second Vatican Council and had much ecumenical impact. While his work embraces liturgy in many aspects, it was the matter of eucharistic theology and the nature of the presence of Christ in the celebration that was to be prominent. It found its particular flowering in the Constitution on the Sacred Liturgy, especially in terms of the notion of presence wider than in the consecrated elements that was set out in section 7, to which reference has already been made; the Constitution, however, did not wholly adopt Casel's ideas about the objective presence of the saving mysteries of the Incarnation, Passion and resurrection themselves. Despite his influence Casel was until recently relatively little studied, but works in English that have sought to bring him to greater prominence include George Guiver's study, *Pursuing the Mystery: Worship and Daily Life as Presences of God* (Guiver, 1996). Casel's influence on some strands of earlier Anglican liturgical thought can be seen in Christopher Irvine's study of the Anglican monk and theologian Gabriel Hebert (Irvine, 1993).

Liturgy and doctrine

The assertion that liturgy is 'primary theology' finds classic expression in the approach to the study of theology taken by the British Methodist scholar Geoffrey Wainwright in what is now regarded as a seminal study: *Doxology: The*

Praise of God in Worship, Doctrine and Life – A Systematic Theology (Wainwright, 1980). As the title and subtitle suggest, this is a systematic theology approached from the perspective of liturgy and which assumes worship, and what it means to be a worshipping person, to be the foundation of systematic theological study: therefore it is, as Wainwright states, also a theology of worship. Its importance as a landmark of liturgical study is encapsulated in Wainwright's conviction that 'the relations between doctrine and worship are deeper rooted and further reaching than many theologians and liturgists have appeared to recognize in their writings' (Wainwright, 1980, Preface). Wainwright's work has been the catalyst for a whole generation of writing on the relationship between liturgy and doctrine, including many of the contributions referred to here.

Recent studies have drawn attention to two further vital theological aspects of liturgy: the place of Christ in liturgy and the relationship between liturgy and the work of the Holy Spirit. The most recent work in this area is represented by and most conveniently accessed in the wide-ranging collection *The Place of Christ in Liturgical Prayer: Trinity, Christology and Liturgical Theology* (Spinks, 2008) and the equally comprehensive collection published as *The Spirit in Worship – Worship in the Spirit* (Spinks & Berger, 2009). Both these collections address both historical and contemporary themes and contain contributions from scholars representing a wide range of traditions.

TRENDS

Change and revision

The dynamics of liturgical change have received increasing attention in recent years, and the foundation of modern study of these is Anton Baumstark's *Comparative Liturgy*, first published in English in 1958. As the title suggests, it is a study of method in liturgical study, and incorporates Baumstark's 'laws of liturgical evolution', for example the proposition that the most ancient forms survive at the most solemn seasons, such as the Easter liturgy (Baumstark, 1958, p. 27). As with the theories of Gregory Dix, there has been much debate about and revision of Baumstark's work, but overall he succeeds in simply alerting the student of liturgy to the fact that there are dynamics of liturgical evolution and change. Some of these are attributable to processes of official revision of liturgy, but this does not wholly account for how and why liturgy changes – social, political and cultural factors and historical context play an equally important part. Some of these are discussed, for example, by George Guiver, who seeks to demonstrate

> a sense that worship never stands still, either at the level of ground events and changes, or at the more elusive level of local and period character . . . the irrepressibility of life's sources ensure that liturgy continues to change.
>
> (Guiver, 2009, p. 9)

One of the contexts for liturgical change and revision in recent years has been the worshipping church under the conditions of postmodernity, and this has been examined from a number of angles by the contributors to the collection *Liturgy in a Postmodern World* (Pecklers, 2006), while Graham Hughes has examined the consequences of late modernity for the worshipping assembly in relation to theories of meaning (Hughes, 2003).

Methods and approaches

Like liturgy itself, the study of liturgy has evolved over many centuries and has employed changing methodologies. The major shift in the past half-century, with increasing emphasis in the immediate recent past, has been that from the broadly historical to the thematic approach to liturgical study which might typically begin with the question 'What does it mean to be a worshipping person?' Thus, the starting points tend to be the theology of liturgy and worship, the language of ritual and the grammar of symbol, the approach adopted by this volume. This is not to diminish the continuing importance of historical study but rather to use its considerable fruits to evaluate and appreciate the place of liturgy and worship in contemporary Church and society. In recent years a more interdisciplinary approach to liturgical studies has emerged. As well as considerable work in the field of ritual studies, this has included the study of the evolution and celebration of liturgy from anthropological and sociological perspectives, for example in the work of Martin Stringer and Kieran Flanagan. The phenomenon of alternative liturgical forms as a response, or series of responses, to the complexities of contemporary culture has also begun to attract the attention of liturgical scholars, most notably Bryan Spinks in a recent comprehensive and challenging study (Spinks, 2010).

Further reading

Chupungco, A. (2010), *What, Then, Is Liturgy? Musings and Memoir* (Collegeville, MN: Liturgical Press).

Guiver, G. (2009), *Vision upon Vision: Processes of Change and Renewal in Christian Worship* (Norwich: Canterbury Press).

Kavanagh, A. (1992), *On Liturgical Theology* (Collegeville, MN: Liturgical Press).

Schmemann, A. (1966), *Introduction to Liturgical Theology* (Leighton Buzzard: Faith Press/New York: St Vladimir's Seminary Press).

Vogel, D. W. (ed.) (2000), *Primary Sources of Liturgical Theology: A Reader* (Collegeville, MN: Liturgical Press).

Wainwright, G. (1980), *Doxology: The Praise of God in Worship, Doctrine and Life – A Systematic Theology* (New York: Oxford University Press).

Chapter 3

Ritual

Paul F. Bradshaw and Katharine E. Harmon

WHAT IS RITUAL?

'Ritual' is a difficult word to define, but is usually said to involve a series of actions (a) performed mainly for their symbolic value and (b) that tend to be repeated with some regularity, if not frequently, within (c) a particular social group. Some scholars restrict the term to religious activities alone (though they sometimes describe non-religious equivalents as 'ritual-like'), while others extend its use to encompass all human actions of this kind. One should not assume on this broader definition that ritual is absent from modern culture, or is no longer necessary to define, establish or maintain particular social groups. The conviction that moderns are 'ritual-less', which was held widely by theologians and anthropologists alike in the last quarter of the twentieth century, does not accurately describe the contemporary situation. Far from being a ritual-less wasteland, modern Western society contains a rich repertoire of ritual practices, even though many of them no longer derive their symbolism from the Judaeo-Christian tradition. Family therapist David Kertzer has observed with regard to contemporary American culture:

> Even in the case of the transition to adulthood, rather than witnessing the demise of rites of transition, we see the continued central role played by such rites. The high school graduation ritual ... provides a key reference point for many of the country's youth, publically signalling their change of status while celebrating a variety of both official and unofficial values.
>
> (Kertzer, 1989, p. 22)

Kertzer goes on to note that public rituals have actually become more rather than less elaborate as the surrounding culture has grown more complex and diverse, and have become even more important in maintaining family and ethnic identity and solidarity now that societies have become more mobile. Families that are no longer centred on a particular neighbourhood, city or even state find various cycles of ritual as the chief times that define their family ties or kinship: weddings, baptisms, anniversaries, funerals, Thanksgiving dinner and Christmas (see Mitchell, 1995, p. 123).

Ritual permeates societies from the ordinary to the special occasion, and ritual interactions define a person's cultural context. At the same time, with the advent of technology, the ritual understanding of an event has potential to conform to another culture's ritual norm. The contemporary wedding, for example, has become more complex as various media (cinema, social networking, bridal magazines) have prescribed what is necessary for the wedding to 'come off' as a complete celebration. Elements which were at one time quite foreign to it, from lighting unity candles to the appropriate combinations of dance partners for the reception, have gradually accrued cultural expectations as being 'normal'. And globalization has also affected understandings of how a wedding ritual should work. For example, while in England bridesmaids have traditionally walked behind the bride in the entry procession, clergy are now beginning to receive requests for them to copy their American cousins and precede the bride into church.

THE HISTORY OF RITUAL

Not only is the notion of ritual notoriously hard to define, but its history in a Christian context has been tainted by a dichotomization between a faithful response to God's word and a supposed preoccupation with the externals of religion. Historian Peter Burke suggests that, for Reformation-era Christians, ritual became equated with 'artifice' and a purposeful mystification of faith by powerful leaders, while simple elements of faith or word alone spoke to honesty, directness and the kernel of faith (Burke, 1987, pp. 223–4; also Bell, 2005, p. 267). With the responsibility of faith resting on the Word, the demise of a powerful church structure, and the increasing number of literate faithful who could read words for themselves, religion became an increasingly private experience (Douglas, 1970, pp. 1–18). Its new locations became the home and family, and it was no longer as conducive to elaborate, prescribed, communal rites. An emphasis on reason and the rise of modern sciences further dismantled general Western comfort with, and reliance on, ritual. Ritual was seen as the opposite of reason; reason was an enlightened way of accessing religious faith, a way pursued by Reformed Protestant traditions, in contrast to the more primitive or superstitious Catholics who relied on 'hocus-pocus' (Bell, 2005, p. 267; also Preus, 1987, pp. 3–103).

Meanwhile, Christian denominations that retained a more elaborate 'ritualized' structure had a somewhat narrow or fixed way of understanding what ritual meant. The ritual itself was strongly connected to how it was spelled out in the rubric; performing a ritual meant to complete a task, to execute a text correctly, or 'get through' the liturgical act. The study of liturgy was confined to text and rule, with fledgling clergy learning it in the hope of doing it correctly. Emphasis on ritual as performing a rubric correctly tended to create a rather one-dimensional experience. In fact, such an understanding of ritual rendered the role of the congregation somewhat moot – or mute: ritual acts could be completed with or without participants. If the faithful wished to express their spirituality during worship, their job was to offer individual devotions, simultaneously, but privately.

Thus, changing socio-historical circumstances of Western culture caused the meaning of ritual to shift. For example, the editions of the *Encyclopaedia Britannica* between 1771 and 1852 defined ritual as a 'book directing the order and manner to be observed in performing divine service in a particular church, diocese or the like', and 'rite' as 'the particular manner of celebrating divine service, in this or that country', like the Sarum Rite or the Mozarabic Rite. After 1852, however, there are no appearances of the term until 1910, at which point ritual no longer meant a script for regulating practice, but 'a type of practice' found in religion, or outside of religion, using symbols which reflect people and their society (Asad, 1993, pp. 56–7; also Bell, 2005, p. 273).

With the rise of academic anthropological studies, the consideration of ritual centred upon cultures radically different from the Euro-American Christian experiences. Fed by a disparagement of ritual as the antithesis of reason, ritual was not how Christians thought of their own worship, but how one described the fetish, the freak and the fantastic *rituels sauvages* of 'other' cultures. While 'advanced' societies had rationalism, economic structures and institutions to negotiate religion, society and the like, 'primitive' societies tended to cling to childish play or superstitious practices to negotiate meanings and relationships:

> This attitude is most manifest in the invention of the convenient distinction between 'religion' (where communication with the deity takes place rationally through the word) and 'magic' (regarded as an irrational belief in the power of human beings to coerce the powers believed to rule the world).
>
> (Searle, 1992, pp. 51–8)

Ritual was also interesting to the field of social psychology, and persons such as Sigmund Freud and Emile Durkheim focused on the contrast between the openness of public religious ritual as a counterpart to private and, potentially, obsessive practices of the individual.

However, the study of ritual moved from the marginal, magical and obsessive to a new place of interest in the 1960s, and the contributions of anthropologists such as Victor Turner, Mary Douglas and Clifford Geertz developed the notion of ritual as key to how a society (be it Christian or not) establishes its identity in the world. Meanwhile, psychologists such as Erik Erikson moved the understanding of ritual from that which marked obsessive personal behaviour to an analysis of ritual behaviour as deeply involved in the normal emotional development of the individual. Ritualization 'seems to be grounded in the pre-verbal experiences of infants while reaching its full elaboration in grand public ceremonies' (Erikson, 1966, p. 337). The contemporary field of ritual studies, then, draws on a wide variety of related areas – from anthropology to semiotics to religion. The result is a field which is multidimensional and in which ritual could be identified as a basic behavioural act for human societies. From this perspective, rituals do not always point to worship or the control of religious authority, but can also reflect national identity, or define stages within a person's life:

> Ritual is now more likely to be seen as a medium of emotional, intuitive expression that is able to express the spiritual states, alternative realities, and the incipient connectedness in which individuals and communities are embedded. While ritual once stood for the status quo and the authority of dominant social institutions, for many it has become antistructural, revolutionary, and capable of deconstructing inhuman institutions and generating alternative structures.
>
> (Bell, 2005, p. 271)

Ritual has come to be recognized as a universal act of humans, not simply something that 'less civilized' persons practise. So, studying rituals practised by groups of persons can reveal elements of that group's identity, history, values and purpose. As Catherine Bell quips, to 'conceive of ritual as a panhuman phenomenon rather than simply to point and gawk at the strange activities of another culture must constitute some form of progress' (Bell, 2005, p. 273).

RITUAL AND WORSHIP

One of the first liturgical scholars to consider the import of work in the social sciences for the interpretation of Christian ritual was Aidan Kavanagh. He saw that the tools of social sciences, which studied multiple dimensions of human persons as individuals and in groups, could be applied to the action of persons coming together in religious assemblies:

> The whole purpose, as I see it, of assembly, of coming together for public ritual engagements, religious or not, is so that individuals may communicate those experiences that are most incommunicable, publically, in standard symbolic patterns agreed on by the group so that those experiences can be entered into, 'put on,' affirmed, and appropriated by the group as a whole. Such standard symbolic patterns are richly ambiguous, but they are also invariably and rigorously judgmental. The point at which the group does, in fact, enter into, finally affirm without reservation, and wholly appropriate the incommunicable

life-experiences of its members is that at which judgment falls away in the face
of solid affirmation and conviction.   (Kavanagh, 1973, p. 158)

As ritual studies emerged under the umbrella of 'liturgical studies', some of the
classical ways of approaching the definition of ritual were connected to Christian
worship, such as the descriptions 'formal', 'functionalist' and 'symbolic'. If one
were to think of ritual in terms of 'form', one would focus on the pattern of
action – actions which are repetitive, have distinctive features, are prescriptive and
readily identifiable. However, limiting 'ritual' to a formal understanding can be
too broad, encompassing 'everything from the nesting habits of the weaver bird
to the coronation of the emperor of Japan' (Searle, 1992, p. 54). A functionalist
definition, on the other hand, focuses not only on the action but on how the
action serves the needs of an individual or community. It asks one to identify
things about the community – whether it is experiencing change, whether it is
in conflict, whether it wants to solidify its identity. It enquires how the ritual
facilitates the state of the community by expressing a transition, resolving a conflict
or memorializing a culture. Finally, a symbolic approach asks that one look at the
ritual as a means of communication. It combines the formal and the functional
definition, by defining 'ritual' as an activity that conveys meaning. This, too, can
be very broad, as any activity could have meaning, and many people interpret
the same act/gesture/word in different ways. Ritual in the symbolic sense, then,
can mean different things for different people, or fulfil different functions for
different people, even if the action or form is the same. A liturgical ritual might
serve to solidify a community's group identity, facilitate an individual's personal
prayer to God, identify structures of leadership versus participants, and remember
the teaching of Jesus in the gospel.

CULTURE, EMBODIMENT AND CHANGE

Although the adjectives 'formal', 'functional' and 'symbolic' (or other adjectives,
such as 'traditional' or 'fixed') are helpful in understanding the different aspects of
ritual, it is now recognized that one of the most important qualities of ritual is its
location in culture. Ritual tradition is 'a fully cultural, historical, and embodied
process – and so is characterized to a remarkable degree by inventiveness,
creativity, change and variability' (Mitchell, 1999, p. 46). While classical views
might insist on 'form' or 'function' associated with repetition of past events,
Ronald Grimes describes a more dynamic approach to ritual as an evolving means
of communicating experience:

> Body and culture, self and society, are not merely opposites; they are dialectical
> pairs. Taking seriously one term in each pair always leads to the other term. For
> this reason I reject much that is assumed about ritual and the individual, for

example, that ritual is by definition collective. It is necessarily collective only in the sense that anything human is: nothing, not the body, not the self escapes culture. And culture has its most persistent root in the human body itself.

(Grimes, 1990, p. 25)

Liturgy, after all, is not made up of ideas, but of things – words, materials, gestures, tastes, noise, sight and smell, and human persons. It is not only our brains that we take to worship, but our whole selves, which we trundle through or around a series of words, materials, motions, noises, sights and other human persons. Because humans are not simply intellectual and rational, but emotional and embodied, ritual helps the human person experience religious worship as more than a cerebral activity; ritual by its nature asks the worshippers to do more than one thing at once: to pray while they kneel, to sing while they walk, to read while they listen. One could thus describe ritual as a 'behavioural pattern', but it is important to note that it is a *social* behavioural pattern. Ritual is concerned with relationships, and uses 'things' to illustrate these relationships. Doing things together is an important aspect of ritual: not just individuals, but communities act together, following a pattern that through routine repetition becomes a tradition.

But, while we may like routine, we also like to be entertained. This is difficult to accomplish if ritual purports to do the same thing every week. As Margaret Mead suggests,

> this phenomenon of boredom with anything done more than once is particularly acute among Americans, and is probably one of the reasons why we find it impossible to ritualize. One cause for this phenomenon, I submit, is that Americans are conditioned to accept and expect a high degree of irregularity in their lives. We live in so many different types of housing, and move so often, and drive so many kinds of cars, and smoke so many types of cigarettes, etc., that change, in certain areas, has become part of our lives. This is a very different type of life from that lived by people who have been reared in one house, and have died in the same bed in which they were born.
>
> (Mead, 1973, p. 98)

Certainly, the shifting needs of particular locations and culture, and to what extent culture and liturgy should affect each other, have long been challenges for Christians. For example, should Christian worship mesh with contemporary culture, thus being more familiar and accessible, or should it offer a distinct counterweight to what culture usually impresses upon its members? Richard Gaillardetz has described this tension among contemporary Christians as a divide between those who want a 'community without transcendence' or 'transcendence without community'. While some Christians prefer worship which is friendly, low-key, warm or relaxed, other Christians gravitate to that which is formal, structured, reverent or awe-inspiring. While one set seems to stress communion with the community, the other seems to emphasize communion with God. Yet, the challenge for the Christian, and the intent of Christian ritual, is to emphasize both aspects:

> This liturgical rift can only be healed by a return to the Trinitarian and Eucharistic foundations of the Christian faith and the liturgy. The formal and social dimensions of liturgical life, when properly celebrated, remind us that human connectedness is written into the very structures of our personal existence and that when we realize ourselves as persons who live the life of communion with others we are, at the same time, living the life of communion with God. The celebration of the liturgy is the privileged ritual expression of what is in fact true every moment of our lives: every authentic act of human communion is by that fact communion with God.
>
> (Gaillardetz, 1994, p. 416)

EMERGING RITUALS

Although ritual is often thought to be timeless, even rites which may appear to be preserving the past unchanged are actually subject to change and creativity:

> just as language is always being invented in the process of using it, so ritual is always in the process of being created as ritualists enact it. The history of any rite known to us always reveals it as changing, and these changes are typically congruent with others, which suggests that ritual is a fully historical, fully cultural process.   (Grimes, 1992, p. 24; see also Bell, 1989, pp. 31–41)

For the same reason, brand new and even temporary rituals can appear. The most fertile location for such ritual development often lies more at the margins of a culture rather than at its heart, among those who are disenfranchised from the mainstream (Mitchell, 1999, p. 47). It is here that one encounters what scholars like Ronald Grimes have termed 'emerging rituals', rituals that do not need to have existed from time immemorial or to last for ever but may be improvised and be practised for a limited time and purpose and then discarded. They exist to define membership of a group, interpret reality in a specific way and become the means of effecting social change. They are meaningful not by reference to something outside or beyond the performance itself but by virtue of what they actually do, individually and socially. As Catherine Bell has observed of political rituals, they 'do not *refer* [emphasis mine] to politics ... they *are* politics. Ritual is the thing itself. It *is* power; it acts and it actuates' (Bell, 1992, p. 195). Sociologist Frits Staal has gone further and argued that something similar is the case during the actual performance of all ritual:

A widespread but erroneous assumption about ritual is that it consists in symbolic activities which refer to something else. It is characteristic of a ritual performance, however, that it is self-contained and self-absorbed. The performers are totally immersed in the proper execution of their complex tasks. Isolated in their sacred enclosure, they concentrate on correctness of act, recitation and chant. Their primary concern, if not obsession, is with rules. There are no symbolic meanings going through their minds when they are engaged in performing ritual.   (Staal, 1979, p. 4)

These rituals, though they may be transient, are in no way less effective. Consider, for example, the power of ritual in political revolution. The revolution in Egypt in 2012, with the ousting of President Hosni Mubarak, began with citizens gathering in the streets, which soon became a repeated practice, each day, with growing numbers of men and women who identified with the group that gathered. The protesters also engaged in communal activities, singing protest songs composed on the spot and chanting in unison. The ritual of gathering, assembling and singing together placed the political situation in Egypt in the realm of the popular. Far from being divorced from the political manoeuvrings of the Egyptian government, ritual involvement offered a powerful venue for people to respond emotionally to the situation, develop a sense of community with fellow Egyptians and effect a change.

MULTIPLE MEANINGS

It is important to keep in mind that, because ritual is multivalent, it can also have multiple meanings. In fact, it can be dangerous to assume that any ritual is only capable of a single meaning, that there is such a thing as *the* meaning of the rite that can be easily identified. The Jewish liturgiologist Lawrence Hoffman in particular has argued that religious rituals have several meanings that are present at the same time. First, there are **private** meanings. These he defines as 'whatever idiosyncratic interpretations people find in things', which religious officials usually ignore and fail to investigate. Second, there are **official** meanings: 'the things experts say that a rite means'. Hoffman cites as an example the interpretation of the Sabbath light as 'the symbol of the divine' in the *Union Prayer Book*, 'invented (for all we know, accidentally or unwittingly) by some unknown prayerbook editor in 1940'. Such an interpretation 'may be wrong, but it is agreed upon and safe'. Third, there are **public** meanings:

> agreed-upon meanings shared by a number of ritual participants, even though they are not officially preached by the experts. In the Jewish world, family solidarity at a Passover Seder is such a value . . . For the average American Jew, Passover may or may not be Exodus time; but it is family

time, the most pervasive public meaning of the Seder rite, whether the officials say so or not.

To these three, Hoffman adds a fourth, **normative** meaning: 'a structure of signification that ritual affixes upon the non-ritualized world that participants re-enter when the rite has been concluded'. When participants exit the ritual event and re-enter ordinary time and space, they see things differently, because the rite has changed them, or formed them in a particular way of being which causes them to act differently in the world. Officials like to think that it is the official meaning of the rite that transforms the way that people see things outside the rite, but

> as often as not, it is any of the other meanings that carry the day, the public understandings that everyone except the experts recognize as the rite's message, or the private meanings that individuals hold, perhaps only inchoately but certainly nonetheless.   (Hoffman, 1993, pp. 79–82)

Hoffman's classification could be refined still further. His 'official' meanings could be subdivided into (a) the intentions that the original compilers of a rite might have had, and (b) the meaning subsequently attached to the rite by later generations of ecclesiastical authorities. The eucharistic rite of the Anglican Book of Common Prayer provides a good example of the distance that can separate these two groups. It is clear, both from the shape that the rite itself took in 1552 and from the known views of those responsible for its composition, that it was intended to give liturgical expression to a very 'low' doctrine of the sacrament. However, a considerable number of leading Anglican divines in the seventeenth century were able to convince themselves that a much 'higher' doctrine could be read out of the rite. And the Book of Common Prayer has continued to be interpreted in that way by many prominent church leaders ever since, by highlighting the few small rubrical changes made to the text at its revision in 1662 and ignoring its historical roots, general shape and 'low' sacramental language. This example should stand as a stern warning not to assume that those who authorize a rite must necessarily share the meaning held by its original promulgators or even that articulated in the text itself. The meaning of the rite may change, according to cultural, historical and social circumstance.

TYPES OF RITUAL

Just as scholars have a number of ways of describing the meaning of the word 'ritual', so too do they have a number of ways of describing the *types* of ritual, some admitting only as few as two, others many more, some even up to 12 separate categories. Bell settles for six main types (Bell, 1997, pp. 93–137):

1 What are known as rites of passage, a concept advanced by the French anthropologist Arnold van Gennep in his classic work, *Les rites de passage* (1909). These rituals mark a person's transition from one stage of life to another, sometimes linked to a biological change like birth, puberty or death but also to a change in social status like coming of age or retirement. Van Gennep distinguished three phases in such rituals: preliminary rites of separation intended to ease the individual undergoing the ritual away from his or her former social position; the marginal or liminal phase when the individual has broken with his or her former status or identity but has not yet assumed a new one; and the post-liminal phase incorporating and integrating the person into a new role or status. Victor Turner later developed and popularized the terms 'liminality' and 'communitas' – the egalitarian relationship that exists between persons stripped of status during a rite of passage (Turner, 1969). Various Christian liturgical practices would fall into the category of rites of passage, chief among them adult baptism and ordination (although in theory one should include infant baptism here too, in practice it often lacks a strong ritual expression of separation). Weddings, funerals and confirmation rites also share these elements to a greater or lesser extent, as do rites of excommunication and reconciliation.

2 Calendrical rites. Just as rites of passage mark significant stages in the life of a person, so calendrical rites mark the passage of time, recurring periodically and predictably weekly, monthly or annually, and bringing order to human life. Some of these celebrations are seasonal, and were traditionally rooted in the rhythms of agriculture, such as sowing and harvesting, although in modern societies they may instead be governed by the dictates of the advertising industry. Others are commemorative celebrations that recall significant historical events, even though the designated day may not always be factually accurate. Revolutionaries often attempt to supplant traditional observances and replace them with new patterns and celebrative days in order to mark a clear break between the old order and the new. Most Christian churches have acquired quite an elaborate cycle of calendrical rites, based primarily upon Sunday and the seven-day week but including many annual seasons and festivals, in some cases inherited from earlier centuries, in others related to current activities within the congregation (e.g. Sunday school anniversary, Bible Sunday, Week of Prayer for Christian Unity) and its outreach to the world (Sea Sunday, Christian Aid Week).

3 Rites of exchange and communion. Under this heading Bell places rituals in which people make offerings to the deity with the expectation of receiving something in return, a practice often summarized in the Latin tag, *do ut des*, 'I give so that you may give.' Fundamental to rituals of this kind is the concept of some sort of reciprocity between the action of the worshipper and the action of the one worshipped, whether in immediate benefits bestowed or in longer-term favour. Although some form of sacrifice is found in nearly all religions,

the notion of communion – the uniting of the divine and human worlds usually through the consumption of a meal understood to be shared with the deity – is more characteristic of the Judaeo-Christian tradition than of others. In Christianity, the Eucharist is the supreme ritual expression of this.

4 Rites of affliction. Rites in this category might more appropriately be termed rites of healing and purification, as their purpose is to seek to mitigate whatever is afflicting human beings with misfortune or pollution by means of exorcism or other forms of purging and restoration. Among rituals of this type commonly or historically practised by Christians are confession and forgiveness, which rids a person of sin and restores him or her to proper relationship with God and community, and the anointing of the sick, which seeks to instil grace and fortitude in the sick and dying through the use of blessed oil.

5 Feasting, fasting and festivals. It might be thought that such practices had already been covered under the headings of Communion and calendrical rites, but Bell recognizes a separate category in which the primary motive is somewhat different, to express publicly people's commitment and adherence to basic religious values. One might alternatively call them rites of identity, because those who participate in the feast, fast or festival define themselves as 'us' and those who refuse to do so or who are excluded from doing so by the community are identified as 'them'. On this basis, all acts of public worship contain an element of this classification – that assembling to worship together in itself is a form of agreement or creed, whether or not worship involves an explicit confession of faith. Such rituals may also involve a reinforcing of the differing status held by individuals and sub-groups within the community.

6 Political rites. This category comprises those rites that create, define and give legitimacy to the exercise of power and authority, and would include such diverse occasions as the coronation of a monarch, a state funeral, a public execution, and the display of military might on a national holiday. Some of these are rites of passage, others symbolize and celebrate the status quo, while public demonstrations that challenge those in power might also be added to the list. Although they may be seen by some as purely symbolic rather than functional, they are normally taken very seriously by those contending for power, because they demonstrate and construct relationships of political dominance and submission more effectively than coercive force itself.

It should be obvious from the above that these categories are not rigidly differentiated from one another, and any one ritual act may contain overlapping dimensions from two or more types, sometimes even in tension with or contradicting one other. But such imprecision should not blind us to the fundamental truth that rituals do achieve their aims – they work, and not just among 'primitive' peoples who believe in magic or religious communities that accept the reality of divine intervention. And by developing a consciousness of ritual and its role in Christian worship, it becomes possible to see that seemingly empty or simply repetitive actions fulfil the function of actively involving the faithful in a relationship with God in the only way humans know how – through symbolic actions, words and objects.

Further reading

Bell, C. (1997), *Ritual: Perspectives and Dimensions* (New York: Oxford University Press).

Bradshaw, P., and Melloh, J. (eds) (2007), *Foundations in Ritual Studies: A Reader for Students of Christian Worship* (London: SPCK/Grand Rapids, MI: Baker Academic).

Grimes, R. L. (rev. edn, 1995), *Beginnings in Ritual Studies* (Columbia, SC: University of South Carolina Press).

Mitchell, N. D. (1999), *Liturgy and the Social Sciences* (Collegeville, MN: Liturgical Press).

Chapter 4

Sign and symbol

George Guiver CR

The word 'symbol' is most commonly used today of a pictorial design that stands in for words. A smoking cigarette crossed by a red line is immediately recognized to mean 'no smoking'. If we move on from the world of simple facts to the more complex dimension of imagination, feelings and intuitions, then two words, 'sign' and 'symbol', are most frequently used by writers on this subject to make a distinction clear. At this level of discourse the cigarette with a red line is a 'sign', conveying a precise piece of information, full stop. A 'symbol' on the other hand does more – there is a surplus that cannot be identified or described with precision. A symbol sets off associations and often engages emotions but you cannot put your finger on all it evokes (e.g. a keepsake of someone who has died). The smoking cigarette would only pass from being a sign to being a symbol if, say, your best friend were killed by a falling no-smoking sign. Then, every time you saw such a sign your friend's tragedy would be evoked and the sign's literal meaning would fade into the background.

The word 'symbol' comes from two Greek words meaning 'thrown together'. Two realities are set in relationship: the symbol itself and the deeper and richer reality it evokes. In most symbols there is a direct connection between the symbol and what it evokes, so that it is often difficult to draw a clear distinction between the symbol and the thing symbolized. The embrace the father gives the prodigal son is part and parcel of its 'meaning': as he threw his arms around his son he would not be thinking, 'By this embrace I am conveying this and this', as if he were outside the symbol. The symbol and the thing symbolized become one thing, a whole absorbing experience.

Symbols fall into different categories:

- Some symbols, such as a smile or the giving of flowers, can normally speak for themselves, primordial gestures belonging to the common stock of humanity.
- Some are determined by their culture: in England the picture of a village nestling in green countryside with its church at the centre is a strong symbol whose nearest equivalent in Italy would probably be a hill town in the midst of a drier countryside, topped by a church campanile. For an English person that would not speak the same volumes.
- Some symbols depend on background knowledge: a poppy in the lapel needs to be explained to people from countries other than the UK. The explanation, however, is only an introduction, as the newcomers still have the task of getting under the skin of what it evokes.

Symbols operate at different levels simultaneously: a good joke can be like a symbol in that it evokes things not said but implied, making us laugh partly because a host of implications are just that – implied, without being directly mentioned. An example would be the joke about my own religious community that if one of the brothers were murdered, the police would be faced with considerable difficulty as they would discover that everyone had a motive. It is unreal, incongruously hilarious, but at the same time conjures up a host of possible real-life scenarios in life together in a group – more than we can imagine, probably. Jesus' teaching and actions were many-layered in this way, on this symbolic principle. Think, for instance, of a large, bedraggled crowd of ordinary people and country folk, fishermen and beggars, to whom he says, 'You are the light of the world.' We are so familiar with the words that we need to stop and imagine them spoken in that situation to appreciate the incongruity. What would the original hearers make of it? It is hilariously odd; it's exciting; but it would also leave them scratching their heads. The overall effect in the context of what Jesus on that occasion was saying, however, is to make you want to be a really good person. 'Let your light so shine before others . . .' This is how symbol works, touching many levels at once, and motivating us. As well as using striking images, Jesus was also given to symbolic actions, among which the poignant and many-layered action of washing the disciples' feet is a fine example. In the liturgy an obvious such symbol would be the cross. If we think about it, this is a gallows, but at the same time it evokes joy, confidence and much more.

Because symbols are alive, they are prone to change. The Easter egg, originally a fertility symbol, came to evoke the resurrection, but has now lost that meaning as well for most people. Symbols can die: the dance called the hokey-cokey was originally a Reformation skit on the gestures of the Mass, but this is now entirely forgotten. It was not forgotten by the vicar where I was a child – if at a parish social we started dancing the hokey-cokey he would stop it immediately. The opposite can also happen: symbolism can evolve out of something that was not a symbol. One of the most powerful moments in the liturgical year is the stripping of the altars on Maundy Thursday, when the whole church is stripped at the moment of desolation as Christ goes out to the Garden of Gethsemane; this originated in spring-cleaning for Easter but became a very powerful and moving symbolic act.

One of the most common things to happen to symbols is that they shrink – the Christian liturgy is full of examples. Baptism, intended as a dramatic submersion in living water, gradually shrank to a few drops on the head while suspended over what amounts to a bird-bath. The big tablecloth dramatically thrown over the altar at the offertory shrank to become a small handkerchief (the corporal), necessitating a duplicate linen cloth that stays on the altar permanently. The solution is to abolish the corporal and simply use the large linen cloth. There is a moral question here: if fundamental Christian symbols shrink for the sake of convenience, what does that say about what we think of them and the person they are for? Is convenience (a polite word in this context for laziness) compatible with love? One of the main tasks of liturgical reform today is to un-shrink our symbols.

SYMBOLS AND WORDS

The relation between symbols and words is complex. Symbols cannot be 'explained'; we cannot describe their 'meaning'. If we can, they are not symbols but signs. Our understanding of a true symbol always remains incomplete – there remains 'more' that dances tantalizingly beyond our grasp. Symbols take over where words are not up to the task.

There are ways, however, in which words do have a part to play. First of all, some symbols need background information. The kiss of peace might be thought self-explanatory, but many people reject it simply on the basis of the self-explanatory part, not realizing that a few words will open a door to further dimensions. We need to read all those New Testament texts, surprisingly many, in which it is mentioned. That begins to give a feel for its setting in the culture of the first Christian communities. We then need to know about the Church's further reflection on the kiss of peace, seeing there not only a making of peace with our brother and sister before going to the altar, but still more: a reverencing of the presence of Christ in the people around us. Pope Paul VI said that there are three real presences in the Eucharist: in the bread and wine, in the proclamation of the gospel, and in the people. The Peace is therefore more than a natural human greeting, and the 'surplus' needs to be discovered by looking into its background.

Most symbols benefit from the attempt (always only partially successful) to analyse and explain their significance. This, however, is subject to a universal rule: simultaneous explanation kills symbols, silences them, truncates their complex evocations. It is a golden liturgical rule never to explain a thing while we are doing it. This is because, as we have said, symbols have more to communicate than can be caught in words, and the 'more' is quickly silenced by human talk. In baptism preparation, for instance, there is a need to help people respond fruitfully to the anointings, where they are done. This might be achieved by looking with them at all the descriptions of anointing in the Old and New Testaments – simply reading the stories without much comment perhaps – and then letting the symbol speak for itself at the subsequent service without further preparation. Other symbolic areas linked with oil could be looked at: prophets, priests, kings, bodily health, food, light. All of that can be done without ever saying, 'This anointing means . . .'. Such an introduction to the world of a symbol is called 'mystagogy' (see Richter, 1990, pp. 54f.), a word which means 'leading into a mystery'. Mystagogy is the deeper teaching that should follow the sacraments of initiation, but it is also recognized as something that happens continuously with all of us, as we are transformed by participating in worship. Through the years we gradually delve into symbols, or they delve into us.

We ought to add that sometimes there will be a need for some sort of emergency explanation, if the people present are completely in the dark about a symbol being used. We need to be very careful how we do that, and separate it as far as possible from the actual performance of the symbol.

Liturgy loves to accompany symbolic actions with appropriate biblical texts, like 'Zadok the Priest' sung at the anointing of the British monarch. At least some of the time it can be good to resist this temptation – the simple placing of bread and wine on the altar, for instance, without any prayers, in complete silence, can allow the act to speak with great eloquence.

We have to remember, however, that words are always to some degree symbols themselves rather than signs. Semiotics has taught us that a word is never a capsule that transmits a tidy 'meaning' unmodified between speaker and hearer. Much is lost on the journey from speaker to hearer, much is changed, much leaves us wondering or uncertain. Take the word 'furniture', for instance. How many things does that evoke, and which come to the fore for you? You as the speaker might intend one of those meanings, while the hearer grasps another. Words are slippery because they are symbols. A Russian writer has said of this incapacity of language to do justice to our thoughts: 'Every thought expressed is a lie.' The words of the liturgy in particular are nearer to poetry than to scientific description. We hear them so often that we are brought to relate to them in a symbolic state of mind even though we might not register the fact. More lurks behind them than behind most everyday conversation, and they need to be treated in a similar way to that in which we relate to visual and other symbols.

CHRISTIAN IRONY

One characteristic of Christianity is that it regards its symbols with varying degrees of irony. Unlike a religion where graven idols are identified with the gods, in Christianity that ultimate identity is not there. Even Christians who regard church buildings as very sacred know that if necessary they can celebrate the sacraments in a field, on the battlefield for instance, or during the summer for a church festival. This 'irony' does not mean that the church building is a mere help or support, an optional extra: there is a strong sense for many Christians that the church building participates radically in the truth to which it is dedicated, and enables our own participation to profound effect. But it could be said that the church building belongs not to the Church's *esse* (being, or essence) but to its *bene esse* (well-being). Once we are back from the field, however happy we were there, we will want as soon as we can to build a church. There was a move away from this in the later twentieth century in a desire to connect worship with the ordinary things of every day. The Eucharist on a kitchen table will speak profoundly of Christ's engagement with people in normal life. But we have come to realize that, without the contrast with a sense of the holy place, the power of the kitchen Eucharist will get lost. We will lose the dialogue between two levels of symbolization. The shock of mixing the sacred with the pots and pans will in due course become simply the familiarity of the pots and pans. Today we need both worship in church and a certain amount of worship that engages with daily life by being planted in it.

SACRAMENTS

There is a level at which it becomes increasingly difficult to view a symbol in this ironic way. This is so with the sacraments, where we find symbols raised to a new order. The realism potential in symbols is here fully realized – according to traditional theology, sacraments effect that which they symbolize (hence the language about 'real presence', for instance). It is not possible to treat the sacraments with irony. The martyrs of Abitina in the persecution of Diocletian in the early fourth century were asked to renounce celebrating the Eucharist, but one of them replied, '*Sine Dominico non possumus*' (We cannot exist without the Lord's sacrament), and so they died. The same can be said of baptism. It is interesting to use this category of irony in testing sacraments out. The narrowing of the number to seven in the Middle Ages has always been precarious: we cannot, for instance, speak categorically of confirmation as a separate sacrament divorced from baptism. In the early centuries sacraments were recognized to be many more, one of them being monastic life. We can say of that, that for a monk or nun who is truly called it is impossible to be deprived of it without an essential violation. The symbol is so closely identified with the reality symbolized that it is no longer possible to separate them: the father, after all, could have greeted the prodigal son joyfully yet keeping away from him and giving no embrace, but something fundamental would be lacking. That embrace was not a sacrament, but you could call it a natural sacrament, one of those things in daily life that are so essential that to omit them will undermine relationships.

One characteristic of sacraments is that they always include the spoken word. As Augustine put it, '*Accedit verbum ad elementum, et fit sacramentum*' (the word comes upon the element, and a sacrament comes to be): the Trinitarian formula in baptism, the Eucharistic Prayer in the Eucharist, the absolution in confession, and so on. (This is not to say that other symbols do not require words, as in the kiss of peace, where we need to say 'Peace'). Here we begin to stray into the realm of ritual, which has a chapter of its own in this book. Ritual could be called extended symbol, symbols enacted in time.

We are left with a threefold progression: sign – symbol – sacrament. There are no clear dividing lines, but gradations on a scale, from a server pointing to the place on the page where an officiant should start reading (sign) to the two supreme sacraments of baptism and Eucharist, all within the fundamental sacrament of the People of God.

THE CHURCH AS SACRAMENT

Just as the Church is called the foundational sacrament, so the Church is also the basic symbol. The disciples knew Christ the flesh-and-blood human being, which we who come after cannot do. After his resurrection the scandal of particularity disappeared, and the risen and ascended Lord became accessible to anyone anywhere, but not in flesh and blood. In order to relate to him, as to any person, however, we need to engage with all our faculties: mind, spirit and body, sight, sound and touch. This is met by the sacramental and symbolic order. Four aspects stand out here: the people, the Scriptures, the things of the Church, and the tradition.

First of all, we encounter Christ in one another – in this, the People of God are symbol and sacrament. The weakness of much contemporary Christianity arises partly from an inability to distinguish between what is purely human in Christian people, and what is symbol. Dislike or disagreement in the congregation can lead to ruptures because the standards operating are purely secular – if we had a strong enough sense of the symbolic nature of the People of God (in other words, of the unseen hinterland behind what is apparently purely human) we would be better able to put such conflicts in their place. It is not enough in the Christian community to have a democratic voice, for instance: decision-making needs to be a corporate quest for the will of God, founded on individuals giving themselves to each other. There is a hinterland to the group that is not there in a secular democratic assembly. If the General Synod of the Church of England had a stronger sense of its unseen symbolic hinterland there might be less inappropriate imitation of parliamentary behaviour. Parliament, by the nature of the case, will work on a basis of struggle and cooperation between individuals and groups, while the Church operates on a different basis of giving oneself away, as individuals are brought to unity in charity. That is a gospel truth, but there is a symbolic hinterland to it which is more like music than mere fact. Symbols such as the sign of peace are only outcrops of an underlying Great Symbol, which is the body of Christ and its life of service and love.

The Church, the People of God, is the basic sacrament. We do not meet Christ in flesh and blood in Galilee, but in the people who make up the Church we see Christ, in whom we see the Father, and we squeeze his hand in the Peace. Christ is also present in all other human beings, the distinction being that in the Church his presence is named, not hidden – that recognition enables us to engage fully with the sacrament of Christ's presence because we believe in it, and we are able to give ourselves to one another as people unified by the act of faith.

Second, we engage with the Christ of flesh and blood in the printed pages of the Scriptures and in hearing them read aloud. In both ways they are a physical reality fulfilling our need to meet Christ bodily. In the Christian tradition great emphasis has been laid on the physical business of reading the Scriptures aloud. In them we meet the spiritual through the physical. If symbols have hinterlands, the hinterland of the Scriptures is endless – we will continue finding things in them in a process that is inexhaustible, as any people find who study them regularly. One thing they are is an artefact in this physical world, which is what our human nature needs, and in their performance we encounter Christ in the dimension of the physical world.

Third, we see and touch Christ by means of symbol in the things of the Church: its paraphernalia, its structures, its buildings. The church building is paradigmatic of the whole faith, as I have already implied. A key factor here is the setting aside of space, patches of earth claimed solely for God. This is not in contradistinction to the kitchens, hospitals and buses of everyday life, as if God were not in them; God is in fact in those places if anywhere. Rather is a place set aside as a symbol and sacrament, to focus the divine, in order to sharpen our senses, so that we may grow in awareness of the divine in everything. In buildings and altars and chalices and icons we see and touch, and are moved to see and to love.

In these three complementary ways we meet Christ in flesh and blood and the material of creation, and in the Christ we see and touch we see the Father.

THE GOSPEL IS GENETIC

A symbol lives the more it is embedded in a narrative. Symbols that do not dwell in a narrative lack deep roots, though they do have their uses. Some modern worship makes use of signs and symbols invented for the occasion, or that have arisen in recent years. The use in a particular way of stones, candles or basic elements like water can have its place, but, until they have acquired the depth that goes with being embedded in a narrative through time, they are not enough on their own – they leave us in danger of simply looking at ourselves and what we have put together. Deep symbol is always received from another people and another time. Language is a good example of this kind of tradition (a word that means 'passing-on'). Although the English language shows great versatility in creating new vocabulary, some elements are more difficult to change. It ought to be simple to invent a gender-neutral pronoun to sit alongside 'he' and 'she', but the best we can do is use the not always clear 'they'. Such is the power of tradition. Just as language is in this way genetic, so is the life of the Christian people.

The Christian symbolic world has grown by accretion, taking in new things as it goes along and shedding others, in an organic process of development. In the arts, a central part of the living tradition is the repertoire. If an organist is going to improvise imaginatively and artistically, then he or she needs to be playing plenty of the repertoire. Even a small amount of such playing can transform a person's capacity to improvise. In painting and sculpture it is often said that both understanding and creativity arise out of viewing as much art as you can, and regularly. Good use of symbol in worship depends on familiarity with the repertoire of Christian symbol – this comes through reading, looking, study and regular use. The preparation of lively and imaginative modern worship needs familiarity with the tradition. The best of what is new always comes out of the best of the old.

THE SYMBOLIC IMAGINATION

All these aspects of the People of God as symbol and sacrament – the people, the Scriptures, the things of the Church and the tradition – are interdependent, and the lack of vital force in Western Christianity today may be partly due to a lack of proper symbolic interdependence. For instance the church building might have all the right things in it, but no connection is made between it and the life of the Christian community and world around it. Or both the church building and the Christian community may betray to the beholder a lack of serious engagement with, or awareness of, the tradition. It can be seen in the way a church is looked after, or the way the people relate to one another ('We don't do the Peace here – we're not interested in being chummy'). To follow Christ requires a symbolic imagination, an awareness of the deeper unifying truths that connect the people with the Scriptures with the tradition with the mission with the building . . . The symbolic imagination is the antithesis of liturgical laziness where symbols are shrunk to make life easier. Our habit is to ask the lazy questions. Why have dipping when it is so much easier to have sprinkling? Why perform a fully liturgical daily office when it is easier to sit in a pew and read it? Why make the effort? The symbolic imagination knows why the effort is worth it, somehow in fact demanded whether we like it or not. This rests on having a sustained conviction that God relates to us by means of symbol and sacrament, and that they are sufficiently important to be treated with the utmost commitment.

THE CONCRETE FRAMEWORK OF CHRISTIAN SYMBOLISM

In the physical place of worship there are certain universal symbols:

1 The place of baptism. In antiquity baptism was done out of sight of the main congregation; the font, however, and the building that housed it, were dominant structures, and were used by the whole congregation regularly during the year to revisit the baptismal mystery. Largely for cultural reasons it is better today for baptism to take place in the midst of the people, and so the font (or its smaller substitute, the holy-water stoup) needs its appropriate place.

2 The primeval instinct to bow comes naturally in worshipping God, but it would be strange to bow without a reference point. Early on, the Holy Table became that – the place of the great memorial of the sacrifice and resurrection of Christ. It is God we are bowing to, but the altar's part in that is as complex as the father's embrace of the prodigal son.

3 It is easy to be dogmatic about the place of the Word in the building: sometimes this item of furniture is designed as a symbolic point similar to the altar and the font; history shows it not to be so simple as that – there has been a tendency for the Word to be dispersed in a number of lecterns and pulpits. In an early Christian basilica, the epistle might be read from a lectern, the gospel from the ambo, and the sermon preached from the president's seat. The place of the gospel also doubled up as the place for the choir. It can be by this very multiplication that the Word is presented as a cardinal symbol in the place of worship.

4 There will be at least two distinct spaces: the place of the people and the place of the altar. Modern history has left them squashed into the rigid format of the theatre, and once again the plague of 'convenience' makes it difficult to rediscover what has been lost: the understanding of the church building as an arena in which every corner is used, visited, passed through, by people worshipping with their bodies as well as eyes and ears. The church is, if you like, an icon that we step into. A church interior, by the way it is set out, maintained, looked after and used is overall a symbol that can be either feeble or strong. The main reason congregations are static and church buildings are not powerful arenas for liturgical action by all is, yet again, convenience.

5 A final primary aspect of the place of worship is beauty. The poorer its aesthetic qualities, the less we will be able to give the whole of ourselves.

There is in addition the symbolic repertoire of the People of God in any particular time and place: prayers you say, songs you sing, things you pray with, symbols and activities that encapsulate aspects of the gospel. The parish round of prayer, meetings, study and service is all in itself a symbol, a repertoire of meaning-making.

In a person's life the range might include a personal discipline of corporate-centred daily prayer, icons in the home, a discipline about participation in the Eucharist, a pledging of time to certain activities, a reflective engagement with the Church calendar. All of this can be disparate activities or a single, coherent symbol that as a whole sings, if you like, a music whose full implications cannot be put into words or even fully grasped, but is a deep-down undertow.

SYMBOL IS FOR HUMANS

In many cultures symbol comes naturally and has no need of books to explain it. We live in symbolically impoverished times, and, if the gospel is about becoming fully human in Christ, then a central part of the Church's mission today is to lead our society back to the profound world of symbol, and in it discover what it is to be fully human.

Further reading
Dupré, L. (2000), *Symbols of the Sacred* (Grand Rapids, MI: Eerdmans).

Irvine, C. (ed.) (2007), *The Use of Symbols in Worship*. Alcuin Liturgy Guides 4 (London: SPCK).

Richter, K. (1990), *The Meaning of Sacramental Symbols* (Collegeville, MN: Liturgical Press).

Sagovsky, N. (1978), *Liturgy and Symbolism* (Bramcote: Grove Books).

Stevenson, K. (ed.) (1981), *Symbolism and the Liturgy*, vols 1 and 2 (Bramcote: Grove Books).

Chapter 5

Prayer

Bridget Nichols

INTRODUCTION

'Prayer' is the name of the configurations of speech, song, silence and gesture in which human beings communicate with God. In that sense, it comprehends the whole Godward activity of worship, an activity which itself originates in God. For Christians, following Paul's letter to the Romans, have understood their prayers to be assisted by the gift of the Spirit who dwells in them (Romans 8.9):

> the Spirit helps us in our weakness; for we do not know how to pray as we ought, but that very Spirit intercedes with sighs too deep for words. And God, who searches the heart, knows what is the mind of the Spirit, because the Spirit intercedes for the saints according to the will of God.
>
> (Romans 8.26–27)

In a more specific and pragmatic sense, 'prayer' defines particular forms of words, and the settings – public and private – in which they are used. This chapter will concentrate on the prayer of the gathered assembly, though never losing sight of the close connection between public and private prayer. As George Guiver reminds us, prayer 'is always in the body of Christ'. It is 'impossible for a Christian ever to pray utterly "privately"' (Guiver, 2002, p. 382). Shared forms of words, common concerns and continuity between the prayers of individuals and the prayers of the assembly create a reciprocity that allows each form of prayer to sustain and replenish the other.

The discussion falls into four parts: the first attends to the elements necessary to prayer itself; the second surveys the most common forms and patterns of public worship as the principal setting of prayer; the third considers the subjects, genres, orders and shapes of prayer; and a short fourth section discusses prayer as both expression and creator of communion and community.

THE NECESSITIES FOR PRAYER

While we are exhorted to pray continually and to give thanks at all times (1 Thessalonians 5.17–18), the presence of some basic conditions will assist our response to that injunction. First among these is place. Where do we pray? Scriptural tradition makes much of places set aside for prayer, the temple and the synagogue particularly, but also other places. Jesus, as a preface to teaching the disciples the Lord's Prayer (Matthew 6.9–13 and see also Matthew 6.5–6), recommends going into a room by oneself to pray. He himself goes away to pray periodically in order to place himself in the presence of God without distraction or intrusion, and to recharge his resources for public ministry (e.g. Matthew 14.23; Mark 6.46; Luke 6.12, 9.28). Early in the Acts of the Apostles, we learn that the disciples 'spent much time together in the temple' and 'broke bread at home' (Acts 2.46).

A phrase like 'going to church' is thus more eloquent than it may appear. It speaks of having a place where spiritual resources can be renewed and where prayer can be informed by a thicker context built out of people, Scripture, preaching, sacrament and music. It alludes both to the horizontal relationships that exist among members of an assembly gathered to offer their prayers in a certain kind of setting, and to the vertical relationship that exists between the people and God.

When we think about prayer, we are likely to think first of words, and probably about particular words, perhaps learned by heart in early childhood – the Lord's Prayer, the Grace, the Jesus Prayer, the Hail Mary. This is a reminder that words are the principal form of mediation in common prayer. Many of the words we use in prayer are scriptural in derivation, either directly or through biblically inspired prayers inherited from earlier traditions. They have the capacity to be immensely evocative, because prayer uses a register of language which is different even when it is not conspicuously archaic or unusual, for example, the opening address of the Collect for Purity: 'Almighty God, to whom all hearts are open, all desires known, and from whom no secrets are hidden' – a striking picture of God's knowledge of our innermost being (*Common Worship* (*CW*), 2000, p. 168). This is reinforced by the triplet – 'open', 'known', 'hidden'. Such forceful personification of God is a feature to be found again and again in different forms of prayer and memorably in the well-known post-Communion prayer, 'Father of all, we give you thanks and praise, that when we were still far off, you met us in your Son and brought us home' (*CW*, 2000, p. 182).

Words have often attracted the greatest criticism and dissatisfaction from participants in and commentators on liturgy. They are variously judged to be too old-fashioned, too numerous, too abstract or theologically rarefied, too conventional in their use of images, and too detached from their social or sociological context. These objections usually ignore the deeply scriptural character of prayer and its inherent linguistic and poetic inventiveness. Human beings are not born knowing how to pray and the importance of good models is incontestable. Not only do they assist us in giving shape to our own petitions, desires, fears and gratitude; they also give us a means of approaching God when our own resources have run out and our ability to voice our concerns has deserted us.

Prayer demands more than just our vocal and intellectual cooperation. It involves the whole embodied person. This means that posture and gesture have a special importance, despite the fact that they are often treated with indifference. Posture should be an aid to prayer and should entail conscious reverence. Uniformity helps to lessen distraction. A degree of physical comfort is helpful as a deterrent to fidgeting, but should not extend to casualness. Standing, kneeling and sitting; bowed heads, closed eyes, clasped hands; and making the sign of the cross all have their proper function in liturgical action and historical precedents exist for all three (Haselock, 2002a, pp. 227–9, 2002b, pp. 377–8).

There is a crucial difference between mere technique, and technique that is essential to the activity of worship. Patrick Prétot, a French liturgist, makes this clear: 'Gestures and postures reveal to men and women *that* they are before God, and *what* they are before God. It is by means of the body that human beings discover the true meaning of their being "before God"' (Prétot, 2006, pp. 18–19; my translation and emphasis). His concern with the role of the body, and especially of gesture, in public worship is a concern for what makes public worship possible. Liturgical gestures, he reminds us, belong to their own grammatical system, calling what might be thought of as an assembly of parts of bodies into relationship with God and with the gathered assembly. It is a matter of concern that the instinctive sense of what to do with one's body in worship, once taken for granted as something that liturgical participation taught the participants, can no longer be assumed (Prétot, 2006, p. 29). Prétot identifies three consequences of a vanishing familiarity with liturgical behaviour: the loss of a common memory; general uncertainty about how to behave in gatherings for public prayer; and the lack of any sort of gestural vocabulary that marks the transition from everyday life to a setting which requires concentration on the presence of God. How these matters are to be addressed presents a significant challenge to the churches.

In addition to places, words and gestures, there are more abstract elements which exert a profound influence on prayer, among which the desire to pray claims a pre-eminent place. As we noted at the outset, this desire is, paradoxically, God-given. Nowhere is this better expressed than in the Book of Common Prayer's collect for the Third Sunday after Trinity:

O Lord, we beseech thee mercifully to hear us; and grant that we, to whom thou hast given an hearty desire to pray, may by thy mighty aid be defended and comforted in all dangers and adversities; through Jesus Christ our Lord. *Amen.*

A second attribute demanded by prayer is persistence. It is commended to the disciples by Jesus, who 'told them a parable to show that they should keep on praying and never lose heart' (Luke 18.1 REB), and is a theme of the spiritual tradition. Monica, the mother of Augustine of Hippo, set an example in many years of prayer for the conversion of her son (Augustine, *Confessions*, chs 3, 6, 8, 9).

Related to this is regularity. Prayer is a habit, a part of the rhythm of our being. Many people find that it is much easier to pray with others, and consciously seek the opportunity to meet a group to say a daily office at a fixed time. In such settings, the human dimension will take on its own importance as worshippers learn to recite at the same speed, to respond to other voices, and to recognize one another's mannerisms – even their footsteps as they enter the place of worship. Others will find the discipline of regular private prayer a powerful source of spiritual sustenance and an important way of preparing for the activities of the day or for reflection at the day's end. Ideally, a combination of the two is highly desirable.

PUBLIC PRAYER: FORMS AND PATTERNS

'Worship summons the Church together, making it visible', observes Bryan Spinks (Spinks, 1991, p. 101). This is a succinct definition of what the Church is about in its various gatherings for the purpose of prayer and worship. The field is wide enough to accommodate forms and expressions ranging from an early morning celebration of Holy Communion attended by a few people in a small country church, to a non-eucharistic praise service in a city-centre setting where there is no resident community but a large gathered congregation, to the stately dignity of Choral Evensong in a cathedral. To this might be added worship in schools and house groups.

Until the middle of the twentieth century, the dominant Anglican experience of public worship would have been Sunday Matins and Evensong (Morning and Evening Prayer) and on some, but not necessarily all, Sundays, Holy Communion (possibly called the Eucharist, the Lord's Supper or the Mass, depending on local preference). Since the 1960s, an ongoing programme of liturgical revision has reshaped practice in all the mainstream churches. Concern for structure as well as words has recognized wider possibilities for worship, with the result that 'services of the word', family services and other more or less formal configurations might form the principal act of worship on a Sunday. It is now recognized that shape and structure are as influential as word and image in creating the habit of prayer, and much attention has been given in recent revisions to raising awareness of the structure of liturgical rites.

In addition, the pastoral offices of baptism, funeral and marriage draw people together intermittently to pray in response to what may be termed 'life events'. Responses to national events, such as royal jubilees and military anniversaries, and to natural disasters and violent crimes which have local and global repercussions are more and more often the motive for acts of public prayer. The media offer a further range of forms of participation in worship, from services broadcast on radio and television to daily prayer feeds available on the Internet.

The daily offices follow patterns developed to a large extent by monastic communities, though as Paul Bradshaw's research has shown, monasticism did not have exclusive purchase on daily prayer (Bradshaw, 1995). The writer of Psalm 119 says, 'Seven times a day I praise you' (Psalm 119.164), and this applies to all who approach God in prayer. But from a very early stage monastic communities took this aspiration seriously as the pattern for their own offices through the 24-hour cycle. The writer of the *Didache*, a first- or second-century treatise on prayer and worship, enjoins his audience of lay Christians to pray the Lord's Prayer three times a day (*Didache* 8.2–3, in O'Loughlin, 2010). The importance of a praying community is that prayer goes on, even when individuals do not have a uniformly regular habit of attending.

In current practice, the Eucharist has become the standard experience of public worship for the majority of churchgoers. Guiver suggests that ecumenical developments since the Second Vatican Council, which closed in 1964, have 'come to acknowledge the Eucharist at the centre of the church's life and prayer, with a renewed highlighting of baptism as a model for our discipleship and source for reflection on it' (Guiver, 2002, p. 381). The inexhaustible meditation on the Paschal Mystery, entailed in obeying the command to 'Do this in remembrance' and to 'proclaim the Lord's death until he comes' (1 Corinthians 11.23–26) is its motive, its shape and its object. The emphasis is on *sacrament* rather than on *word*, although the reading and preaching of Scripture in the Eucharist should not be undervalued.

There are no spectators at acts of worship. Common prayer creates opportunities for worshippers to occupy a variety of roles. Properly interpreted, it is led, orchestrated and directed by people with defined roles, whose task is to enable the role of the assembly as worshippers to be fully expressed. Clergy and worship leaders act as directors, animators and choreographers of prayer, which is always the action of the whole assembly (Guiver, 2009, passim).

THE SUBJECTS, GENRES, ORDERS AND SHAPES OF PRAYER

Christian prayer is often categorized under five headings: praise, petition, intercession, confession and thanksgiving. These groupings usefully describe the genres of prayer used in public worship, which customarily includes corporate confession of sin, followed (in Anglican and Roman Catholic practice, if a priest is present) by absolution; prayers of intercession and petition which may combine prescribed and newly composed or extempore forms; prayers of thanksgiving, which include eucharistic prayers and prayers over baptismal water; and praise in the form of hymns, psalms and canticles. The invitation to confession which introduces the Book of Common Prayer's Orders for Morning and Evening Prayer sums up the various functions of prayer. Our purpose, 'when we assemble and meet together', is

> to render thanks for the great benefits that we have received at [God's] hands, to set forth his most worthy praise, to hear his most holy Word, and to ask those things which are requisite and necessary, as well for the body as the soul.

Not all public worship uses prescribed prayers. Many Free Church and charismatic gatherings place the highest value on the inspiration of the Holy Spirit and may in certain circumstances be suspicious of forms composed and handed down. In such settings, spontaneity and freedom are taken as an index of sincerity and integrity. Some churches, the various branches of the Methodist Church, for example, have an authorized worship book but do not make its use compulsory. The Church of England and its sister churches in the Anglican Communion have operated a mixed economy since the first stirrings of revision in the 1960s and are now accustomed to a generous provision of authorized material for worship, amplified by an increasingly wide range of approved resources.

Orders for public worship, where they are provided, divide into two categories: fixed prayers and variable prayers. In the case of the Eucharist, the terms 'ordinary' and 'proper' are used by Roman Catholics and Anglicans to distinguish what is laid down for use each time the assembly gathers, and what varies according to seasons and festivals. In practice, even fixed prayers will now be available in several options. Thus the *Common Worship* Order One eucharistic provision offers eight eucharistic prayers.

What are the basic ingredients? Anglican practice insists that a form of confession be included in public worship. In places where the same group of people gathers regularly, it is likely that the same form, or at least a very small range of alternatives, will be used on most occasions. This would also be true of the Eucharistic Prayer, the congregational post-Communion prayer and, through much of the year, the final blessing.

The prayer that has varied week by week from a very early stage in the formal organization of the liturgy in the Western Church is the collect, the short prayer, usually including a single petition, which concludes the entrance rite. In addition to the provision for each Sunday through the year, collects are provided for festivals and saints' days, and a number of alternatives, authorized and otherwise, are now available. At Matins and Evensong, each of which in its Prayer Book forms has two invariable collects at the conclusion, this variable prayer, the 'collect of the day', is said before the other two.

While Sunday collects are not thematic or particularly related to the lectionary (certainly where the *Revised Common Lectionary* is used), there is an obvious case for thematic compositions when it comes to the seasons of the Church's year and the holy days. The Prayer Book Anglican tradition did not use variable post-Communion prayers, although the early sacramentaries from which many of the collects are derived had parallel sets of post-Communion prayers and prayers to be said by the priest over the gifts before the Eucharistic Prayer commenced. The practice of using a post-Communion prayer has been recovered in recent revisions.

Another variable element is the proper preface, inserted into the Eucharistic Prayer for seasonal and festal occasions. This is optional and not compulsory. The Church of England and the Anglican Church of Australia are unusual in providing long prefaces as well as the short prefaces used elsewhere in the Anglican Communion. Long prefaces, a number of them translations from the *Roman Missal*, replace entirely the section between the opening dialogue (*Sursum corda*) and the Sanctus. Short prefaces add a paragraph to the common preface, immediately before the Sanctus. Some of these are examples of particularly striking and moving liturgical composition. They draw on Scripture and on the riches of early Christian writing to offer a level of theological interpretation which respects the aesthetic as well as the didactic concerns of liturgical prayer. Take the example of a section of the extended preface for use from Christmas Day until the Eve of the Epiphany:

> In this mystery of the Word made flesh
> you have caused his light to shine in our hearts,
> to give knowledge of your glory in the face of Jesus Christ.
> In him we see our God made visible
> and so are caught up in the love of the God we cannot see.
> (CW, 2000, p. 303)

Prayers over the gifts, to be said at the preparation of the table, are optional and come in several variants, most of them based on ancient sources, Jewish and Christian. Final blessings have expanded considerably beyond the basic Prayer Book form:

> The peace of God, which passeth all understanding, keep your hearts and minds in the knowledge and love of God, and of his Son, Jesus Christ our Lord. And the blessing of God Almighty, the Father, the Son, and the Holy Spirit be amongst you, and remain with you always.

Seasonal and festal blessings now exist alongside collects, post-Communion prayers and prefaces. Some of them take a responsive form, often framed to emphasize the Trinitarian nature of God, and provide an alternative to a univocal conclusion pronounced by the priest.

INTERCESSIONS AT PUBLIC WORSHIP

Although every Christian is encouraged to intercede frequently for the needs of the world and other people, the space set aside for intercession in public worship creates particular imperatives. It merits detailed attention here, because, unlike collects, *preces* at the daily offices (versicles and responses deriving mostly from the Psalms), eucharistic prayers, forms of confession, post-Communion prayers and blessings, it is often the intercessions that provide scope for creativity within an otherwise mainly fixed liturgical order. Together with the public reading of Scripture, leading intercessions also offers a central and well-established role for lay members of the worshipping body.

Eucharistic Order One in the Church of England's *Common Worship* outlines five categories for inclusion in the intercessions, which are offered by an individual intercessor on behalf of the whole assembly:

The Church of Christ
Creation, human society, the Sovereign and those in authority
The local community
Those who suffer
The communion of saints   (*CW*, 2000, p. 174)

The same guidance would apply to any principal Sunday act of worship, and to other occasions when an act of public worship incorporates intercessory prayer.

Several models are offered, which tend to come in two varieties. The first is a continuous form, resembling the 'Prayer for the Church Militant Here upon Earth' in the Book of Common Prayer, which is said by a single voice and without interpolation. The second is the litany form, composed of biddings (invitations to pray for particular causes) with a response after each petition such as, 'Lord, in your mercy, hear our prayer' (*CW*, 2000, pp. 281–7). Both forms can be effective vehicles for addressing the range of subjects suggested for attention. The litany form offers the assembly some articulate participation and tends to state concerns in a concise way, while the uninterrupted form offers a fuller description of the objects of prayer. Several litany models can be found in *Common Worship: Daily Prayer* (*CW*, 2005), and there is a wide variety of published collections of intercessory prayers or outlines for their construction.

Preparation is essential, whether the intercessor is a member of the clergy or a lay member of the assembly. This should take account of the Church's year and the readings for the day as a way of keeping the texture of the act of worship consistent. The intercessor should be aware of current events, national and international, though avoiding treating these as informative prayer ('Dear Lord, as you know . . .'). Alertness to the local context is vital and the concerns of the church and civic communities should be recognized. The national church, its international sister churches, and its ecumenical partners are also part of the proper concern of the local church. National church bodies all produce cycles of prayer to be used throughout the year and it is the responsibility of those coordinating intercessions to keep current information to hand. The sick, the recently departed and those whose anniversary of death falls around the time when a set of prayers is being prepared should be mentioned by name. In places where prayer for the dead is controversial, a different view may be taken. Length is an important consideration, and the intercessions should be in proportion to the whole act of worship. Public prayer depends on the ongoing round of private prayer, which is able to lift up matters of concern to God in considerable detail. When the whole assembly gathers, there is a balance to be found between mere mention and excessive detail.

Stock phrases, such as 'places of conflict or tension', 'those less fortunate than ourselves' and 'those affected by the recent hurricane' must be used with care. On the one hand, they are a form of shorthand representing events about which the media will be supplying constantly updated information. On the other hand, they can be excessively bland and inadequate to the suffering undergone by people in the world's war zones, the poor, unemployed and homeless, and victims of natural disasters. They are best avoided if other solutions can be found.

It is not inappropriate to quote hymns or poems in public prayer, though much depends upon the choice of material, the skill with which it is woven into the prayers, and the competence of the delivery. Reading poetry is not like reading one's own scripted intercessions. For those who do write their own intercessions without consulting partly scripted models, the temptations of adventurous metaphor and startling expression are to be resisted unless the intercessor is very confident about their effect. Good examples of composition that is striking in the best sense are to be found in more recent collections of collect-style prayers, such as the *Opening Prayers* produced by the International Committee on English in the Liturgy (ICEL), Janet Morley's *All Desires Known*, and Steven Shakespeare's *Prayers for an Inclusive Church*. One clue to their success is to be found in the practice of seeking the inspiration for prayer in Scripture, and the translation of the Bible used in the composition of prayers is of considerable significance.

Music and singing may be neglected as forms of prayer. Many hymns have a markedly prayerful character, most often expressing praise and thanksgiving, but also at times assuming an intercessory or penitential character.

Public intercessions normally end with a prayer that asks God to accept and respond to our petitions, often invoking Jesus Christ as the mediator. It is therefore desirable that forms of intercession be shaped towards such a conclusion.

PRAYER AS COMMUNITY AND COMMUNION

As well as being an activity which can be isolated, defined and described, prayer is the texture, substance and mode of Christian worship. It is difficult to capture this in a word, which is why many commentators resort to poetry, quoting George Herbert ('Prayer, the Church's banquet, angels' age') or T. S. Eliot, or to contemporary figures such as R. S. Thomas and Carol Ann Duffy. At its best, prayer should bind and unite worshippers into a single body, one in heart and mind and will. In other words, prayer both expresses communion and creates communion. This is a description of a perfect world. In practice, and with fluctuating attendance patterns, lack of familiarity with prescribed forms, and minimal experience of unison recitation, the seamless, harmonious unity of common prayer can be hard to achieve. The definition of 'communion' and 'community' in any case goes beyond the gathered, 'traditional' Church at worship, to prayer groups meeting in other places, family prayers, and individuals whose faithful prayer connects them to others who pray in a way that transcends the conventions of place and time.

But these words have a still larger meaning. Amid all this variety the Church has a distinctive responsibility, a sacred duty, to go on trying to pray. This is because its worship strives to mirror the worship of heaven and to realize the bond that exists between the Church on earth and the Church eternally gathered in the presence of God – the communion of saints – with angels and archangels and all the company of heaven that is captured in the Revelation of St John the Divine and in the Letter to the Hebrews. This is the eschatological imperative of prayer. It expresses our temporal concerns, but as an activity it is not finite. Our prayer is constantly evolving to meet the circumstances of a particular people at a particular time. It is also part of an unbroken continuity, moving in harmony, an unseen and eternal community of 'angels and archangels, and the whole company of heaven' (*CW*, 2000, p. 185).

Further reading

Bradshaw, P. F. (1995), *Two Ways of Praying: Introducing Liturgical Spirituality* (London: SPCK).

Guiver, G. (2002), 'Prayer', in P. F. Bradshaw (ed.), *The New SCM Dictionary of Liturgy and Worship* (London: SCM Press), pp. 380–2.

Guiver, G. (rev. edn, 2011), *Company of Voices* (Norwich: Canterbury Press).

Haselock, J. (2002a), 'Gesture', in P. F. Bradshaw (ed.), *The New SCM Dictionary of Liturgy and Worship* (London: SCM Press), pp. 227–30.

Haselock, J. (2002b), 'Posture', in P. F. Bradshaw (ed.), *The New SCM Dictionary of Liturgy and Worship* (London: SCM Press), pp. 377–9.

Morley, J. (new edn, 2005), *All Desires Known* (London: SPCK).

Shakespeare, S. (2008), *Prayers for an Inclusive Church*, (Norwich: Canterbury Press).

Chapter 6

Word and sacrament

Liam Tracey OSM

INTRODUCTION

Contemporary reflection on the relationship between the word of God and the celebration of the sacrament has tended to ground this interaction in biblical theology, with its emphasis on the word of God as an event of God's self-communication to the whole of creation, and, more especially, in the revelation of the mystery of God in the person and ministry of Jesus Christ. The mystery of the risen Christ continues in the liturgical celebrations of the Church, where he continues to intercede and draw believers to himself in his praise of God. The word of God seen as a creative action, incarnated in the person of Jesus and carrying on in the liturgy of the Church, is foundational to a consideration of the interaction of word and sacrament. This understanding has largely been accepted by contemporary Christian communities after centuries of polemic between Reformed communities characterizing themselves, or being characterized by others, as 'the Church of the Word' and their Roman Catholic neighbours as 'the Church of the Sacrament'. It is quite remarkable how this fracture has been healed and that such a large measure of consensus now exists between Christian communities on the word of God as foundational to the sacrament which gives life and visibility to the same word.

In discussing the interaction between word and sacrament, it is important to clarify what is intended by this pairing. While the link between the two is seen as natural and obvious, it is not always clear what is intended by this phrase: from practical considerations of the correct balance between the Liturgy of the Word, with its readings, prayers and songs, and the liturgy of the Eucharist, with its great prayer and distribution of Communion, in any given Sunday celebration, to a perceived theological opposition between the two which requires some kind of theological reconciliation. Modern theologians have tended to stress that this relationship is more like a continuum than an 'and'. There are other relationships between word and sacrament beside the fact that the word is present in the liturgical celebration; this is usually denoted by the use of the phrase 'the Word of the Lord' and points to the use of Scripture as proclaimed readings, or prayer. This chapter will seek to articulate some of these relationships and suggest that the notion of continuum is a more fruitful one than an 'and' relationship. As Herbert Vorgrimler has noted,

> The Word of God is intensively involved in the sacramental structure: it causes what it perceptibly 'signifies', namely the grace of God through Jesus Christ in the Holy Spirit. Reflection on the salvific quality of the word of God begins, from the nature of things, with the holy Scriptures. It gives special attention to its Trinitarian origins: before time, the expressibility of God implies the eternal Logos who, as word of the Father, became human, and who is in one person, the promise of God to humanity and the acceptance of that word of promise by humanity. (Vorgrimler, 1992, pp. 76–7)

THEOLOGY OF THE WORD OF GOD

Any theological consideration of the word of God begins with an exploration of how we communicate and express ourselves as human persons. In order to communicate with others and indeed with ourselves, we require words. Who are we? What do we desire? What is important and of value to us? What do we believe in? What do we struggle with and find difficult? It is in this speaking of who we are, who we desire to be and who we are not that we come to be as human subjects. This is more than offering the hearer some notional information about me; it is the offer of who I am and who I strive to be. From this human experience of the word, an insight can be gained into the meaning of the word of God. The word of God is both communication about God, or more crudely put, information about God, and also communication of God's self, who God is for us. The communication of God is more than information but is a self-disclosure of God in human history and especially in the history of the Jewish people; Christians believe that God's self-communication happens in a unique fashion in the person of Jesus Christ, the Word of God.

The renewal of biblical theology in the twentieth century enabled a greater insight into the word as an event. If, in the past, theology has tended to focus on the objective content of the word as offering concrete information about something, biblical scholarship has focused on the creative, living and effective word of God. The word is powerful, living, forceful, an event of salvation, piercing, revealing, discerning (see 2 Thessalonians 3.1; Hebrews 4.12). This is rooted in the Hebrew *dabar* (word), which is not just an ordinary word but is an event, a deed; more than an expression of thought or a piece of information it is dynamic and active. This word, coming from the very mouth of God, shows forth God's will and power. This is the very word that created the universe at the beginning of time; it is the word that gives the law and directs the course of history towards fulfilment in God. In the course of the history of Israel it is perhaps most associated with the activity and ministry of the prophets. The prophet is one who has devoured the word and is called now to deliver it to the people; a word that challenges and consoles, that instructs and condemns, that builds up and tears down (Jeremiah 1.9–10). The word given to the prophet is dynamic and living, demanding to be proclaimed and creating the reality it announces.

This dynamic sense of word is carried over into the Greek *logos* of the New Testament. The ministry of Jesus is characterized by his preaching and teaching, not just in terms of instruction but his words are powerful and effect what he announces. His words expel demons, heal the sick and even control nature. His words are salvific; they reflect the very word of God. Scriptural scholars have noted how in the New Testament there is a movement from the preaching of Jesus to preaching about Jesus, or a word of Jesus to a word about Jesus. The word comes to signify not just the words of Jesus but the whole Christ event. It is in the Johannine tradition that this is seen clearly: Jesus is the very Word of God; filled with the Spirit, he is the saving Word of God, who witnesses to everything that he has seen and heard (John 3.34). He is indeed the Word of truth and life, the one through whom the glory of the Father is revealed.

God's creative word is an event, a moment and a person which reveals the purpose or plan of God for the whole of creation. In this sense, because the word is given and revealed in a mediated way, it is sacramental. The word is spoken to human persons who are in time and space, in particular historical moments with particular life histories and all the limits of human history. Renato De Zan has described this action as 'Scripture preserves the memory of the foundational saving Event. This Event is essentially Word' (De Zan, 1997, p. 36). But it is the very word that is spoken that allows believers in the power of the Spirit of God to see in these simple events and things the very mystery of God revealed and which invites a response. As Louis-Marie Chauvet has noted, language is no longer seen as an attribute but is the very ground of human existence.

> Like the body, language is not an instrument but mediation; it is in language that humans as subjects come to be. Humans do not pre-exist language; they are formed in its womb. They do not possess it like an 'attribute', even if of the utmost importance; they are possessed by it. Thus language does not arise to translate after the fact of human experience that preceded it; it is constitutive of any truly human experience, that is to say, significant experience.
>
> (Chauvet, 1995, p. 87)

The word of God comes in a language that human persons can understand and is mediated in a worldly way. The activity of Jesus, who gives himself for us in his life and words, is now continued in the words of the Church called to extend the message of salvation to all peoples. The word of God is given in words, sounds, metaphors, images and experiences, and human life is linked to the saving action of God through this self-communication of the divine. This is the drama of the Christian understanding of revelation: God creates in us a desire to hear the word spoken by God, but it is the human person who responds or not to this divine initiative.

Word and revelation are often used in an interchangeable way, but they are not the same, in that word implies content and revelation is an activity, but both tend to the self-communication of God; it is God who speaks, who unfolds a plan for the salvation of humanity. As the *Dogmatic Constitution on Divine Revelation, Dei Verbum* 2–3, notes, this is the person and mystery of God who offers salvation, not just ideas and abstract truths:

> This plan of revelation is realized by deeds and words having an inner unity: the deeds wrought by God in the history of salvation manifest and confirm the teaching and realities signified by the words, while the words proclaim the deeds and clarify the mystery contained in them.

This word heard must also be proclaimed; it is not given to be kept by oneself. In responding to the word heard, women and men are gathered and formed into the Church, a community built on the word of God, which is invited to communicate to others what they have heard. This word is offered in freedom; it can be accepted or rejected, but those who accept it are formed into the Church. 'In the hearing of God's word the Church is built up and grows, and in the signs of the liturgical celebration God's many wonderful, past works in the history of salvation are symbolically presented anew' (*General Introduction to the Lectionary for Mass*, 1981, p. 7). In hearing the word, the Church gives thanks, especially in the great action of thanksgiving that is the eucharistic celebration. The Eucharist by its nature sends those who hear the word in the celebration to bring the word constantly forward to those who have not heard or scarcely heard it.

> From the earliest days of the church, the reading of Scripture has been an integral part of the Christian liturgy, an inheritance to some extent from the liturgy of the synagogue. Today, too, it is above all through the liturgy that Christians come into contact with Scripture, particularly during the Sunday celebration of the Eucharist. In principle, the liturgy, and especially the sacramental liturgy, the high point of which is the eucharistic celebration, brings about the most perfect actualization of the biblical texts, for the liturgy places the proclamation in the midst of the community of believers, gathered around Christ so as to draw near to God. Christ is then 'present in his word, because it is he himself who speaks when sacred Scripture is read in

the church' (*Sacrosanctum Concilium* [1996], 7). 'Written text thus becomes
living word.'   (Pontifical Biblical Commission, 1993, pp. 307–8)

This text from the Pontifical Biblical Commission recalls that, first, the word
is Christ, the Word of God; he is the Word uttered by God and, taking human
flesh, reveals God's purpose and plan for humanity. Second, the word is codified
and announced in Scripture and, third, the word is proclaimed in the preaching
of the Church. The goal is always to proclaim the self-giving of God to humanity
and invite the full response of believers. This is a goal that will only be reached in
the fullness of God's time, when creation is fulfilled in God. Human utterances of
the word and human responses are always partial – there is always more; the full
reality and power of the word can only belong to the *eschaton*. This is the reason
why liturgical celebrations and especially the sacraments are important: God's
word, which is efficacious, reaches its fulfilment in the sacrament, and a human
response, while only ever partial, is called forth.

> When God shares his word with us, he awaits our response, that is, our listening
> and our adoring 'in Spirit and in truth' (John 4.23). The Holy Spirit makes
> our response effective, so that what we hear in the celebration of the liturgy we
> carry out in the way we live: 'Be doers of the word and not hearers only' (James
> 1.22).   (*General Introduction to the Lectionary for Mass*, 1981, p. 3)

It is in this context that an opposition between word and sacrament is seen not to
be true; the veracity of Augustine's comment that the sacrament is a visible word
is shown to be true. The word given is from God but responded to by humans;
it follows the human rules of communication and the human ability to create
signs and symbols to speak of life and experience. Don Saliers, a contemporary
liturgical theologian, puts it as follows:

> Christian liturgy, we have claimed, is the ongoing prayer, proclamation, and
> life of Jesus Christ – a sacrifice of thanksgiving and praise – offered to God in
> and through his body in the world. That is, Christian liturgy is our response to
> the self-giving of God, in, with, through the One who leads in prayer.
>   (Saliers, 1994, p. 86)

This rich sense of the word as an event, an encounter with the risen Christ, was lost,
largely when the Jewish sense of the word as an action and activity was forgotten,
as the Jewish roots of Christianity faded away. When the word comes to be seen
as the communication or transmission of intellectual truths and polemics rather
than a proclamation of what God has done in the past and continues to do in
this worshipping community today, the importance of the word is soon obscured
and seen as not even essential. As we will note later, it is only in the twentieth

century that this attitude is finally challenged and a more rounded sense of word and sacrament grows among Christian communities. The word is constitutive of the sacrament; one points to the other and always points back, hence the concern among liturgical reformers of the twentieth century to adequately reform the various lectionary traditions and to provide each sacramental celebration with its own proper lectionary. This is an integral element of the celebration and is treated in the *General Introduction to the Lectionary for Mass*. Chauvet offers a fine summary of this dynamic interaction of word and sacrament:

> The word of God does not reach us except through the sacramental mediation of the Scriptures read in church; conversely, the sacraments are like the precipitate (in the chemical sense) of the Scriptures as word. Of course, sacraments are rites, and we cannot understand them theologically without most carefully taking into account their ritual modality. However, although every sacrament is a rite, the rite becomes a sacrament only if it is converted by the word and the Spirit. (Chauvet, 2001, p. 47)

This leads us to a consideration of the sacrament and its celebration.

SACRAMENTAL THEOLOGY

If the various disciplines and divisions of theology are reflections on Christian practices, it is not surprising that a theological reflection on the liturgical celebrations of the Church is found. Traditionally this split in the general early modern breakdown of theology into various parts saw the sacraments being considered part of dogmatic or systematic theology, and the practice of liturgy as more akin to canon law and the art of rubrics. Medieval theologians and more especially those of a scholastic background began their consideration of the sacraments with a course or a treatise on the 'sacraments in general'. Only after they had explained what a sacrament was and, in their terms of matter and form, what made it valid, did they move on to treat the various sacraments. Their writings considered issues of validity, the effects of grace, the number of the sacraments and who could administer the particular sacrament. Little or no attention was paid to the history and development of the actual celebration or practice of the sacrament. The reformations of the sixteenth century sharpened the division between Christians and, while much of the reformers' theology is in continuity with late medieval thinking, a sharp divide opened in the realm of sacramental theology. Their suspicion of any rituals that seem to suggest humanity can make its relationship right with God led them to reject any sacraments that were not clearly instituted by Christ, and to insist on the primacy of faith. It is faith that opens the way to God's saving action in Christ. Chauvet has commented on the disastrous results of this split:

Although the distinction between word and sacrament is a legitimate one, their dichotomy has had disastrous results [although initiated] by the Reformers of the sixteenth century in the context of excessive sacramentalism, against which a reaction in favour of returning to the word is easily understandable

(Chauvet, 2001, pp. 48–9)

He goes on to caution against seeing the word as the source of true and authentic faith, while viewing the sacraments as magical or little more than superstition. This view forgets that the word is given to us through the mediation of a body of texts, which themselves are material, and are equally open to manipulation. It also exposes a dualistic notion of the word in opposition to the sacrament; all liturgical proclamations of the word have a ritual dimension, and the sacrament is a particular modality of the word.

Sacramental theology underwent a remarkable renaissance and reform in the twentieth century. Among the influences on sacramental theology and practice was the impact of the modern Liturgical Movement (alongside the earlier biblical and patristic revivals), and its call for full, conscious and active participation by the congregation in the celebration of the liturgy. Added to this movement are important writings on the sacraments by Karl Rahner, who moved a sacramental discourse away from a sacrament as thing to sacraments as symbols embedded in an event, and Edward Schillebeeckx, who sought to restore to sacramental theology the concrete experiences of contemporary men and women. Schillebeeckx introduced the language of personalism into sacramental theology, focusing attention on the sacrament as an encounter with Christ and requiring an embodied faith response. Finally in the twentieth century are the ritual reforms (which include the proclamation of the word of God as an essential element), set in train by the Second Vatican Council. The teaching of the sacraments themselves underwent a revolution. In many seminaries and schools of theology no longer were sacraments the domain of systematic theologians but they were now taught by liturgists from the perspective of liturgical practice; sacraments were first and indeed foremost actions of the assembled Church, celebrations of the Christian community gathered together by Christ in the power of the Spirit to give God glory, and they themselves are made holy. As Chauvet has noted,

Sacramental theology is the theory of a practice. Its object is the church's celebration itself. It has nothing relevant to say that does not stem from the way the church confers the sacraments. If one had always obeyed this golden rule many deviations would have been avoided.   (Chauvet, 2001, p. 48)

The sacramentality of Christian existence has once more become the foundation of sacramental reflection. Only in the last 25 years has a totally recast idea of 'sacraments in general' become again a fruitful topic for theological reflection, especially with Chauvet's work becoming more readily available in English translation. Along with the Italian theologian Andrea Grillo (2008), Chauvet has relocated sacramentality within the domain of fundamental or foundational theology; together with Scripture and ethics, he argues, sacraments form the kernel of Christian existence and identity.

THE WORD OF GOD IN THE LITURGICAL CELEBRATION

The best introduction to how the word of God functions in the celebration of the liturgy is to be found in the *General Introduction to the Lectionary for Mass* (1969) from the Roman Catholic tradition, which was expanded in the second edition of 1981. The first ten concise articles of the Introduction offer some general principles on the celebration and the significance of the word of God in the liturgy. 'That word constantly proclaimed in the liturgy is always, then, a living, active word through the power of the Holy Spirit. It expresses the Father's love that never fails in its effectiveness toward us' (*General Introduction to the Lectionary for Mass*, 1981, p. 4).

Not only does the word proclaimed return to what it was originally – a word – but, in the liturgy, the word is embodied in the person of the one who proclaims it in a definite time and place, a reader (lector), a deacon or a presbyter. It is embodied in the community who welcome the word, a community formed by this word and gathered together as an assembly by the same word. Key to understanding the interaction between word and sacrament is the Church, the gathered community celebrating the liturgy. This particular and concrete community has the gifts and the limits that being located in history brings; in this context the word is proclaimed and becomes a word for now, not just a word from the past with information about the past, but a word for today which challenges, consoles and constructs a community, a worshipping assembly, participating in the prayer of Christ in the power of the Spirit, the inspiration of the word that has gathered them together. Chauvet comments that one cannot exist without the other:

> Book and community are recognized as inseparable. The book is nothing without the community, and the community finds in the book the mirror of its identity. The norm is thus not the Book alone, but *the Book in the hand of the community*. The Church thus represents the impossibility of *sola scriptura*.
>
> (Chauvet, 1995, p. 209)

The biblical pericope or passage is taken from its original context in the Bible and moved to a new context: that of the assembly gathered to celebrate the liturgy. For Chauvet this is a return to the crucible of where the Scriptures came to birth. Thus, this change of context changes in some way the meaning of the text, and a new strategy of interpretation is required. The context is now one of prayer, song, non-verbal gestures and movements, and art works that may reflect the text proclaimed. This is alluded to in the *General Introduction to the Lectionary* 3 note 7:

> Thus the same text may be read or used for diverse reasons on diverse occasions and celebrations of the liturgical year; this has to be remembered in the homily, pastoral exegesis, and catechesis. The indexes of this volume will show, for example, that Romans 6 or 8 is used in various liturgical seasons and celebrations of the sacraments and sacramentals.

The changes are not just ones of context: they can also be the addition of words to the opening and closing of passages, the omission of certain verses, and breaks in the passages that do not always make sense to exegetes. This is particularly true of those churches that have a lectionary system where Scripture is organized in a different way from the Bible hermeneutic that is familiar in other Christian communities. This leads Chauvet to claim that

> [t]he Bible never comes into its truth as Bible as much as when it is read within the celebrating *ecclesia*. The latter is the premier sacramental milieu for the *a-letheia* (truth as uncovering) of the former; it reveals the Bible's invisible ecclesial essence, always in danger of being forgotten (*lethe*). Therefore, we can say in a completely literal sense that *the liturgical assembly* (the ecclesia in its primary sense) *is the place where the Bible becomes the Bible*.
>
> (Chauvet, 1995, p. 212)

CONTEMPORARY REFLECTIONS

Renato De Zan has argued that 'Scripture is for faith that celebrates': it is only in the liturgical celebration that the Scriptures reach their full expression. He recalls that a test for canonicity among early Christians was not only that the writing was held to be apostolic in origin; it also had to be read at a liturgical celebration. This is also forcefully brought out in the *General Introduction to the Lectionary* 4: 'Moreover, the word of God unceasingly calls to mind and extends the plan of salvation, which achieves its fullest expression in the liturgy. The liturgical celebration becomes, therefore, the continuing, complete, and effective presentation of God's word.' The unfolding of the liturgical year or the seasons of the life of the Christian community is marked by the proclamation of the word. How does the time of year or the particular circumstances of a given community add to our understanding of that word? Is there or can there be a celebrative hermeneutic of the word of God?

The many riches contained in the one word of God are admirably brought out in the different kinds of liturgical celebration and liturgical assembly. This takes place as the unfolding mystery of Christ is recalled during the course of the liturgical year, as the Church's sacraments and sacramentals are celebrated, or as the faithful respond individually to the Holy Spirit working within them. For then the liturgical celebration, based primarily on the word of God and sustained by it, becomes a new event and enriches the word itself with new meaning and power. Thus in the liturgy the Church faithfully adheres to the way Christ himself read and explained the Scriptures, beginning with the 'today' of his coming forward in the synagogue and urging all to search the Scriptures. *(General Introduction to the Lectionary*, 1981, p. 3)

This quotation is as good as any in explaining where the discourse on the relationship between word and sacrament is today for Christians. While some of the terminology may not be common, the inner dynamic alluded to is one that is shared across the divisions of Christianity.

The sacraments allow us to see what is written in the Scriptures, which is an imperative to be lived every day by individual believers and the whole community of the Church. It is precisely the sacraments that are the place of 'transition' from word to lived reality, of the move to mission and just living.

Further reading

Chauvet, L.-M. (1995), *Symbol and Sacrament: A Sacramental Reinterpretation of Christian Existence* (Collegeville, MN: Liturgical Press).

Chauvet, L.-M. (2001), *The Sacraments: The Word of God at the Mercy of the Body* (Collegeville, MN: Liturgical Press).

De Zan, R. (1997), 'Bible and Liturgy', in A. J. Chupungco (ed.), *Handbook for Liturgical Studies 1: Introduction to the Liturgy* (Collegeville, MN: Liturgical Press), pp. 33–51.

General Introduction to the Lectionary for Mass (1969; expanded 2nd edn, 1981) (Vatican City: Sacred Congregation for the Sacraments and Divine Worship).

Grillo, A. (2008), *Grazia visibile, grazia vivibile: Teologia dei sacramenti 'in genere ritus'* (Padua: EMP-Abbazia S. Giustina).

Pontifical Biblical Commission (1993), 'The Interpretation of the Bible in the Church', in D. P. Béchard (ed.), *The Scripture Documents: An Anthology of Official Catholic Teachings* (Collegeville, MN: Liturgical Press 2002), pp. 244–317.

Saliers, D. E. (1994), *Worship as Theology: Foretaste of Glory Divine* (Nashville, TN: Abingdon Press).

Vorgrimler, H. (1992), *Sacramental Theology* (Collegeville, MN: Liturgical Press).

Elements

Chapter 7

Language

Juliette Day

Worship is more than words, as the chapters on ritual and music in this volume make clear, but words dominate the worship event and they are often what remains in worshippers' memories when the event is over. Christianity has placed a great emphasis on words: Jesus Christ is the 'Word of God' made intelligible by the Incarnation; the gift of the Spirit was publicly demonstrated by the apostles' preaching in all the languages of those present; when, in the Gospels, the disciples ask Jesus how to pray, he gives them the Lord's Prayer as a text in itself and as a model for the content of prayer in general. Language is more than just the words themselves; at the very least, it is the combination of words (vocabulary) in conventional structures (grammar) in order to convey some sort of meaningful message. Our choice of language is determined by the mode of communication and by context: whether in speech or writing, to many or to one person, in the lecture hall or the playgroup, to someone we know or whom we do not know, and so on. In this chapter we will consider what is distinctive about the context of a worship event and how that affects the language used, and how language might function in worship, before concluding with some reflections on whether there is something which can be called 'liturgical language'.

LANGUAGE IN THE CONTEXT OF WORSHIP

As the focus of this volume is on public worship, primarily that using set liturgical texts, the language of private prayer will not be discussed, but it is worthwhile to ask whether there is, can or should be a relationship between the private and personal response to God in prayer and the public and communal formulae used in liturgical worship. For churches with set liturgical forms, the worship event has been prioritized as a communal activity in which we respond to God as the body of Christ and not as individuals, and this affects the way language is used in the authorized texts.

Collective speech

What distinguishes liturgical language from any other type of speech event in our culture is that it is collective speech; it is not the speech of an individual or of a collection of individuals, but it is the speech of a group. This has two stylistic effects: that in syntax, rhythm and vocabulary it may be easily spoken; and that the meaning conveyed has the potential to be assented to by all. It is normal in all churches, whether using a set liturgical text or not, for people to participate in liturgical events using words which they have neither chosen nor composed; in order to do so, they have suspended the very subjectivity which they may employ in everyday life in other cultural and social activities. The liturgy is shared prayer, shared speech, never the possession of an individual or a group composed of individuals asserting their individuality. But the responsibility for ensuring that this shared collective prayer may take place is not just on the participant, but also on the liturgical composers and leaders. Liturgical texts should preferably use language which can be easily spoken in a physical sense by participants, but they also need to employ language which the participants are able to say because they assent to its contents.

Spoken

Liturgical language is spoken, but the composers of texts have not used the style of language we might use in conversations between friends, or even in more formal situations, such as a public speech. Although texts are written for speech, they are not intended to replicate ordinary speech in the way that the script of a television soap opera may be; a closer parallel might be theatre – a much more stylized speech, but even that is neither like ordinary language, nor exactly like written language.

Contemporary worship, on theological grounds, has placed an emphasis on the 'full, active and conscious participation' in the liturgy by the people, and consequently comprehensibility and speakability have become key concerns in the provision of all liturgical texts, but particularly those for the congregation to speak. Congregational texts are usually intended for choral recitation, which, in order to avoid cacophony and barriers to participation, requires attention to rhythm, 'speakability' and opportunities to breathe, even before one attends to the accessibility of the meaning. 'Speakability', here, describes what remains when any barriers to physical speech are removed, that is, avoiding words of five or more syllables, or avoiding awkward sequences of consonants and tongue-twisters. Choral recitation also works much better when sentences are broken up into short phrases with a regular rhythm which can be easily memorized. The printed text may indicate when the congregation can breathe by presenting the text in broken lines with disregard to the normal written-language conventions, particularly the integrity of the sentence and punctuation. This can be most obviously seen in the text and performance of the longer congregational texts: the Gloria, Creed and Lord's Prayer. The latter, in particular, is most often recited with little regard to sentence construction and the pauses bear little relation to punctuation.

But, despite this injury to sentence construction, for the benefit of speech, liturgical texts do not reflect normal speech patterns: they avoid contractions such as 'isn't' and 'won't', inarticulate interjections like 'um' and 'er', and the sort of incomplete utterances that we find in conversations. When worship leaders depart from the 'script', such as in extempore prayer, intercessions or when giving notices about community events, then some semblance of normal speech patterns may return, although even here conventions about the type of language proper to each communication activity may displace normal speech. There is what may be called a 'formality' to what people are expected to say, even when using the contemporary idiom.

Distinctive, too, is the manner of speaking: choral recitation requires a much flatter intonation than one might use when reading aloud or speaking in other contexts. This flat intonation is also present when the minister speaks alone or an individual reads extracts from Scripture, even when there is dialogue or strong emotion. The speakers opt for clarity over meaning, corporate seemliness over personal expression: think what it might sound like if the congregation did, in fact, 'bewail [their] manifold sins and wickedness' as the general confession from the Book of Common Prayer suggests they ought. So, another feature of liturgical language is that the performance of the text may not be connected to its content or intended meaning.

In most acts of worship, the words which are spoken or sung have not been written by the speakers, and, unlike a play intended to be performed by professional actors, the speakers in worship are likely to be an extremely diverse group in terms of, for example, age, race, culture, education, regional accent. This poses particular problems for those charged with providing those words. They may choose a style of language close to contemporary speech patterns while still exhibiting some formality; or indeed, acknowledging that the language of the liturgy will always display features alien to a particular group at any one time, they may self-consciously adopt a style which is quite different from normal. Perhaps the recognition that liturgical language continually departs from everyday language, and of the attendant risks of losing comprehensibility, is indicated by the emphasis of historical as well as contemporary liturgical reform movements. Thus the Preface to the 1662 Book of Common Prayer justifies the changes from the earlier books because of the need

for the more proper expressing of some words and phrases of ancient usage in terms more suitable to the language of the present times, and the clearer explanation of some other words and phrases, that were either of doubtful signification, or otherwise liable to misconstruction.

THE RANGE OF COMMUNICATION ACTIVITIES

Not only are the speakers diverse in themselves, but liturgical worship also employs a very broad range of communication activities, and, despite these common features already mentioned, the form and style of language changes with each activity. First, ministers or leaders speak alone in addresses to God on behalf of the congregation or on their own behalf, or to the congregation; there may be dialogues with the congregation; the congregation as a whole or a single representative may address the minister, or each other or God. The purpose of the communication varies considerably: to praise God, to make requests, to express sorrow or joy, to convey instructions, to tell stories, to state beliefs. Even when the content may change from week to week, texts often follow established patterns (genres) which affect the way the information is presented and the choice of vocabulary; this is most clearly demonstrated by collects or eucharistic prayers or certain forms of intercession. Spoken texts can follow prose patterns, but texts intended for singing are often in metre where the music's demand for rhythm and rhyme may override even further normal syntactical conventions. In addition to music, the words may be accompanied by rituals which extend the meaning beyond what the words at face value indicate; an obvious example of this would be the Eucharistic Prayer, or, at baptism, where the meaning of 'I baptize you in the name of the Father, and of the Son, and of the Holy Spirit' can only be completed by a ritual action involving water. Such diversity might not even be found in the entire output of a speech radio station, but in churches it is contained within a single worship event.

Technical vocabulary

In common with all other groups in society, the Church employs 'technical language' either by using certain words or phrases which are not used anywhere else, or by giving a distinctive meaning to ordinary words. Examples of such technical vocabulary include theological terms like 'consubstantial', 'redemption', 'bless', but also ordinary words such as 'bread', 'cup', 'peace', 'man'. Additionally there are partially anglicized loan words from languages perhaps unfamiliar to the congregation, like 'baptize', 'Eucharist', 'presbyter', and so on, and it is not unusual for many diverse congregations to be comfortable with the Greek prayer *Kyrie eleison, Christe eleison, Kyrie eleison*.

Other 'exclusive' language exists because of the heavy borrowing of imagery and metaphors from biblical texts. These might be used in direct quotations, such as 'Holy, holy, holy Lord', in a modified form like the institution narrative in the Eucharistic Prayer which conflates the versions in the Gospels and 1 Corinthians 11, or just as allusions. Although the predominance of agricultural imagery may seem archaic in (post-)industrial societies, its presence is legitimate because it is drawn from the community's primary narrative, the Bible, which it owns and celebrates every time it worships. Attempts to provide contemporary imagery have had a polarizing effect: for example Richard G. Jones's 1968 hymn, 'God of concrete, God of steel', or the 1979 Eucharistic Prayer C published by The Episcopal Church in the United States of America (ECUSA), dubbed the 'Star Wars prayer' because of the thanksgiving for 'the vast expanse of interstellar space'. These are considered unusual. Liturgical texts employ, then, vocabulary and imagery which is not common in the surrounding culture but which is used without comment by worshippers because it is part of their culture infused by Scripture and their own traditions. But is this an indicator of a distinctive language, or simply a style of language belonging to a subculture?

In addition to vocabulary and imagery, worshippers employ forms of greeting which are unusual outside the worship context. Many liturgies begin by the minister addressing the congregation with 'The Lord be with you' to which the response is 'and also with you/and with your spirit', rather than 'Good morning' or 'Hello'. In English Anglican practice, this brings about the curious feature of the vicar 'greeting' the congregation at the church door after the service with 'Hello' and a handshake, where 'The Lord be with you' would be considered extremely inappropriate. And whereas it would not be considered appropriate to say 'Hello' to someone several times during a conversation, this liturgical address may be used three times in one service without attracting comment. Similarly, the liturgy may close with 'Go in peace', rather than 'Bye, then' or 'See you next week'.

Again unlike normal speech situations, the one addressed is almost always named in the liturgy, often with additional epithets. The most common form of the addressee is 'God', 'Father', 'Lord', to which can be added 'almighty', 'merciful', 'God of love', 'eternal'. The epithets may be doubled to produce, for example, 'Almighty and everlasting God', and then subordinate clauses may further elaborate the characteristics of the addressee, e.g. 'Eternal God, giver of love and power' (*CW*, 2000, p. 477). Only in liturgical texts is the distinctive form of address 'O . . .' retained, even in contemporary liturgical books. It is not just God, but worshippers too who are directly addressed and named in unique ways. The Book of Common Prayer, for example, contains some quite distinctive forms of address for the people, the best known of which would be from the opening to the Marriage Service: 'Dearly beloved, we are gathered together'. Modern English texts, though, have tended to remove such terms when these introductory paragraphs are revised, and worshippers are now often addressed impersonally. Thus the same text in the 1980 *Alternative Service Book* opens with 'We have come together' and so too in *Common Worship*, which, by and large, removed the prefaces. Such a change is more than simply about modernizing the language; after all one might easily expect partners to address each other with something like 'John, dear, pass me the newspaper'. Social and ecclesial changes are indicated where those present at a marriage service may well not be members of this or any worshipping community and thus an ambiguity is introduced about their place in it – can they truly be 'dearly beloved'? It is noteworthy that, in the disestablished Church in Wales, where these social pressures may be less acute, the most recent liturgical texts contain the address 'Brothers and sisters in Christ'. A further distinction between the forms of address in the liturgy and outside is the absence of 'politeness formulae' such as 'Would you be so kind as to', or the ubiquitous 'please' and 'thank you' of much British English; mostly absent too are deferential terms (Sir/Madam) used between the participants (a rare example might be any scripted exchanges between a deacon and a bishop in the orthodox liturgy), and formulaic terms of endearment which are used regardless of kinship – 'Dearly beloved in Christ', 'My brothers and sisters' and not 'Ladies and gentlemen', for example.

THE FUNCTION OF LITURGICAL LANGUAGE

In light of the entire worship event, what is it that language specifically contributes?

Articulates experience of God

Liturgical language is not just about God, but it is addressed to God and brings those who use it into the presence of God such that God may speak through the liturgy. These last two are not solely functions of the liturgical text, but are affected by the very gathering of the worshipping assembly as well as by non-verbal or non-scripted liturgical elements; however, we should not thereby ignore the contribution which language makes in this regard. The language we use in public prayer enables us, to a variable extent, to articulate our experience of God; it provides us with vocabulary for 'God-talk'. It may also provide us with a language for our own prayers, the manner of addressing God, or making petition; it presents to us attitudes to God and about the world which we may model in prayer and in our lives, attitudes of gratitude, praise, love, repentance, for example (see the chapter on Ethics). It is not surprising, then, that those charged with the provision of liturgical texts have such a challenging task, nor that their results prompt quite diverse and strongly felt opinions, precisely because the liturgical texts facilitate the personal as well as the communal relationship with God.

Makes present that of which it speaks

Liturgical texts are composed on the basis of theological presuppositions about God, about humanity, about the ordering of creation, about the relationship between people, and between people and God. Exclamations like 'Lord, have mercy' are not just requests made in hope and are not commands, but are pre-fulfilled requests made in the knowledge of God who is merciful, derived from promises in the Gospels and validated by the experience of worshippers or the community. Through language, distinctions between God and humanity are established. Traditionally, this was done by reserving 'Thee/Thou/Thine' for God after these forms had fallen out of use between people in spoken and written English, but even now certain epithets are reserved for God which are not used of humans or even heavenly beings – 'ineffable', for example. When used in the liturgy, an epithet like 'ineffable' does not describe God or conjure up God by clever wordplay; rather it asserts that the God who is present in the liturgy is recognized as ineffable, or immortal or almighty, and so on. These words restate for the community what sort of God it is who hears and answers their prayers.

Jean Ladrière has used the term 'presentification' for the way in which liturgical language makes present for the worshippers that about which it speaks. The words do not describe; they manifest, and thus for him they are endowed with a sacramentality because some of these words spoken now in the liturgy have the same efficacy as when they were spoken by Christ. Thus, in the liturgy through language, the Church makes assertions about a reality perceived by the participants; it wishes for that which it believes is achievable (healing or the kingdom of God, for example). Within the conditions created by the liturgy these things are true and real, and the liturgy creates the context where these can credibly be requested. To pray 'Thy kingdom come' presumes an existing notion of what the 'kingdom' is, to acknowledge its desirability and to place oneself within it; this kingdom exists already, but paradoxically will also come. To speak about it in the liturgy is, then, to make it a present reality. In worship, participants, both speakers and hearers, assent to the reality of what is said potentially or actually, whether or not they experience the fulfilment of what is prayed for or about.

Identity formation

The Church is established by its liturgy, primarily through the sacraments of baptism and Eucharist and through the normative status of Scripture. In worship the Church realizes itself, and Christians are formed. As words dominate worship, they do therefore become the means through which the community understands itself, worshippers create bonds between them, and individuals find articulated their place in the body of Christ. In certain secularized Western cultures, a worshipper's identity may be acutely formed and distinguished by the use of an exclusive language. The social linguist Tabouret-Keller has remarked that 'Members of a group who feel their cultural and political identity threatened are likely to make particularly assertive claims about the social importance of maintaining or resurrecting their language' (Tabouret-Keller, 1998, p. 318). The role of language in identity formation and preservation may well be the principal driver of the somewhat intemperate language debates in some churches. To maintain a preference for Church Slavonic, or Latin, or sixteenth-century English as the language for public prayer may well be about a reaction to contemporary society and/or its threats to the Church, rather than theological or aesthetic arguments. However, as we have seen in the earlier part of this chapter, even worship in a contemporary idiom uses language in distinctive ways which mark out the activities of the worshipping community from those outside the worship context.

IS THERE A LITURGICAL LANGUAGE?

Does the liturgy employ *normal* language in a specific way? Or, does the liturgy provide such a unique context that it has given rise to a *distinctive* language? Indeed we might also ask, and some have asked, whether communication with the divine requires a *sacred* language?

For many centuries the language used in worship was a 'given': for Anglicans, the Book of Common Prayer in a form of sixteenth-century English aimed at edifying the worshipper; the Latin of the 1570 *Missal*; Byzantine Greek and Church Slavonic for many Orthodox Christians. Those in other Reformation churches emphasized worship in the vernacular, which did not always mean using the most contemporary idiom. The renewal of worship in the twentieth century and the requirements for evangelism in secular Western societies focused attention on the comprehensibility of the language of worship, giving rise in the latter decades of the century to the translation and modernizing of historic liturgical texts, and the composition of new liturgical texts. For revisers, translators and composers, the questions just posed became key issues, and recently, with the second-stage revisions of the early twenty-first century (e.g. the 2011 *Roman Catholic Missal*, or the Church of England's *Common Worship*), the initial decisions about the language for the liturgy have been open to scrutiny and in many cases rejected. Probably the clearest statements about the principles to be adopted in translation (although the same concerns affect revisers and composers working in only one language) are found in two Roman Catholic texts: the *Instruction on Liturgical Translation (Comme le Prévoit)* issued by Pope Paul VI in 1969, and *Liturgiam authenticam* issued by the Congregation for Divine Worship in 2001.

In the former, 'The language chosen should be that in "common" usage, that is, suited to the greater number of the faithful who speak it in everyday use, even "children and persons of small education"', and the vocabulary was to 'normally be intelligible to all, even to the less educated' (*Comme le Prévoit*, 15). While not disagreeing with this principle, *Liturgiam authenticam* required that the liturgical texts should be 'free of an overly servile adherence to prevailing modes of expression' and that following the guidelines might lead to the development of

> a sacred style that will come to be recognized as proper to liturgical language. Thus it may happen that a certain manner of speech which has come to be considered somewhat obsolete in daily usage may continue to be maintained in the liturgical context. (*Liturgiam authenticam*, 27)

If we return to the questions posed just a few paragraphs back, these two brief quotations from lengthy documents present quite different responses: in *Comme le Prévoit*, the liturgy should use 'normal language in a specific way'; for *Liturgiam authenticam*, the liturgy is such a unique context that only a special language will do, which through use might take on the characteristics of a 'sacred language'. And although lacking the sort of clear authoritative directions of the Roman Catholic Church, these similar considerations are evident in the fruit of liturgical revisions by Anglicans, Lutherans and other Reformation churches over the last 50 or 60 years.

This chapter began by setting out what makes liturgical worship different from other communication activities; it is difficult to think of any other context in which these characteristics are displayed. Additionally too, it is not just that the words should be worthy of repetition on a weekly or daily basis, but that, whether they are worthy or not, they will be repeated. The words will be memorized and recalled by worshippers; they form a bedrock for individual and corporate spirituality and theology. By necessity, texts which are owned by a group are less fluid than our own speech, less prone to change, and thus the language of liturgical worship will always and necessarily be out of step with contemporary speech patterns and idiomatic use. This may not be problematic, so long as criteria such as edification, comprehensibility and participation are not compromised. This does not mean that the language should be turgid and prosaic, however; once these basic criteria are rejected or diluted, the issue ceases to be one of language choices, but is rather about the Church's vocation in the world.

Further reading

Comme le Prévoit: On the Translation of Liturgical Texts for Celebrations with a Congregation (1969), Consilium for Implementing the Constitution on the Sacred Liturgy (Vatican City).

Day, J. (forthcoming, 2014), *Reading the Liturgy* (London: T&T Clark).

Jasper, D., and Jasper, R. C. D. (1990), *Language and the Worship of the Church* (New York: St Martin's Press).

Ladrière, J. (1973), 'The Performativity of Liturgical Language', *Concilium* 9, pp. 50–62.

Liturgiam authenticam: On the Use of the Vernacular Languages in the Publication of the Books of the Roman Liturgy (2001), Congregation for Divine Worship and the Discipline of the Sacraments (London: Catholic Truth Society).

Ramshaw, G. (2001), 'The Pit, or the Gates of Zion? A Report on Contemporary Western Liturgical Language', *Worship* 75.1, pp. 12–19.

Tabouret-Keller, A. (1998), 'Language and Identity', in F. Coulmas (ed.), *The Handbook of Sociolinguistics* (Oxford: Blackwell).

Walsh, C. J. (2000), 'Minding Our Language: Issues of Liturgical Language Arising in Revision', *Worship* 74.4, pp. 482–503.

Chapter 8

Proclamation

Rosalind Brown

To proclaim is to announce, declare, make known, assert, broadcast or pronounce. There are many forms of Christian proclamation but, in the context of this book, the focus is on proclamation as expressed in preaching within the liturgy. That gives proclamation an immediate framework – people are gathered to worship God and are participating in the liturgy within which the sermon or homily is part of the proclamation of the word. This is not a speech or lecture where the attention is on the speaker, where the talk is perhaps the main item on the agenda and the reason people have attended; instead the sermon is a part of a larger whole that is focused on God and needs to fit seamlessly within the liturgy, drawing on its scriptural, seasonal or specific themes, being addressed to this particular congregation gathered for worship on this particular day.

What do we proclaim? Jesus came proclaiming that the kingdom of God has come near, and essentially we proclaim that God reigns; God's kingdom is coming. So the Church of England charges its priests with proclaiming the word of God and spells that out in terms of being called to be messengers, responsible to teach and admonish, to feed and provide for God's family, to guide God's children through the confusions of the world, to be formed by the word, to tell the story of God's love, to nurture new disciples in the faith, to unfold Scripture, to preach the word in season and out of season and to declare the mighty acts of God. In proclaiming the kingdom of God, doctrine and praxis meet, and our responsibility is to inhabit and interpret the larger Christian tradition for and with the people who have gathered to worship so that everyone is better able to fulfil the commission given at the end of many services to 'Go in peace to love and serve the Lord.'

The kingdom of God is incarnational – God has taken human flesh; Jesus proclaimed that the kingdom is at hand. So Christian proclamation is incarnational, related to daily life whether locally, nationally or internationally; otherwise we deny the mystery of Emmanuel, 'God with us'. We live in an ambiguous world – so beautiful and yet so broken – and preaching dares to enter and inhabit that ambiguity with the assurance that God is present. In that incarnational place, proclamation is about redemption – through the death, resurrection and Ascension of Jesus Christ we have been made children of God and, through the indwelling of the Holy Spirit, we are empowered to live holy lives. Indeed, Paul says that if Christ is not raised then our preaching is in vain and our faith is empty (1 Corinthians 15.14). So our preaching proclaims God's redemption in saving us and the Christian way of life to which we are called. The kingdom of God is also eschatological: there is more to come as we await the time when God's kingdom has indeed come on earth as it is in heaven. So we proclaim God's kingdom coming: we give an account of the hope that is set before us and hold out that overwhelming hope to others, letting that enlarged horizon shape life now.

PROCLAMATION IN THE CONTEXT OF LITURGY

Liturgy not only gives preaching a context – people gathered for worship; it also gives preaching a place within that worship which includes spoken words, music, silence, movement and symbolic action, all of which need to be taken into account by the person preaching. The sermon at the Eucharist comes as the climax of the Ministry of the Word, ideally followed by silence, leading to a response of faith (the Creed) and the Prayers of the People, before the Ministry of the Sacrament. That position is critical: proclamation of the word does not upstage the Eucharist, which is itself proclamation – of the Lord's death until he comes (1 Corinthians 11.26). The Ministry of the Word has established a framework through its fixed elements and through the hymns and readings for this particular day. It is jarring if the sermon goes off at a tangent, leaving people struggling to re-enter the liturgy that follows. So the Scriptures that have been heard are the catalyst and chief dialogue partner for the sermon which explores them, applying them in the life of this congregation and of God's wider world. In practical terms this means that the sermon interacts with the Scripture readings people have heard and with the wider context in which people have gathered; most of the time this is the ordinary life of this church in this locality, but it would have been a strange sermon on the Fourteenth Sunday after Trinity 2001 that did not take account of the events of September 11. So we consider everything – the Scriptures and the life stories we bring to the service – in the context of worship and interpret life in the light of Scripture, rather than the other way round. The role of the preacher is to bring all these elements together on behalf of the congregation and to offer, in the context of the liturgy, a message that proclaims the kingdom of God, is life-giving to those who listen, and gives them a way to respond and make what they have heard their own (remembering that what they have heard is not always what we have said).

Proclamation in the context of worship does not have to do everything in one go but is part of ongoing formation of the people of God. The liturgy can carry much that might otherwise be said in the sermon, and simply pointing people to that can be enough. If we are preaching regularly to the same congregation we can plan ahead and know what will save for future weeks, especially if the set Scriptures are a continuation of those set for this week. If we are preaching to a congregation that we will not meet again, we still do not have to do everything in one sermon; one or at most two themes from the readings are adequate; otherwise our hearers will get spiritual indigestion and we may go on for too long.

In Matins, Evensong and some Services of the Word, much Scripture has gone before the sermon, not just in the readings but also in the Psalms and Canticles (which are often proclaimed in song and might be proclaimed in a sermon occasionally), and the sermon comes as the climax of the service, something to be kept in mind in helping people to respond. Pastoral Offices are different again; at a funeral, the homily is shorter than a sermon, and the challenge is to make the homily personal but not a eulogy, and to proclaim the gospel of hope in the resurrection of the dead and comfort for the bereaved. Mourners listen for help in their grief in a way that few congregations gathered at other times listen so attentively to the preacher; in contrast, at some weddings the homily may be perceived as an irrelevance to be endured before the partying begins. In both cases, as at baptisms, the liturgy can do much of the work and may suggest themes or imagery to be picked up in proclamation.

Liturgy is the context of the sermon but, within that, there is also a form to the sermon to take into account. Fifty years ago the form was unquestioned: the preacher began from a text or a theme and constructed (the word is significant) a sermon with a recognized framework – perhaps three points, perhaps more, often with subsets of points. He would announce the text or theme and the conclusion to be drawn, and would then proceed to prove his point. The move was from universal truth to specific application and, depending upon the tradition of the preacher, there could be an element of teaching, of biblical exposition, of engagement with world and cultural issues, or of preaching for response whether expressed in evangelistic conversion or in moral reformation. But the destination of the sermon was never in doubt and the route to it was familiar to hearers.

Beginning in the late 1960s all that changed and there was a radical shift from the former deductive preaching (deducing the particular from the universal) to inductive preaching; 'inductive' being used, as in scientific experiments, to describe the movement from particular experience to general conclusion. The sermon shifted from being a tightly structured thesis proving a preannounced conclusion to a largely passive congregation to being a shared journey led by the preacher with the congregation as active participants who develop their own insights as the sermon progresses. The destination is not announced at the outset, so there is an element of discovery and, as in any journey, time for moving forward, time to pause and look at the view, time for recalling the route taken thus far. In this approach, theologically the locus of authority shifts from the preacher to the whole Church, as preacher and congregation interact together with the biblical text; hence the title of a book on preaching by Fred Craddock, one of the leaders of this shift, *As One Without Authority*. In the last 50 years there have been many contributions to the development of the inductive sermon, notably but not entirely from the USA. Other early contributors to the 'new homiletic' include David Buttrick who focused on rhetorical structures in preaching, Thomas Long who developed the idea of preaching as bearing witness and drew attention to the sermon's focus and function, and Eugene Lowry who shifted the focus from the text's contemporary meaning to the felt need of the hearers and identified five movements the sermon should make. Others, for example Richard Jensen, have stressed the need to recover narrative in preaching while Thomas Troeger has identified issues raised by society's shift to a multimedia culture. More recently, the distinctive contribution of African American preachers (for example, James Earl Massey) and women (from the UK, Susan Durber and from the US, Barbara Brown Taylor) have been heard and, post Vatican II, the Roman Catholic Church has given new attention to preaching (see the essays edited by Michael Monshau). The distinctive elements of many of these contributions are drawn together in my book, *Can Words Express Our Wonder?* (Brown, 2009, pp. 30–56). There are many methodologies and enormous scope for the preacher today to find his or her own voice within the overall concept of the sermon as a shared journey.

However, if the preacher no longer has the unquestioned authority once ascribed to him, epitomized in the idea of a man sounding forth in a pulpit six feet above contradiction, he or she retains responsibility for proclamation, and to that responsibility we now turn.

THE RESPONSIBILITY OF THE PREACHER

It is a big responsibility to be charged with proclaiming the word of God in the context of worship. The Church rightly looks to those it calls to ordained ministry not only for sound learning (which we need to develop in depth but should wear lightly in our proclamation) but also godly life. So proclamation asks us to be willing to grow in wisdom and not to settle for mere knowledge, however important that is. In this we follow the example of Jesus who grew in wisdom, and divine and human favour (Luke 2.52).

Proclamation is essentially communication. We communicate the gospel and so, while Paul could write, 'we do not proclaim ourselves; we proclaim Jesus Christ as Lord', he went on to say 'and ourselves as your slaves for Jesus' sake' (2 Corinthians 4.5). Although he was not the subject of the proclamation, he was active in it as a slave of his hearers because faithful proclamation is not an excuse for an ego trip or to get something off our chest but part of our service of God and God's people. Although preaching is an oral form of communication, and growing confidence and competence in speaking in public is part of ongoing ministerial formation, it is more than that. We all proclaim a message with our lives long before we open our mouths, and a major part of preparation to proclaim the kingdom of God is the way we tend our own lives day in, day out. People who have not met us before we enter the pulpit can read our body language, while people who know us well will filter all we say in the pulpit through what they see of us when we are out of it and, if there is dissonance, our lives will trump our words every time. Implicit in that is the need to be present in the pulpit with integrity, to be ourselves, not some persona we assume for 15 minutes, because otherwise the words we say will not ring true. We are called to be self-aware but not self-obsessed, people who say something to our fellow Christians that is worthy of attention without being attention-seeking. That brings the responsibility to know the gospel, knowing it in the biblical sense of knowing intimately, not only academically or knowing of it. A good preacher does not simply refer to Scripture but inhabits Scripture, unobtrusively day by day, so that the resulting sermons similarly inhabit rather than just quote or are clever with Scripture. That is the work of a lifetime, but it is a work to which we can and should give ourselves joyfully. For an example of proclamation that does this beautifully, in contexts ranging from small parish churches to Westminster Abbey, see Michael Mayne's sermons (Mayne, 2010).

All sermons need to be shaped by engagement with Scripture even if, when preached, they do not start from Scripture or refer to it pedantically throughout, and that engagement is the preacher's hidden responsibility. So, once we know which particular Scriptures we are to preach from, we need to immerse ourselves in them so that God can speak to us through them as part of our own ongoing formation. In one sense it does not matter if we never preach the sermon; we will still be being formed ourselves. But if we do preach a sermon then it springs from our own life with God. So it is good practice, starting perhaps three weeks before the sermon is to be preached, to read the Scripture passages through daily, aloud if possible because hearing the words adds a new dimension. That way we have time to inhabit them and let them inhabit us. We may be reading two or three sets of Scriptures for successive weeks at the same time, but no shaping of the sermon is needed at this point, just prayerful exposure to God through these particular verses from the Bible. Gradually we can bring into this prayerful dialogue with the Scriptures the people to whom we will preach and the world around us so that, nearer the time, possible sermon themes begin to emerge and ideas can be explored in more depth. In these early stages of preparation for proclamation, our responsibility is simply to be people who know and love Scripture and are ourselves formed by it. In terms of proclamation, it is our hearing afresh the good news we are to proclaim.

Faithful proclamation requires us to know and be comfortable with our tradition. That does not mean being unquestioning of it, but it does mean respecting it and being able to draw from it appropriately. The Anglican heritage of proclamation is a rich one, as are those of the other traditions, and we should be aware that each one of us worships and preaches within a tradition. The differences may be highlighted when someone from another tradition preaches in a church but, more fundamentally, drawing on the tradition in proclamation means we can access the corporate memory of the congregation – a memory that embraces both the tradition of the denomination, which may go back centuries if they have been exposed to it by wise preaching in the past, and also the tradition of that particular congregation, and build on both heritages for their future hope. There are rich resources in the Christian tradition for preachers, and our libraries should include well-read copies of spiritual classics old and new. Keeping a file of quotations is essential for preachers; it used to be called a Commonplace Book and written carefully by hand but now can be a computer file that is added to every time we read something that strikes us as worth saving for future reference.

In addition to familiarity with Scripture and tradition, people charged with proclamation need to stay abreast of what is happening in the world to which God's kingdom comes. While sermons are not commentaries on the latest news, people who are preaching should always listen to the news before preaching in case there is something new of import that will be distracting the congregation. This can be addressed in more depth in the prayers but may need to be acknowledged in the sermon by a brief reference, even if the sermon is not primarily about that. In doing this, we indicate that we are all at the same starting point; otherwise our hearers will be lost in their own thoughts and will not come with us on the sermon's journey. If proclamation is to be incarnational we also need to know this particular congregation – not every personal situation that people bring to church each week, but well enough to supplement pastoral knowledge of individuals with informed guesses about what is going on in their lives based on knowledge of the wider local scene, including the local economy and significant local events. Leonora Tubbs Tisdale has written helpfully on this. Again, we do not have to preach directly to that situation every week, but knowing our hearers will shape our interaction with Scripture during our preparation. People will know, without us telling them, if we have been faithful in our preparation on their behalf and can help them to make connections for themselves between God's kingdom and their lives when they go from worship to serve God in the world.

As people called to proclaim God's kingdom, we are also responsible for ourselves; so is God's kingdom coming in our lives? Are we being nurtured or burning the candle at both ends? What brings us joy in life? What stresses are we facing that take up more of our energy than usual? Do we know and are we comfortable with ourselves as people? David Schlafer's workbook, *Your Way with God's Word*, can help us to find our own preaching voice which is distinct from that of others but within the long tradition of people called to proclaim the kingdom of God.

Knowing our preaching voice can help us to work with it and also to recognize and address our blind spots and weaker areas.

Sometimes sermons just 'come' easily and we feel that we have something to say to the congregation that has life and joy in it; at other times we have to struggle to form a sermon and it feels more like a duty that has to be fulfilled – we have to stay with the hard work of preparation and then trust that God will somehow take our faithful efforts and make more of them than we imagine to be possible. And that, of course, is the factor that distinguishes preaching from any other form of public speech: God is involved; this is proclamation in the context of worship where God is present and active. Most preachers can tell of sermons that felt dry, if not lifeless, to them, for which someone thanked them afterwards because God brought them life through a part of it. This is not an excuse for shoddy sermon preparation, but a glorious reminder that we proclaim the gospel of a gracious God who takes and uses our human efforts in ways we cannot imagine.

Words matter immensely in proclamation: they are the raw material available to us and we can listen to words with discernment and an inquiring spirit into how other people use them to best effect, so that good words come more easily to us. It is our privilege to clothe God's word in human speech of the twenty-first century, choosing wise and evocative words that allow it to pulsate in the world today. God is gracious and the words we use to speak of God should be gracious and beautiful. We can relish words and meanings, and a good dictionary and thesaurus are essential tools because we cannot settle for the mediocre or merely functional in our choice of words; it is good practice to check sermons for dull words and find replacements that make the sermon sparkle without being obscure or verbose. Poetry exposes us to words used carefully for full effect, often evoking images and ideas that pedestrian language would stifle. Well-written novels are another source of inspiration; two that are beautifully written and have the bonus of being about a life given to preaching are Marilynne Robinson's *Gilead* and its sequel, *Home*.

Imagination is a significant gift in proclamation; we can let our imagination loose on Scripture, on the world in which we live, on the people who will listen. We can enter imaginatively into worlds that are not our own, walking in another's shoes and experiencing the world differently; we can explore new perspectives on the familiar, for example by giving attention to minor characters in a story or noticing things we normally just glance at; we can, as Emily Dickinson wrote, 'Tell the truth, but tell it slant'. However, our imagination needs to be yoked to Scripture and tradition rather than being given totally free rein, and it is wise to check that the sermon and the rest of the liturgy do not undermine but instead shed new light on each other. Music can interpret words in new ways, transcending the intellect as, in worship, we stand on the edge of mystery.

Preaching is oral communication, and the insights of rhetoric, which are being recovered in part thanks to President Obama's rhetorical skills, can help us to say what we want to say in a way that will have an impact. We should not fear that rhetoric will demean or dilute our proclamation of the gospel. When we write the sermon, we write for speech, not for a research paper or Twitter, and there are practical considerations about writing for speech which draw on the insights of rhetoric both in the structure of the whole message and the details of sentences (Brown, 2009, pp. 170–4). The greatest content is rendered powerless unless we can entice people to listen and come with us on the sermon's journey. For books that provide an overview of how to prepare a sermon, see works by Rosalind Brown, David Day, John Killinger and John Stott.

When people gather for worship and to hear the word of God proclaimed in that context, their eyes are gazing on God. The role of proclamation is to help them focus their gaze, to draw closer to God, to be guided in what to believe and what to hope for as Christians, to be strengthened for life in the coming days, to help them grow in holiness and godly living. Taking our cue from the Old Testament prophets and from Jesus, sometimes proclamation is primarily pastoral and sometimes it is prophetic, but very often it is both together, because without the pastoral element we cannot connect with our hearers and without the prophetic element we deny them the opportunity of transformation. That takes us back, full circle, to where we began: proclamation in the context of liturgy takes the words of Scripture, interprets and applies them for this particular congregation gathered to worship God in this particular place on this particular occasion, and leads them further on their journey towards the knowledge and love of God and thus to transformation and increased maturity in their Christian lives.

> What can we say? Can words express our wonder?
> How shall we live? Can we reflect your grace?
> Come Spirit, come, disturb our cautious living,
> be known in us, your human dwelling place.
> (Brown, 2009, p. 189)

Further reading

Brown, R. (2009), *Can Words Express Our Wonder? Preaching in the Church Today* (London: Canterbury Press).

Day, D. (1998), *A Preaching Workbook* (London: SPCK).

Day, D. (2005), *Embodying the Word: A Preacher's Guide* (London: SPCK).

Mayne, M. (2010), *To Trust and to Love*, ed. J. W. Huffstetler (London: Darton, Longman and Todd).

Robinson, M. (2006), *Gilead* (London: Virago).

Robinson, M. (2009), *Home* (London: Virago).

Taylor, B. B. (1993), *The Preaching Life* (Cambridge, MA: Cowley Publications).

Chapter 9

Ministries

Thomas O'Loughlin

At first sight, the issue of 'liturgical ministry' would appear to be simple. Every religion, and every Christian denomination, has religious leaders, and these take the leading roles at its rituals. Thus we talk about 'priests' in various religions, and, even in a religion like Islam where the term has no strict meaning, we still speak about 'Muslim clerics'. Moreover, ritual requires expertise, and the amount of expertise required is usually a direct function of the length of the group's remembered tradition. These experts, nowadays usually formally trained, are its liturgical ministers. Thus a presbyter in an Eastern Orthodox Church needs to know about a complex ritual harbouring elements that have grown up over a period of perhaps 1,700 years; the leader of a contemporary Western evangelical church, while eschewing any inherently sacral status, still needs to claim special expertise as a biblical teacher. Such expertise is then seen as the empirical basis for ministry (either parallel with or apart from some notion of authorization such as 'ordination'), and then those experts 'minister to' the other church members, by either carrying out the rituals, leading the group in its liturgies, or acting as its teachers during worship. In each case there is a binary model at work: a sole minister or small ministry group which acts, leads and preaches/speaks/teaches on one side, and opposite them a much larger group which attends/listens/receives ministry. We see this model in a nutshell in the statement 'The clergy administer the sacraments', or the funny pub sign with the parson alongside other functionaries and the label 'I pray for all'. This is a valuable and widely appreciated model because it fits well beside other expert service providers in society (e.g. medics providing healthcare to the rest of the community or accountants providing financial services), and, therefore, full-time 'ministers of religion' are aligned by society, and often by themselves, with those other experts. And, indeed, trained ministers do have a great deal of expertise, honed by experience, in comparison with most other church members, and this, coupled with a service ethos, thrusts them into leadership positions such that ministry takes on the shape of 'active' giving by leaders, while the rest are 'passive' receivers. The dynamics of ministry in the liturgical space are, therefore, not unlike the dynamics of actors/audience in a theatre: both groups are participating, one by giving a performance, the other by receiving and responding to it. Moreover, in society many tasks are carried out on behalf of the whole group by a specialist cadre (e.g. politicians or police) and the small group acts with deputed authority; a religious variant of this can be found in the notion of a 'priesthood' or a 'clergy' in many religions which have a specialist temple personnel (e.g. the Levites in ancient Jerusalem). Thus, because society needs a 'chaplaincy' service, we have a justification of clergy and of their liturgical ministry within society. This kind of justification for ministry is now rarely proposed by Christians when living in multicultural situations, but was widely used when they imagined their societies as homogeneously Christian.

For Christians, in stark contrast to such highly structured notions of ministry or priesthoods are the memories of the first disciples of Jesus. Jesus was not a Levite, his ministry barely engaged with the formal religious expert systems, and, when those structures are recalled (e.g. Luke 10.31, 32; John 4.21), they are the objects of criticism or presented as transient. Moreover, while Jesus was presented as appointing messengers/preachers (apostles), there is no suggestion that these were thought of as liturgical ministers. And, while leaders emerged in the various early churches (with a variety of names, e.g. 'elders' (*presbuteroi*) or 'overseer-servants' (*episkopoi kai diakonoi*), which was originally a double name for a single person, but which later on would divide into two ranks: 'bishop' and 'deacon'), it took generations, until well into the second century in fact, for those patterns to be harmonized between communities and then systematized into authority structures. There is no suggestion in the first-century documents that leadership at the two key community events, baptism and Eucharist, was restricted in any way or the preserve of those who were community leaders, much less a specially authorized group. The link between leadership of the community and presidency at the eucharistic meal (a linkage that would drive much later thinking on ministry, and even today is a major source of Christian division) would not be forged until the third century, and only later again would 'the history of its institution' by Jesus be constructed. Even more explicit was the remembered teaching upon leadership in the community where there was to be radical equality among church members, for example in this story:

And Jesus . . . said to them, 'You know that those who are supposed to rule over the Gentiles lord it over them, and their great men exercise authority over them. But it shall not be so among you; but whoever would be great among you must be your servant, and whoever would be first among you must be slave of all.' (Mark 10.42–44 RSV)

This vision of equality is also found in the third 'do this' story in the Gospels (the other 'do this' commands relate to baptism and the Eucharist) in John 13.3–15 where the relationship of leaders in the community is modelled on that of washing the diners' feet by Jesus, a task normally done by a female slave. Significantly, this action, despite the injunction in John 13.15, did not develop into a regular community practice. The followers of Jesus were to be a 'priestly people' (1 Peter 2.9: 'a priestly kingdom' (*basileion hierateuma*; my translations)) where all shared by baptism in Christ who was uniquely their priest (*hiereus*) (Hebrews 2.17).

This tension between, on the one hand, the empirical need for organization within groups, coupled with the fact that power tends to concentrate and to be seen as a sacral faculty – a development facilitated by using a combination of Old Testament models and terminology and cultural assumptions taken from Graeco-Roman culture (e.g. *pontifex* or *ordo*), and on the other hand the memory of what distinguishes the new priestly people in Christ where ministry was both more embracing (the whole community is the minister) and less structured (each can potentially take on any service for the others), can be seen as underlying all the later disputes about ministry and priesthood. Those disputes, which still continue for many Christians, were made all the more intractable by the conviction on each side, in each dispute, that an explicit answer could be derived from their authoritative foundational sources.

It has long been an illusion of the various Christian denominations that a study of history – and particularly the first couple of centuries or the texts from those times they held to belong to the New Testament canon – could provide either a blueprint for ministry (e.g. 'the threefold structure of order': bishop, presbyter, deacon) or a conclusive answer to questions relating to ministry that have arisen in later situations; for example, what 'power' can be seen as coming from Christ to the priest at the time of the Reformation, or whether a woman can preside at the Eucharist today. This is an illusory quest, for not only does it fall victim to the anachronism inherent in all appeals to a perfect original moment, a much-imagined period in the past when all was revealed (at least *in nuce*), but it assumes that ministry as it later developed was not itself the outcome of multiple, often conflicting, forces in the particular societies, as well as adaptations by Christians to well-known inherited religious structures. So, for example, the clerical system, within which was/is located liturgical ministry, for much of Christian history related originally to the political needs of the Church as a public body within the Roman Empire; and as that imperial society had highly organized priesthoods, so people took it for granted that similar groups would exist in the Church. Likewise, the monastic elements that became linked with liturgical ministry can be seen as a result of the place of monasticism as the ideal of holiness in late antiquity; while the notion of 'hierarchy' (i.e. sacred power descending through intermediaries from higher to lower levels of reality, such that the holier leader (the 'hierarch') offers sacrifice 'on behalf of' or performs liturgy *for the others* as an effect of his special election and superior powers) can be seen as the result of fitting Christian theology within a Neoplatonic world view within a rigidly layered social environment.

Given that there was no 'original' plan for liturgical ministry in the Church, and as a result of centuries of disputes there are many conflicting views of what constitutes someone within ministry, it is quite impossible – except within the mythic spaces of particular denominations – to produce a systematic basis for liturgical ministry. However, given that ministry occurs and is needed, one can set out some criteria which can help individuals and communities to develop a pragmatic theology of liturgical ministry. A balanced approach, both in practice and theologically, needs to take account of five factors.

First, every specific ministry is a particular variation of the ministry of all the baptized, and in baptism there is a radical equality: 'There is neither Jew nor Greek, there is neither slave nor free, there is neither male nor female; for you are all one in Christ Jesus' (Galatians 3.28 RSV). This radical equality is a characteristic of the new creation brought about in Christ; therefore, any subsequent distinctions such that particular ministries are not potentially open to every baptized person are tantamount to a defective theology of baptism by which all ministry is brought into being. It is baptism that constitutes the people who manifest the work of the Christ in the world.

Therefore, making further demands for 'signs' of particular divine election (e.g. being able to speak in tongues or handle snakes) as indications of suitability for ministry fly in the face of the incarnational dispensation seen in baptism. Likewise, regulations that restrict ministry to particular states of life (e.g. demanding celibacy as a condition for the presbyterate in the Roman Catholic Church or for the episcopate in the Orthodox churches) have to be seen as an undue concern with the status of certain ministries, implying that baptism is merely some basic entry requirement for 'Christianity' rather than that which creates the new person who can minister, and in that new creation no such distinctions exist. Similarly, the notion that women, as such, can be excluded from ministry on the basis of some pragmatic historical appeal (e.g. 'Jesus did not ordain women' – assuming such a pre-critical view of 'history' has any value) fails to take account of the fundamental role of baptism in all Christian existence and action. The slogan 'If you cannot ordain 'em, you shouldn't baptize 'em' may seem crude, but it does capture the fundamental insight that incorporation into the risen Christ (i.e. baptism) is the source of all liturgical ministry and of every particular act of liturgy.

Second, it must respect the awareness that all action and ministry by Christians is *Christ*-ian in nature. Christians form a people – they are not simply a collection of individuals – and this is a priestly people because it acts in union with its unique High Priest, Jesus. It is the work of the Christ in blessing the Father that constitutes the reality of liturgy of the New Covenant, and the worship of the disciples is only *Christ*-ian liturgy in so far as it is through, with and in Jesus. So individuals do not offer praise and petition except as part of the community, and the community only does so in so far as it acts in Christ. This fundamental dynamic becomes actual in the liturgy of particular gatherings. It is as a church, a real community, that we gather to celebrate our common meal of thanksgiving, and it is the church which blesses the Father. This desire of the assembly is given voice by the one presiding within the community, and this prayer of thanksgiving is made in, with and through Jesus who makes us his people in the presence of the Father.

We all too often, and too easily, lose sight of the fact that Christians must think of their liturgy in a way that is radically opposed to that commonly found in other religions, of a 'religious service' due to God or the gods. In that paradigm, the divine is the opposite of the world in which we live and to which something is owed, presented, transferred, and this constitutes a mode of contact with the divine realm, which might constitute a debt of loyalty/praise/petition or appeasement. Making this connection, whether by an individual or a group, assumes a technical knowledge and some sacred skill – usually the work of a special priesthood – such that the divine recognizes that the action performed is the appropriate sacred deed. Christians, contrariwise, conceive their worship on the basis that their priest has come to them and is with them as a community. Therefore, where two or three are gathered in the name of Jesus, he is with them (Matthew 18.20), and so their actions together, such as celebrating a meal, take place in the presence of the Father, because Christ, present among them, is always their High Priest. This theological vision has important implications for individual Christians who find themselves performing specific acts, ministries, within the Church.

First, professional Christian 'ministers' need to remember that, although in common perceptions they will be seen as the 'religious service experts' and as yet another variant of the religious phenomenon of 'priests' (a word designating sacred functionaries in most world religions, and understood as such in religious studies), this is not a good starting point for their own self-understanding. Christian history has too much distracting baggage resulting from its ministers taking over their understanding of their role within the Church by analogy with the role of priests (*sacerdotes*), temples and sacrifice in both the Old Testament and Graeco-Roman religions. Within Christianity, the ministry is that of the whole community – and so for that matter every Christian can, and perhaps should, own the designation 'minister of religion'; therefore, the difference between any two Christians (even if one has the most gaudy liturgical wardrobe and uniform, while the other wears none) is only a matter of external perception, accepted learned skills, and designated functions within the community. Second, it is worth remembering that language plays us false in understanding 'priestly ministry' in particular. In the Old Testament the *cohen* (which we render by the word 'priest') performed special tasks – as a matter of divine appointment – on behalf of the rest of Israel (see Leviticus and Numbers). This was rendered in the Septuagint by the word *hiereus*, a word commonly used for pagan temple officials, and then, later, into Latin by *sacerdos*, which was a generic word covering all the various special temple 'priesthoods' such as *flamenes* and *pontifices*. The early Christians did not use these words for their leaders: *hiereus/sacerdos* belonged to Jesus alone in the heavenly temple. Christian leaders were designated *by their relation to the community*: as the one who oversaw, led or served it. Later, the *hiereus/sacerdos* language was absorbed and became the basis of Christians' perceptions of their presbyters. So our word 'priest' is etymologically from the word '*presbyter*', but conceptually it relates to the sacerdotal functions. One consequence of this is that those so designated think of themselves as 'ministers of God' – they perform a service to him – but it is the community in Christ that is the minister of God, and specific individuals are functionaries, such as presbyters, and ministers to the community. Third, another consequence of Christian officials taking over a sacerdotal self-understanding was that they explained their work (by parallel with Old Testament *cohenim*) in terms of its distinctiveness from that of the rest of the baptized, or as did pagan priesthoods (*sacerdotia*) as being specialists acting on behalf of ordinary people. Once this had occurred they had to ask what made them different and what special religious quality they had which others did not possess: the answer came with the notion of a power 'to consecrate', and then this power (itself the subject of rhetorical inflation) became the basis of 'ontological difference' between them and 'ordinary Christians', or between their 'ordained priesthood' and a nebulous, and often ignored, 'common priesthood'. Not only is this 'priesthood defined by difference' theologically flawed, but it obscures the unique role of the Christ in Christian liturgy, it downplays the role of the Church as 'the people of God', and it creates a 'two-tier' Christianity of the special religious people (e.g. clergy/monks/nuns) and passive 'other ranks' whose ministry is 'praying, paying and obeying'.

After more than a millennium and a half of these confusions in Christianity, both East and West, it is very hard for many who see themselves as 'ministers' in a church – especially those with elaborate sacerdotal liturgies – to break free of this baggage. But for all its complex, gilded splendour, it is still a distracting deviation from core Christian beliefs. Meanwhile, some churches continue to evolve in its wake (e.g. the recent declaration by the Roman Catholic Church that women are absolutely excluded from the presbyterate), while being conceptually cognizant of the problems of imagining ministry in terms of a distinct *sacerdotium*. Tradition can be like a great oil-tanker turning at sea: it takes a long time to overcome inertia, and for the ship to answer the helm.

Third, one of the thorniest questions that beset discussions, particularly between denominations, about ministry concerns the issue of authorization. This usually presents as a discussion about 'ordination' within a sacerdotal model of 'priesthood' such as we have just examined. In such a model the priest must be thought of in terms of some specific 'power' and since this, unlike that of the Levites, does not come with birth, it must come from a specific act of empowerment: 'ordination'. Ordination, in turn, comes to be seen as an act of 'making something'. In such a situation a person is either 'the thing made' or not. So discussions between churches either ignore the issue (which renders the discussion little more than polite window dressing) or search to validate each other's 'orders' (which becomes a matter of arcane history and black/white answers). Such starting points only promote deadlock.

A far better approach is to note that all groups need, at least, some formal organization, while Christians must also work with one another in communities (they claim to be called to love one another), and, then, to treat each such community as a basic church. Next, enquire if the ministry structures are adequate to helping them to pray together, to receive teaching that promotes understanding and discipleship, to keep them together as a group, to answer specific needs a group might have (e.g. the poor, the old, young families) and ensure that the ministers do not behave in a manner that is tyrannous (as can happen all too easily in ministry) or abusive (it is easy for 'religious authorities' to take advantage of the trust given them) or self-serving (a problem already noted in the mid-first century). Whoever fulfils these needs and functions should be seen as 'the ministers' of that community, and respected as such by other churches and groups of ministers. The differences in the styles and structures can be considered subsequently as part of the varied tapestry of the work of the Spirit and historical circumstances; and they can learn from one another which elements from the others' visions of ministry they might import, and which of their own they need to change or drop.

Fourth, most specific expressions of ministry to the community require some level of skill and this, given the way humans develop, will be the result of ability, experience and training. Many churches are not far beyond the older position whereby, if one passed an academic course in theology or was deemed 'fit for orders', then training in liturgical ministry was but a practical afterthought. And in traditional societies where 'going to church' was part of the week, few cared whether a minister had any sensitivity to leading people in liturgy. However, an adequate view of liturgy, and the nature of contemporary Christian belonging, requires far more awareness of the skills needed for this ministry. Thus, someone presiding at the Eucharist needs to have the skills of a host at a great celebratory meal; and if that is a task that fills them with dread (note the number who fear such roles at weddings, for example), then that person should not be called on to preside and give voice to the community. Likewise, someone who dislikes public speaking or lacks aptitude as a teacher will find preaching difficult, and this cannot be remedied by training in 'communication skills'. A basic ministry skill in most communities today is the ability to lead spontaneous prayer, which needs great sensitivity and some of the art of the poet, so someone who lacks this skill is not someone who, simply by virtue of ordination, should presume to be able to lead a community in its prayer. By contrast, those who are good communicators are often poor listeners and will, therefore, not be so good in ministries of reconciliation. And while we can all benefit from growing in sensitivity for those who are suffering, a ministry of healing will fit best with someone with a 'bedside manner'. We should see the Spirit empowering each community with the variety of skills it needs and then aligning each individual's skill to the necessary tasks as the work of ecclesial vocation. After such alignment, formal training (always valuable given the haphazard way humans absorb information) is a case of organizing, developing and drawing out charisms latent in the individual as a member of the community. So rituals like ordination should be seen as actualizing and recognizing gifts already within the Church from the work of the Spirit, rather than the conferring of 'powers' extrinsic to the person.

Moreover, liturgical ministry is *not* a matter of holes and pegs. Rather, it is a community recognizing its needs in Christ, and of individuals deploying, creatively, their range of gifts, insights and skills (a mix unique to each person) in the service of their church. Each liturgical ministry should actualize that person's distinctive contribution to a unique moment in Christian history. Liturgical ministry is an art as much as a skill or a 'vocation'.

The standard one-size-fits-all model of the cleric (usually chosen for other criteria than liturgical ministry) who in virtue of 'ordination' carries out every ministry cannot be justified either theologically, for it ignores the Spirit's workings in an actual church, or practically, as no individual can be presumed to have that skill range or be able to deploy such adaptability on a day-to-day basis. A deeper awareness of the needs of liturgical ministry leads to basic questioning of most ministry training models – many denominations are still too content with that of 'the one-person show' – and this is a major challenge facing churches today.

Fifth, churches grow, and often become vast international organizations with consequent management needs. Down the centuries it has been assumed that those chosen for their skill in liturgical ministry would automatically have management ability (at least at local levels), and it has always been assumed that those with the widest administrative duties would be the most senior liturgical ministers – and sometimes this has been the case. However, just as there are varieties of skill within liturgical ministry, so liturgy as the *Christ*-ian expression of the community is different from church management, and, consequently, there is a difference in the abilities needed between those who perform specific tasks in each sphere. In those churches with highly structured line-management, it is often the case that the leaders, usually bishops 'with the power of jurisdiction', are also expected to be able to take the lead in liturgy, and this is not a problem if liturgy is seen just as a derivative of 'the power of order'. However, experience often shows that such managers (and such are needed) are not those who can either teach adequately or lead worship effectively; and the converse situations are also true: a good academic or a sensitive pastor of a small community may turn out to be a useless bishop. A deeper consciousness of such problems, which come to light most clearly when we consider liturgical ministry, inevitably leads to an awareness of the need in most churches for them to consider afresh the whole set of interlocking structures that come within the bounds of 'church ministry'. There is only one (merely logical) certainty: the future will not be like the past; and, when a present seeks to recede into its past, it is untrue to its own moment.

Further reading

Brand, E. L., and Kühn, U. (2003), 'Ministry, Ministerial Offices', in E. Fahlbusch et al. (eds), *The Encyclopedia of Christianity* 3 (Grand Rapids, MI: Eerdmans/ Leiden: Brill), pp. 539–44.

Cooke, B. (1980), *Ministry to Word and Sacraments: History and Theology* (Philadelphia, PA: Fortress Press).

O'Loughlin, T. (2010), *The Didache: A Window on the Earliest Christians* (London and Grand Rapids, MI: Baker Academic), pp. 85–128.

O'Loughlin, T. (2012), 'Divisions in Christianity: The Contribution of "Appeals to Antiquity"', in S. Oliver, K. Kilby and T. O'Loughlin (eds), *Faithful Reading: New Essays in Theology and Philosophy in Honour of Fergus Kerr OP* (London: T&T Clark), pp. 221–41.

Thurian, M. (1983), *Priesthood and Ministry: Ecumenical Research* (London: Mowbray).

Chapter 10

Music

Thomas R. Whelan

Most churches today consider music to be a structural component of Christian worship, without which it would be an impoverished experience. Different understandings of music have caused debates at various times regarding how music is employed in worship, and the criteria for deciding what are to be deemed appropriate styles of music are still a contested zone in some churches. This chapter serves to introduce the reader to some perspectives on Christian ritual music in the hope that it might generate further discussion and reflection, and stimulate deeper investigation.

DEFINING TERMS

Many terms are used to refer to music associated with worship, and each has its own set of presuppositions (see Foley, 1990, pp. 854–5; Joncas, 1997, pp. 281–3). The first three designations below, sometimes used interchangeably, are still found, even if they are deemed to be rather vague.

Today, the term **religious music** is considered to be too broad, referring, as it does, to any music that has a religious theme or sentiment, whether intended for use in worship or not.

There is a preference in official Roman Catholic writings for the designation **sacred music**. The first difficulty here is that it presupposes that some music can be, of itself, 'sacred'. The designation is also employed so as to distinguish it from 'profane' music, implying that certain music styles are deemed more acceptable than others for use in liturgy. A second difficulty relates to a lack of clarity about what it refers to, as it is also applied to works such as Bach's *St Matthew Passion* or Verdi's *Requiem*, pieces which are clearly not intended for use in worship.

Church music was once used as an all-encompassing term for music found in Christian worship traditions throughout history. The term, however, refers to the space in which a type of music is to be encountered and does not necessarily describe music that is deemed to be particularly appropriate for use in liturgy. Church music includes devotional hymns, Sunday school singing and other forms of music, not proper to worship but employed in Christian rallies and gatherings.

Found mostly in writings by Roman Catholics since the 1960s, the term **liturgical music** refers to music used as part of the liturgy, and it highlights its functional aspect particularly as it serves liturgical text. Its form and meaning are derived from its association with the liturgical event itself (in the words of the composer and theologian Joseph Gelineau, 'music *of* the liturgy') rather than from the mere fact that it is employed *during* worship ('music found *in* the liturgy'). Unlike 'sacred music', it does not refer to inherent musical qualities deemed to be required of the liturgy, or to aesthetics.

Almost synonymous with liturgical music, **service music** is preferred in a few traditions to refer to the singing of parts of the service such as the Gloria, Sanctus or anthems and hymns which form parts of the offices and eucharistic liturgies.

Somewhat broader than liturgical music, **worship music** is favoured across a number of church traditions, and does not necessarily carry all the ritual/functional baggage that some see in 'service music'. The emphasis implied is primarily prayer and worship rather than ceremonial or ritual. This term allows for the inclusion of music that serves to carry the praise of the assembly and is addressed to God, as well as didactic hymns whose principal aim is to impart doctrinal truths to the congregation while it performs its act of worship. This term can be employed when referring to music used in the worship of other religions.

A term found in the USA, **pastoral music** indicates a preference for music that is accessible to the assembly in order to facilitate participation, but can also refer to music suitable for Sunday school use, or other occasions of catechesis.

First introduced in the 1980s by Universa Laus (an international and influential study group for liturgical music), **Christian ritual music** emphasizes the role of music in the worship event viewed predominantly as an element of ritual enactment. As this term highlights the functional over the aesthetic, it draws attention to the appropriateness of music to relate to or carry a ritual act, as well as to serve the ceremonial development of the worship event. Some suggest that the term does not sufficiently subvert music to the liturgical rite, understood to be composed of not just ritual, but also – importantly – text.

ELEMENTS OF A LITURGICAL THEOLOGY OF MUSIC

Many writers propose ways in which to understand worship music theologically, and they variously use, as a springboard for their theological reflections, considerations from anthropology, biblical studies, history or ecclesiastical writings on music in worship (see, for example, Ferguson, 1993; Foley, 1990, pp. 868–9; Foley, 1995, pp. 107–26; Joncas, 1997, pp. 312–20; and Joncas, 2002, pp. 326–9).

If the designations 'liturgical/service/Christian ritual music' are taken seriously, then it is not unreasonable that music would be theologically interrogated as a ritual element of the worship process itself. If music serves not just as an ornament to worship, but as an actor at the heart of the salvific and worshipful event that transpires when believers assemble to 'actively act', then it can be legitimately expected that the contours of a 'liturgical theology' will emerge. These contours will vary according to what different churches consider to be central to their worship. Whether the emphasis is placed on word proclaimed, sacramental encounter or personal testimony, all churches assemble in order to witness to the wonders of God (*mirabilia Dei*) and to offer unceasing praise and glorification for what Christ continues to do in their midst, through the Spirit. *Sacrosanctum Concilium* section 112 states that, because of the pre-eminence of music over any other form of art in liturgy, it 'forms a necessary or integral part of the solemn liturgy', to the extent that it is 'more closely connected with the liturgical action'.

Employed properly, music, along with text and other ritual elements, facilitates the assembly in its doxology, efficacious remembrance, and ecclesial and Spirit-led actualization of the Paschal Mystery of Christ. A brief consideration of these aspects will guide this outline of a liturgical theology of music.

Paschal Mystery

One of the great insights of liturgical theology of the twentieth century was that all worship is centred on, and is a participation in, the Paschal Mystery of the salvific life of Christ, which found its most intense expression in his death and resurrection. Memory is kept of this entire Mystery, at least implicitly, every time Christians gather to worship, and not just during the classic 'high seasons' of, for example, Christmas or Easter.

If music is integral to the liturgical action of the assembly and its ministers, then it cannot but facilitate the sacramental action of worship. While the medieval *opus operato* served to protect the integrity of the salvific working of God from the sinfulness of ministers, appeal was rarely made to the *opus operandi* – the requirement that the assembly cooperate with the working of the Spirit of God so that liturgy will take effect in their lives. Music, appropriately chosen, can serve to carry the assembly into the heart of the Paschal Mystery of Christ being celebrated, thus making it disposed to the self-implication that true worship requires.

Among the many musical tools which could be employed to help this is the choice of music that can carry something of the liturgical texture of different times of the year or occasions. Normally certain hymns, anthems and psalms have the 'once-a-year' character that facilitates bringing the assembly into the liturgical season (say, Christmas or Lent) or occasion being celebrated. However, in those liturgical traditions which emphasize a preference for singing the actual text of the liturgy, musical settings can be employed which allow the penitential dimension of Lent, the festive character of Christmas, the paschal spirit of Easter or the celebratory quality of a local patron come to the fore. Over a number of years, the very employment of a repertoire of music associated with one or other liturgical cycle will assist the assembly to access worship memories and associations that should help predispose their emotional and spiritual participation. This in turn can have a positive effect on other levels of their active participation in the liturgical ritual – and thus in the mystery of God.

Word

All traditions uphold the centrality of the proclamation of the word of God in worship, giving pride of place to the saving ministry of Christ as set out in the Gospels. In one way or another, all express the active presence of God in Christ through the word proclaimed and announced in the assembly.

To the extent that music can encompass biblical text with appropriate melody and rhythm, it assists in the proclamation of the word. The dialogic dynamic that is ritually embodied in some liturgical traditions – whereby the assembly uses God's word in psalms to respond to God's word proclaimed – characterizes the age-old way in which God related with people. Appropriate use of music, especially with settings of the Psalms (using psalm tone, metric or other forms of expression), helps to embody aspects of the dialogic nature of the word. Good music settings will aim to express the inner truth of the word, including the tensions inherent in our inadequate response to the claim that the word has over us. The challenge that God's word makes on believers was experienced in Old Testament times: the Hebrew term *nâbâ* means 'to make music', but can also mean 'to prophesy' (this association is found in Exodus 15.20; 1 Samuel 10.5–10; and 2 Kings 3.15). The prophetic role of the word continues to operate today as a condition for the very proclamation of the good news.

Because of the irreplaceable nature of the Scriptures in Christian living and worship, all churches have considered hymns that are biblically based to hold pride of place in worship (see Dunstan, 1992), to the extent that some reverse the meaning of Prosper of Aquitaine's adage and require that the *lex credendi* be articulated clearly and served by the *lex orandi* of hymns and songs employed in liturgy. Some churches take great care to ensure that all that they sing is at least biblically based, if not a setting of parts of Scripture itself. This care is not misplaced because the songs of the assembly are, in a real sense, those of the body of which Christ is the Head, addressed to the Father in the Spirit.

In Pauline literature (especially Ephesians 5.18–20 and Colossians 3.14–16), singing is to be Spirit-filled, and the assembly is to be permeated with the 'word of Christ'. This 'word of Christ' is not to be confused with *kerygma* (addressed to those not yet followers of Christ), but is directed by the liturgical assembly *to itself* so as to build up the community (Ephesians 5.19; Colossians 3.16) and instruct.

Church

Almost without exception, all churches presuppose as normative the ecclesial or communal nature of its regular worship. As the living body of Christ gathered around the tables of word and Eucharist, the assembly identifies itself with Christ and is conscious of the active presence of the Spirit in its midst as it offers praise and thanksgiving to God. Anthropology of music identifies such ritual contexts, in which fellowship and unity are expressed, as occasions which seem to find natural expression in music and song. From New Testament times, congregations used 'psalms, hymns, and songs' (Ephesians 5.19 REB) as part of their corporate worship. By engaging with the same music (even if enriched through added rhythm and harmonies), singing has the effect of not just giving expression to unity but also helping to bring this about and affirm it. Thus, if we can assert that we engage in worship, not just as individuals but primarily as the living body of Christ, and that this embodiment is crucial to the celebration of the Paschal Mystery, then we can also assert that music, although not essential, serves as an actor at the heart of the assembly's efficacious and salvific engagement with Christ.

Eschatology

The community's act of worship is intrinsically eschatological. Worship places the community, baptized in Christ, in the 'last days'. It must negotiate in its public life (with its social, political and economic dimensions) the tension that is created by the salvation achieved completely by and in Christ (the 'already'), and the acquisition of this that each community makes in its concrete human and cultural reality (the 'not yet').

The term 'new song' acquired a messianic sense after the exile and is found six times in the Psalms (33.3; 40.3; 96.1; 98.1; 144.9; 149.1) and also in Isaiah 42.10. In the New Testament, this 'new song' of praise and thanksgiving found its fulfilment in Christ (see Revelation 5.9; 14.3; 15.3). It is a cosmic song that involves both heaven and earth (see Revelation 5.9–10), and it is the song of the 'elect', incomprehensible to those who do not know the Lamb (see Revelation 14.3). The Lordship of the Lamb is acknowledged *by all creatures* in this acclamation of praise. So, if the 'Song of Moses' was in praise of the Lord for deliverance from Egypt (Exodus 15.1ff.), then the Song of the Lamb (the Redeemed) celebrates the deliverance of God's people from slavery to sin (Revelation 15.3–4). The Song of Moses is transposed and gives a christological significance to the salvific act of the Father.

While the biblical phrase 'new song' must be understood to refer to the fulfilment of the promise made by the Father in Christ and not simply to a musical phenomenon, it does help to realize that singing is particularly well suited to giving expression to the eschatological reality within which liturgy is located. Singing requires the human voice itself to articulate melodious sound, and the ensuing music is not tangible (music exists only in terms of sound and time), but points beyond itself. It has the potential to help the assembly transcend itself in order to consciously participate in its negotiation, in Christ, with the implications of its final destiny (partaking in the life of the triune God who saves).

Doxology (praise)

All worship is characterized by its doxological dimension. Indeed it can be rightly asserted that, if the tone of the service is not doxological, then it is not an act of worship and self-offering. Doxology permeates everything, even the daily life of the worshipper (see Romans 12.1–2). The psalmist saw that the act of doxology is self-implicating (see Psalms 1 and 2), so the act of singing in praise and thanksgiving must be such that it places the assembly on a trajectory that links the gospel (and sacrament) with ethics.

AN ANTHROPOLOGY OF CHRISTIAN RITUAL MUSIC

Genesis (4.21) speaks of the origins of music as it recounts God's developing creation. Its incomparable importance is located in its being a primordial means of human expression. Singing, as a vocal act, connects with the Hebrew concept of 'word' (*dabar*) with all its materiality and dynamism, and is revelatory of the depths of human existence. Apart from its entertainment and aesthetic values, an anthropology of music proposes that music has the capacity to expose the ultimate truth of the person, as well as to regulate human engagement with the world. In the service of this transaction, music performs a social function and is also a principal actor in most ritual performance.

Social function

Music has the potential to create associations: connections can be generated between melodic figures/rhythmic patterns/harmonic progressions, and text/ emotions, and events. While these correlations are often culture bound, and to that extent tenuous, they do offer a framework for considering music in a functional way. Western musicians are generally agreed that, within certain cultural contexts, some types of musical expression are judged appropriate for funerals, others for joyful occasions, or to accompany processions, or to create a reflective moment in ritual. Though less obviously today, with the unsolicited ubiquity of music in almost every social and commercial context, music still functions as an element of social formation and manipulation.

In liturgy, music makes a contribution to the stability of the faith community because it affirms the ritual pattern accepted by the worshipping community, primarily through familiarity with the sung text that is chosen, and melodic and harmonic patterns already known to the assembly. Musical associations confirm and 'validate' for the assembly its ritual action, and in this way uphold, through musical expression, the 'social norms' (i.e. 'gospel norms') of the assembly, the result of which is a contribution to the integration of the group. In theological terms, this refers to the potential that music has to contribute to the creation of unity and a degree of cohesion in the community, a local manifestation of the body of Christ. This power of music to perform and assert ritual and social functions is rarely fully appreciated.

Music as a ritual component

The very fact that a group of believers decides to assemble in order to proclaim the word, and to offer praise and thanksgiving to God, implies ritual. It is of the incarnational nature of liturgy and worship which in turn is predicated by the incarnational nature of God's word. We are bodily people. Our communal worshipful encounter with the saving Mystery of God in Christ happens in an embodied way – through gestures, symbols, movement, speech and music. So ritual is not something added to worship: it is precisely the mode we employ in communal worship. And certain things can only be done ritually. Nothing else can be substituted for the central role of music in the process of ritual enfolding: 'Music is not indispensable to Christian liturgy, but its contribution is irreplaceable' (Universa Laus, 1980, Part II.21).

Three of the 'ritual norms' which apply to music reveal how it serves worship.

1 Music highlights a moment. To make one part of a service or ceremony stand apart, it is marked musically by either singing the prayer text itself, or by employing a hymn or chant to accompany the action. Music can also be employed to function as a 'stand-alone' moment in itself (e.g. the Gloria). The converse is also true: music can also be used, unhelpfully, to highlight a worship moment that is of little ritual importance.

2 A second ritual norm applies to the cultural (or subcultural) context of worship, and to whether the local Christian assembly understands its relationship to be counter-cultural or fully bound with contemporary cultural forms of expression. Either way the appropriateness of musical styles needs to be considered in terms of how they serve the assembly's liturgical celebration of the Mystery of Christ. Churches seem to be in general agreement that worship cannot make claim to any single musical style to the exclusion of others.

3 The quality of worshipful engagement in liturgy is not changed by whether it is festive or not. However, of its nature, human ritual involvement requires that events are differentiated and therefore the 'progressive solemnization' of liturgy can assist the assembly to mark high and low seasons as well as moments of

local importance. Greater festivity can be marked through the use of more elaborate song or an enhanced use of instruments; parts of the service normally spoken could be chanted or sung (as appropriate within a church tradition).

MINISTRY OF MUSIC

It is normally the responsibility of the local assembly to arrange and resource its music ministry. Many factors (financial resources, availability of highly gifted musicians, whether it is a cathedral church, and so on) will influence music performance, but the principal criterion must rest with the fact that Christian ritual music reflects the praise and glorification of God by a *particular localized* assembly of believers. What is of primary importance is the living praise of the assembly, not the musical standard of the performance. When it is considered that the rendering of praise to God is first and foremost the task of those people who have actually gathered together in worship, then thought needs to be given to the appropriateness of using atmospheric or environmental music in worship that is pre-recorded and reproduced through CDs or with the help of other forms of digital media. What this statement does not question are the requirements of liturgical aesthetics. A balance must be achieved between the desire for musical excellence and the possibilities available to an actual assembly whose musical worship and praise is rooted in their cultural and human reality.

Assembly

The primary liturgical subject is the assembly, in Christ. Each church tradition has its own sense of the musical importance of the assembly, some excluding, or only permitting by way of exception, choral anthems or instrumental/vocal solos. While developing its own worship music requirements, the Roman Catholic Church benefited from the large repertoire of congregational material available to it from its post-Reformation brothers and sisters (e.g. some hymns by the Wesley brothers and from the Lutheran tradition). Churches continue to produce appropriate music that is capable of functioning liturgically while facilitating the active musical participation of the assembly. All traditions seem to agree that, no more than any other liturgical ministry, music ministry has as its sole purpose the service of the worship of the entire assembly (see McKenna, 1990, p. 852–4).

Some musical roles

The **presiding minister** can sometimes be invited to enter into dialogue with the assembly through chant or to employ a form of cantillation (a type of simple chant) when praying a presidential prayer. Assemblies that do not have the service of a choir are often served musically by the **cantor**, probably the oldest of all music ministries, as it is found in ancient synagogue worship (see Foley, 1995, pp. 65–87). Known as a **precentor** in some traditions, this person sings verses to which the assembly responds in refrain, or performs the liturgical role of **psalmist** in the ministry of the word and the offices.

An important ministry in almost all worship traditions is that of the **choir**. Often employed to simply support (and maybe embellish) the singing of the assembly, the choir performs an enabling ministry. In some churches it is permitted so long as it never substitutes for the assembly, while other churches provide a place in their worship for the choir to sing music that is more demanding vocally than that expected of the assembly (e.g. Anglican cathedral music). These latter traditions exploit a huge repertoire of music, ranging from polyphonic settings to anthems and elaborate chorales. Many of the best composers in the Western tradition have written magnificent choral music for use in their own liturgical traditions. While spatial or liturgical contexts can dictate otherwise, it is normally appropriate that musicians and singers do not occupy a space apart from the assembly, but ought to be seen to perform a particular ministry *within* the assembly.

For many reasons the **organ** is deemed to be the normative musical instrument in most worship traditions, although the employment of other instruments has always been taken for granted, especially in cathedral worship. Today different traditions hold varying views regarding the acceptability of certain musical instruments (e.g. electric guitars, worship bands). Some churches admit the use of solo instrumental music at designated parts of the service to support and facilitate the singing of the assembly. Listening to music does not have to be a passive activity but can be a form of 'co-performing', allowing the hearer to be carried into a deeper consideration of the Mystery through the splendour of text or sound, beautifully rendered. **Composers** are rarely considered in writings on music ministers, yet there would be no music without their God-giftedness (as Luther emphasized) and their writing skills. The 'power' that composers have is rarely considered. They are the people who decide, through their employment of pitch, rhythm, harmony and melody, how the assembly uses, feels or musically embodies their faith in their worshipful response to the proclamation of the word and enactment of sacrament. It takes good musicianship for composers to write excellent music that can be easily sung by the assembly while also being liturgically appropriate.

All music ministers exist to serve the worship needs of the entire assembly. With the assembly, their task is to offer their obedience to God in Christ, to witness to the work that God continues to accomplish in their midst, and to become an embodiment of the Mystery of Christ in and to the society of which they form part. Like liturgical art, musical ministry is not for its own sake, but for the sake of the reign of God. The solo work of choirs, singers and instrumentalists is never a performance, and musical talent is at the service of God through the assembly, and is therefore nothing more, or less, than a ministry.

CRITERIA FOR WORKING WITH CHRISTIAN RITUAL MUSIC

A recent American Catholic document proposed that there is a threefold judgement to be made when choosing worship music for a liturgy (United States Conference of Catholic Bishops, 2007, pp. 126–36). These judgements, it suggested, are liturgical, pastoral and musical. While the ordering of these assessments is significant, the document notes that 'no individual judgment can be applied in isolation from the other two' (United States Conference of Catholic Bishops, 2007, p. 126).

Liturgically proper

Music should relate to the literary form of a text, and serve the ritual place that this occupies in a celebration. Ritual function, for example, requires of dialogues or litanies musical forms different from those employed for chorales or acclamations. Music must be within the performance capacity of an assembly when its full participation is liturgically required, and must be such as to enable a liturgical minister to chant parts proper to him or her. More challenging music can be used for the choir, as long as this serves the liturgical tradition and expectations of a particular church denomination.

Pastorally appropriate

The question implied by the pastoral judgment is, 'Does this choice of music ultimately serve the congregation and its needs?' Just as choice of biblical readings and prayers is guided by the pastoral reality of the baptized gathered in worship, so too are musical choices, however good other music options may be in themselves. Pastoral appropriateness includes a consideration of local circumstances, the cultural and sociological make-up of the assembly, and the duty to serve the faith needs of the given worshipping community. Music must ultimately serve the community which assembles in order to facilitate its engagement with the salvific Mystery of Christ through word proclaimed and sacrament celebrated, being always conscious of Christ's presence in their midst as they gather in his name (see Matthew 18.20).

Musically good

Musicians are the most competent people to apply a judgement in relation to the quality of the music employed; however, this must be carried out in deference to liturgical and pastoral concerns. A distinction needs to be made between musical styles and the quality of music, as these are two very different aspects of the art form. Music should be chosen that is aesthetically appropriate (whether in folk, popular, jazz, classical or contemporary styles) and that is accessible to a non-musically competent assembly. Music styles are culturally determined and an assembly will choose the extent to which it deems various modern or older styles appropriate to its own worship, while resisting music that is trite or clichéd. Music must be deemed capable of assisting the assembly to achieve its worshipful purpose, and must serve the ritual unfolding of the worship event. It must also appeal to aesthetic taste.

The Lutheran, Anglican and Roman Catholic traditions, in particular, constantly need to consider how and when it is appropriate to incorporate the great musical heritage, some of it of inestimable value, which belongs to these traditions. The challenge is created by the difficult negotiation that must be made between the desire to employ musical forms (that is, when musical resources permit this) that have emerged from, and partly informed, a liturgical tradition, and a contemporary theology of worship that makes different musical demands and has new cultural and pastoral contexts and requirements. The liturgical renewal of different churches since the 1960s makes new claims of composers and musicians, and these need to be responded to in a spirit of fidelity to traditions as well as in a creative engagement with contemporary music styles.

Further reading

Duchesneau, C., and Veuthey, M. (eds) (1992), *Music and Liturgy: The Universa Laus Document and Commentary*, tr. P. Inwood (Washington, DC: Pastoral Press).

Kubicki, J. M. (1999), *Liturgical Music as Ritual Symbol: A Case Study of Jacques Berthier's Taizé Music* (Leuven: Peeters).

Saliers, D. E., and Saliers, E. (2004), *A Song to Sing, A Life to Live: Reflections on Music as Spiritual Practice* (San Francisco, CA: Jossey-Bass).

Studia Liturgica 28 (1998), entire volume.

Ward, P. (2005), *Selling Worship: How What We Sing Has Changed the Church* (Carlisle: Paternoster Press).

Westermeyer, P. (1998), *Te Deum: The Church and Music – A Textbook, a Reference, a History, an Essay* (Minneapolis, MN: Fortress Press).

Chapter 11

Space

Christopher Irvine

MODELS AND METHODOLOGIES FOR THE STUDY OF LITURGICAL SPACE

Among the many approaches to the study of liturgical space, the earliest were unapologetically historical, and focused on the architectural forms of church buildings and the ordering of their interior spaces (see, for example, Addleshaw and Etchells, 1948). This architectural approach was extended in the late 1960s and 1970s by scholars such as J. G. Davies who promoted the design and reconfiguring of interior church spaces in the light of the perceived liturgical needs and missional challenges facing the Church in what was regarded as an increasingly secular society. Since then, architectural studies of cathedrals, abbeys, churches and chapels have proliferated. These have tended to be largely historical in their approach to the subject, with only a sideways look at how these buildings reflect the culture and social setting of the different epochs and geographical locations in which they were built. This approach was significantly broadened by Nigel Yates in the UK and James White in the USA, who in their respective work approached churches in the light of their primary purpose as the architectural setting of the liturgy, and examined architectural function and liturgical form together. More recently, Allan Doig (2008) has published an interdisciplinary study setting out the different liturgical rites which were celebrated in a broad range of historic architectural settings.

Many of these studies have also sketched out the theological principles which have been articulated by the different architectural styles of churches, abbeys and cathedrals, but there are as many theological models of liturgical space as there are architectural styles. Some recent US studies have fully recognized the multiplicity of theological models for places of worship, and have set out in a systematic way to elucidate these differing theologies through a survey of contrasting architectural forms and styles of building. Two studies, in particular, merit further attention, namely those of R. Kevin Seasolz (2005) and Richard Kieckhefer (2004). Seasolz writes from a Roman Catholic post-Vatican II perspective and begins his study with a serious engagement with the question of the relationship between faith and culture. How the Church negotiates different cultural expressions is played out in relation to the development of places of worship in the Western Church, and moves towards a conclusion which underlines the symbolic nature of the worship space, its fittings and decoration. Architectural case studies also feature in Kieckhefer, but the weight of the enquiry falls in this more ecumenical view on the ways in which architectural styles both articulate a theology of worship and give concrete expression to the self-understanding of a church being a church. Different chapters of the book deal with the dynamics and configuring of the interior space of a church building, the visual and liturgical foci within the building, the aesthetic impact of the building and its symbolic resonance.

A church building, of whatever denomination, is an intentionally ordered symbolic space, designed to give concrete expression to the Church, the *ekklesia*, to those 'called together' by the word, and constituted by the 'invisible word' of visible signs and sacraments, such as Bible, baptismal font and table. But what of the physical building itself? What might we say about the particular places in which Christians gather for prayer, teaching and worship?

MAPPING SACRED SPACE AND HOLY GROUND

There has been a spate of books in recent times on the significance of place and sacred space. John Inge's erudite study (Inge, 2003) persuasively pleads for equal attention to be given to sacred geography (place) as has been given to sacred history. In seeking to map sacred geography Inge proposes a triangulation of God, people and place, and such a model certainly understands a God who engages with, and has a purpose for, the physical world of time and space. The re-enchantment of what may appear as an abandoned world is a topic that is magisterially and comprehensively covered by David Brown, in *God and Enchantment of Place: Reclaiming Human Experience* (Brown, 2004). The very title of his book headlines the need to both recognize and appreciate 'holy places', not least, as he pointedly says, among some of the official custodians of our churches. Other writers (for example, Sheehy, 2007) seek to establish the possibility of 'sacred spaces' on more explicitly theological grounds, such as the *a priori* principle of incarnation. But such a claim is difficult to maintain, given the strong scriptural strand of tradition which insists that God 'does not dwell in houses made by human hands' (1 Kings 8.27; Acts 7.48). At best, it is problematic to designate any walled and enclosed space as being intrinsically a 'holy place', as the ubiquity of divine presence resists containment and eludes localization (Psalm 139). But perhaps what is required here is a definition and elucidation of the term 'holy'. The root meaning of the

Hebrew word for 'holy' (k-d-sh) is that which is separate, 'set apart' or 'ordered', but something of a speculative hare has been set loose by anthropological studies which too easily regard the 'sacred' and the 'profane' as being oppositional terms. In the Christian narrative, the dichotomy is exploded by the fact that Jesus was crucified outside the city of Jerusalem, that is, beyond the bounds of designated holy space. The history of early Christian liturgy also seems to tell of a porosity between the sacred and the secular worlds. In the urban and cosmopolitan centres of Rome and Constantinople, from the fourth century until the eighth, the city was claimed through the movement from place to place in stational liturgy and processions through its streets, as being a sacred *polis* (Baldovin, 1991, pp. 5–8, 11, 18, 22).

The relation between the sacred and the profane is not of one set against the other, but is more of a gradation. Such a gradation of the holy is well illustrated in the design and construction of the temple complex in Jerusalem. The temple was architecturally zoned by a series of courtyards. The 'holy of holies', entered only by the high priest once a year, was at the centre, but a capacious courtyard, the courtyard of the Gentiles, provided space for those who were not strictly counted as being 'holy'. So, the zoning of 'sacred space' in this model is not intended to exclude the profane, but on the contrary to give access to the holy. An interesting parallel may be drawn to features in Christian architecture, such as the medieval chancel screen, or the iconostasis (icon screen) of Eastern Orthodox churches. These can easily be construed as separating the holy from the common, but this would be to miss the point of their primary function, which was not to be a barrier but a marker, marking, as in the 'holy of holies', the condensed presence of the holy. The zoning of the holy place, in other words, has more to do with signalling the promised presence of God than seeking to contain and cabin the divine.

When the first urban Christians met for teaching and worship in domestic settings, they did not meet in any house, but in those which were sufficiently spacious to accommodate the Christian community living in a given locality. Gradually, as archaeological research, such as the famous discovery of the 'church house' in the Syrian border town of Dura Europos demonstrates, early places of Christian worship were intentionally adapted and decorated to serve the purpose of sacramental worship, and, on this basis, we cannot draw the inference that worship in the primitive Church was domestic, with all the connotations that the term carries for the contemporary reader. Again, following the conversion of the emperor Constantine when Christian practice could become more public, the kind of building chosen for its place of worship was the public meeting space of the *basilica*, which literally means 'the royal hall'. The basilica, usually a colonnaded longitudinal space, was again adapted for the worship of the local community, and by the late fourth century became the most common architectural form for the Christian place of worship in the Roman Empire. The Syrian basilica typically had a centrally placed bema, a raised platform from which the Scripture readings were proclaimed and prayers offered, with a free-standing altar for the Eucharist at the east end of the building. In Italy and North Africa, the bishop's throne was placed behind the altar, often following the line of a semicircular apse, with benches on either side for the presbyters (Irvine, 2013, Chs 1 and 5). Alongside this development of the hall plan there was also the rotunda, or the domed architectural space, the *thoulos*, which is constructed as a series of ascending concentric circles. Whereas the basilica shape draws the eye of the worshipper, a domed roof lifts the eye and heightens the sense of space. Such a domed space was classically represented by the Roman mausoleum, and became the favoured church design of the Christian East, where it was regarded as a microcosm of the visible and invisible universe, the worship space in which heaven was liturgically mirrored on earth. A particular example of this type is the Christianized pagan temple in Rome, the Pantheon, which was dedicated to St Mary and all Christian martyrs, and later we have Charlemagne's Palace Chapel at Aachen, which incorporated spoils from the imperial palace in Ravenna.

These architectural forms, (a) the single room, 'church house' or hall, (b) the basilica, and (c) the domed, circular or circle in a square space, became the three basic models of church architecture though the ages. The first is arguably seen in the ornately decorated baroque churches of the Counter-Reformation, the classically ordered churches of seventeenth-century England, and the hybrid Classical/Gothic shape widely adopted across Protestant America in the nineteenth century (White, 2006, p. 806). The second is seen in the basic 'hall' shape combined with a designated 'holy space', such as a shrine, or saint's tomb constructed below the altar. The basilica form achieved a greater verticality and increased the natural light in Gothic and later neo-Gothic architecture, and thereby became a pathway into the transcendent. The third basic shape was classically expressed in Justinian's magnificent Byzantine church of Hagia Sophia in what is now Istanbul, and came to influence some early twentieth-century church building, albeit on a smaller scale, such as the Great Chapel at Kelham, which was locally known as 'the Dome'. These three architectural forms provide us with three distinguishable models of liturgical space. The first model emphasizes the essential ecclesial nature of Christian worship, as the church gathered by the word around the Lord's table. The second highlights the corporate and celebratory dimension of worship, and the third heightens the sense that Christian worship is something of 'heaven on earth'. For what is enacted there, in that place, does not so much mirror as link the worship of the local community at a particular time and place to the eternal worship of heaven around the Lamb who was slain. Each architectural style marks out, in its own way, a 'holy place', that communicative space which is experienced by worshippers as being the locus of an interaction of the human and the divine in the particularity of a place, a place that is constructed, ordered and consecrated for the purpose of worship in particular locations, and which, in each place, visibly represents the invisible presence of God 'in our midst'.

TOWARDS A LITURGICAL READING
OF WORSHIP SPACE

So far we have acknowledged the indisputable tension in the scriptural reading of what may be deemed to be a 'holy place'. The multiple biblical voices and witness seem equally balanced between a negative critique and an affirmation of holy places. But our enquiry should resist any hasty foreclosure. Jeremiah warned against seeing the temple as a guarantee of security (Jeremiah 7.4). God's presence there was a gift and not a possession; the location was God's gratuitous choice (Deuteronomy 12.13). But, as God chose the place, so he could equally absent himself (Ezekiel 10.18) and abandon the place. And yet, the divine presence was surely seen and known in the temple (Amos 9.1; Isaiah 6.1; Habakkuk 2.20). The divine presence was invoked in Solomon's temple (Psalm 132), and the vision of God being present in the restored temple was the prophet's eschatological hope and expectation (Ezekiel 43). The promise of the divine dwelling with humankind persists and intensifies, and although in the Christian scheme of things the temple and its *cultus* is superseded by the person of Christ and the living temple of his body, the Church, the image of a heavenly temple appears in the vision of John the Divine in Revelation, and the language of temple and its cult comes to be reappropriated by a number of early Christian writers. The temple, the holy place, it seems, cannot be simply written off the Christian map, as it recurs as a key theme throughout Christian history and experience. The lines of continuity between the Jewish temple and Christian liturgy have been creatively charted by Margaret Barker (Barker, 2003).

A positive evaluation of the temple as sacred space may be read from El Greco's paintings of the so-called cleansing of the temple, which can be seen in the Frick Collection in New York, and in the National Gallery in London. In these paintings, Christ is shown to be wide-eyed and determined. The canvases are full of drama and energy, but there is no sign of fury or anger on the part of Christ who is depicted with his right arm raised to lash the traders already in disarray, as the disciples, on the right of the picture, exchange puzzled looks, and two of their number seemingly offer an explanation as to what the commotion was all about. Was it a kind of demonstration, Christ showing that the temple and its sacrificial commerce were soon to be rendered obsolete and bankrupt by his own self-sacrifice? Without denying this meaning, there may be an equally valid reading of the incident, namely that Christ is claiming his messianic status (see Malachi 3.1b) and, in doing so, repossessing the sacred space. This reading receives some support from Christ's recorded statement: 'My house shall be called a house of prayer', a statement which is, incidentally, doubly attested to in Matthew 21.13 and Luke 19.46 and therefore likely to be an authentic saying of the historical Jesus. At face value we have here a positive evaluation of sacred space as a place of prayer, and, reflecting further on El Greco's *Cleansing of the Temple*, one may see that the dramatic incident was a reclaiming of the space, a deliberate clearing of a space, a 'making of space' as we might say. If this is a legitimate reading of the story, then the question to be addressed is the question of what the space is made for, and for whom. Let me briefly offer a possible threefold answer to this question:

1 A space in which to meet together as an ecclesial body (Matthew 18.20; Ephesians 2.21; 1 Peter 2.5 on Christians as the living temple);
2 A place where we are addressed by God (Revelation 2.29; John 18.37b);
3 A place where the divine presence is encountered (Genesis 28.17b; Exodus 25.22; 2 Chronicles 5.14b).

LITURGICAL SPACE

How we shape the interior space of a church to meet these three criteria of 'sacred space' is the primary question. As we shall see, many modern churches, following either a centralized or a radial space design, may prove to be too narrowly functional and static as a liturgical space. What may be required would be a more differentiated space, one which resonates with Christ's statement: 'In my Father's house are many rooms' (literally, 'stopping places') (John 14.2). In design terms, a church should be a building with related architectural spaces, including a place for baptism, a place for reconciliation, a safe space for quiet reflection and for daily prayer on ordinary weekdays, as well as the larger assembly space for the celebration of Services of the Word and the Eucharist on Sundays and major feast days. Such a building would have an inviting entrance, with architectural features to signal that when one entered the building, one was entering a **liminal** space, crossing a threshold into a space whose very geometry is suggestive of the transcendent.

Like the foyer in a theatre, the entrance of a church could lead people into a meeting or social space, such as a narthex, before they gather within the actual arena of worship, the 'holy theatre'. The theatre director and writer Peter Brooks once said that when a person walks across an empty space and another watches, an act of theatre is being performed. A number of similarities have been drawn between the theatre and the liturgical action performed within a designated space for worship. Interesting and illuminating analogies (respecting both similarities and dissimilarities) have been drawn between the theatre and worship, a subject treated more fully in Guiver (2009, ch. 3).

The world of theatre can certainly help us to understand the significance of space and the correlation of movement through and between the spaces, or, in the terms of our discussion, the loci of liturgical celebrations. A study of a liturgical space would usefully map the pathways through which people make their way into the building and take their place for worship. The kinetics, or spatial relationships between fittings and furniture, and the movement of ministers and people during the celebration would certainly provide a more adequate liturgical map of the worshipping environment. Equal consideration could profitably be given to the spatial relations, the proxemics, between the assembled congregation and the various liturgical loci. Both these methods of reading a liturgical space may well result in a clearer understanding of the kinds of interaction which operate between liturgical ministers and the congregation during a liturgical celebration.

A church building is *both* a *domus dei* (a house of God) *and* a *domus ecclesiae* (a house of the people of God), an ordered space in which people can deliberately place themselves before God in gathering with others among whom Christ has promised to dwell: 'where two or three have gathered in my name, there am I in the midst of them' (Matthew 18.20 RSV). This covenanted presence can, in principle, occur anywhere. But when Christians gather together (the first and constitutive liturgical act of a Christian community – see 1 Corinthians 11.17; cf. Hebrews 10.25), they need somewhere to meet, and they meet 'here' and 'there', that is, in particular locations and architectural spaces. The location or place of meeting is in some sense secondary to the intention, which for Christians is to place themselves attentively before God in prayer. It follows from this intention that the location where they gather becomes a potential site of encounter, a potential place of meeting with the divine. What we are considering here are particular places, and the emerging view is that what makes a place a 'holy place', a specific location 'holy ground' (Exodus 3.5), is what *happens* there (Genesis 28.18). An attempt to elucidate this view would require a broader approach than simply charting the biblical references to places of encounter and the marking of holy places. Indeed, the very notion can only be established by a cross-disciplinary approach, by drawing on other perspectives and disciplines of study. As a possible example of a cumulative argument which may establish a basis for an understanding of 'sacred space', let me marshal three supporting sources, the first, theological, the second, architectural, and the third, philosophical:

1   Augustine of Hippo marshals the reasons why the Christian may admire God's 'wonderful tabernacle'. God's tabernacle on earth, he asserts, is the faithful. What makes and constantly reconstitutes the faithful as the Church, Christ's body, is for Augustine what they *do* when they gather together, namely, to celebrate the liturgy. The celebration of the liturgy takes place in a particular location, here and there, in 'the sanctuary of God', the place where God comes to dwell with his people, and where they glimpse, however fleetingly, something of the constant worship of heaven.

2   The architect John Pawson believes that good architectural design attends to what takes place in any designated space, not in a simple functional way, but in a way that recognizes the importance of the symbolic associations of 'place' and the ritual aspect of human behaviour. What he requires from his brief, in other words, is an account of what happens, or occurs in any given space, for these things, he believes, 'are the rituals that give our lives shape' (Moryadas, 2002, p. 18).

3 In his classic work *The Poetics of Space*, the writer Gaston Bachelard comments on the analogy between the human dwelling and a shell. What fascinates him is not so much the form as the *formation* of the mollusc's shell, its 'dwelling'. 'The mollusc exudes its shell'; it lets the building material 'seep through', 'distil[s] its marvellous covering as needed' (Bachelard, 1969), and so the mollusc's dwelling is constructed as it lives out its distinctive form of life. Its dwelling, quite simply, is the product of the way it lives its life.

The accumulative force of these three points compels us in the direction of seeing that it is what actually happens in a place that gives it its particular shape, character and, one may perhaps also say, its mood and atmosphere. In terms of church buildings, we are constrained to say that it is what happens within the walls of the building, the prayer and worship, that makes that house of the people of God a house of God. Following the logic of our sources, we could quite simply say that the buildings in which Christians worship have been shaped by their ways of worship, by the liturgical celebrations which occur around the font, the ambo and the altar. But alongside this, we must also reckon with the fact that Christians are themselves shaped by the buildings in which they worship; a point which brings us to the question of the reordering and use of liturgical space.

In the late twentieth century, when participation was the watchword in liturgical renewal, visibility took precedence over the symbolic placing of liturgical furniture, and a number of reordering schemes placed the various foci of worship – the ambo, chair, altar and font – on a single axis at the east of the building. More recently, the movement of the people, as well as the ordering of furniture, has become an equal aim in the reordering of liturgical space. On the basis of an earlier study of the architectural plan of ancient Syrian churches and the ordering of church interiors in eighteenth-century England, Peter Doll (Doll, 1997) has set out a case for 'pilgrim liturgy', of the worshipping community moving through the space of a church from one focal point of the liturgy to the other in celebrating the Eucharist (Doll, 2005). Doll fully appreciates that a church building is often a historically layered building, and that many of the fittings and furniture are traces left by previous generations of the local community, and so shifts the emphasis in the reordering of the liturgical space from the furniture to the people. The aim of 'pilgrim liturgy' is for the worshippers to move through the space(s) as the liturgical action unfolds. A more avant-garde way of using the worship space was developed by Richard Fabian at the Church of St Gregory of Nyssa, in San Francisco. The interior space, decorated with a fresco of dancing 'saints' each nominated by the worshipping community, is divided into two distinct spaces. The congregation gathers in one for the Liturgy of the Word, seated in monastic choir fashion, and then in song and through dance moves into the second space where the whole assembly is reconfigured in a series of concentric circles around the altar-table for the Eucharistic Prayer and Communion.

It is commonplace to see liturgy as action, a rite performed in a particular setting, and two late twentieth-century examples of the reordering of liturgical space, Philadelphia Cathedral (USA) and Portsmouth Cathedral (UK), take full cognizance of this. Richard Giles's reordering of the Episcopal Cathedral in Philadelphia is a good example of using space in a way which focuses attention on the principal liturgical loci of ambo, altar and font for the worship of the baptized pilgrim people of God. At Portsmouth Cathedral, David Stancliffe developed a series of spaces, which lead from one to another and then beyond into a further space. From the nave, an ample gathering space, worshippers move through an arch, on either side of a rectangular, coffin-shaped font into a more decorated eucharistic room. The space beyond is a quiet zone for prayer with a hanging pyx for the reserved sacrament. This progression, and the sense of one space leading onward and opening into a further space, invites the physical movement of worshippers from the place of the word to the font, and then to the table, and thereby articulates the Paschal Mystery as it is celebrated at the Easter Vigil. This particular pattern may not best serve the multiple liturgical needs of a cathedral church. But then, it would be folly to suggest that there could be a single plan of the space to cover every liturgical need or set of local circumstances. Nevertheless, in considering these two examples of reconfiguring a building for worship we are reminded again that the worshipper's understanding of Christian faith and life is significantly shaped by the buildings in which he or she worships.

BUILDINGS MATTER

We have argued that it is corporate worship and personal prayer which is generative of the mood and ambience of the building as a church, as 'sacred space', but this does not preclude other legitimate uses of the spaces within a church building. And what has been said about the zoning of holy space supports a flexible use of a church building, such as a concert venue, a forum for public discussion, or an art exhibition. What matters is that, within a related series of spaces, one accessible zone should be designated and visibly retain signs of its being a sacred space. Regarding the placing of visual art and sculpture, whether temporary or permanent, the question needs to be asked as to how the work in question may be integrated into the act of worship, rather than its placing being decided solely on the grounds of where it may best be exhibited and seen.

Every worshipping space, of whatever tradition, has its particular visual foci, and it is instructive, on entering a worshipping space, to register what it is that strikes the eye. How and to what extent does what you see inform you of what is done in worship, of those constitutive acts of the Church which most explicitly express the gospel? Walking into a recently reordered church, I entered what looked like a functional 'worship hall'. Chairs virtually filled the whole floor space. An altar-table the size of a telephone table was placed at midpoint along the north wall, and a Victorian font remained in its original position, but had now lost its symbolic function as a sign of entrance into the community because of the reorientation of the building. The loci or centres of liturgical celebration need to be visible foci with clear sightlines from where the congregation are assembled. Attention may also be usefully given to the spatial relationship between the different foci of worship, the altar-table, lectern or ambo, pulpit and font. Taking each item in turn, one may ask if each focal point, or centre of liturgical action, speaks of the meaning of what happens there. For example, does the altar-table strike the viewer as being the fixed 'centre point' of the building, the point at which the centre of Christian faith, the death and resurrection of Christ is commemorated and celebrated? Does the placing of the lectern signal how Christians at worship gather under the word of God, and attentively listen to the stories and figures of faith? Does the font, again in both its placing and design, speak of how Christians begin their journey of faith, and need to return again and again to the source of Christian life? The placing of the different liturgical foci may well change according to the rite which is being celebrated, or be determined by the particular theme, feast or mood of the season of the Christian year which is being celebrated. An area of the church removed of furniture may speak, for instance, of the wilderness in Lent, and the font in a church could be decorated with lights, flowers and the appropriate icon for the feast of the Baptism of Christ and Pentecost Sunday.

In considering the design, reordering and assessment of liturgical space, a useful checklist is: (a) visibility, (b) audibility and (c) the acoustic of the building. Visibility is very important in relation to both the participation of the worshipping community in the liturgical action, and the placing of the different foci of worship. Lighting is a key consideration here, and the play of natural light within a building through the changing hours of the day and the natural seasons of the year can speak powerfully of the sanctification of time and be a signal of transcendence. Invariably, natural light will need to be augmented by artificial light, but the tendency to over-light modern buildings is best avoided in churches. A good lighting scheme not only provides sufficient light to see and to read, but also contributes to the mood of a building. Modulated light can accentuate its architectural lines and cast shadows in selected corners and arches. A good lighting scheme will also illumine the entrance points and the pathways through the spaces of a building, and will sensitively spotlight the different focal points as the liturgical action unfolds.

Audibility is also a key practical consideration in relation to participation, but let my final remark be about the acoustic of a church building. Many of our historic churches, abbeys and cathedrals were purposely built for singing in, and this may well be instructive for us as we seek to tune our sense of liturgical space. It is not coincidental that one of the two architects of the vast eleventh-century abbey church at Cluny, reputedly the largest church in Europe until the sixteenth century, was also a musician. The soaring vaulting of Gothic cathedrals was designed to allow the chant to reverberate through the building and then to deepen the silence. The architecture serves both sound and silence, and in this sense correlates the coordinates of time and space. Music, we say, is sound in time, but it also completes the architecture of space.

CONCLUSION

Living in a world where so much is disfigured and blighted by brutality, by human violence, natural disaster and poor design and planning, we especially need well designed, built and ordered churches to be markers of memory and meaning in our landscape. As the agnostic poet Philip Larkin recognized, a church building is 'a serious place' ('Church Going'). Churches should be places where our attention can be heightened and arrested, and where we are addressed and questioned by the language that is beyond language in music and the visual arts. Its architectural lines should invite all who cross the threshold to open themselves to that which is beyond, to the mystery of the transcendent. For those who gather for worship, the liturgical space needs to be a resonant place in which the voice of praise may resound, and in whose silence the echo of God's word may be heard. The building should provide a space of welcome for the visitor, an unobtrusive space for the tentative inquirer, and a safe space for the distressed needing 'some space'. In short, we need church buildings to be, as Paul Couturier, the doyen of twentieth-century Christian art and architecture put it, places of enchantment, poetry and deliverance (Couturier, 1989, p. 105).

Further reading

Doig, A. (2008), *Liturgy and Architecture: From the Early Church to the Middle Ages* (Aldershot and Burlington, VT: Ashgate).

Halgren Kilde, J. (2008), *Sacred Space: An Introduction to Christian Architecture and Worship* (Oxford and New York: Oxford University Press).

Heathcote, E., and Spens, I. (1997), *Church Builders* (Chichester: Academy Editions).

Inge, J. (2003), *A Christian Theology of Place* (Aldershot and Burlington, VT: Ashgate).

Irvine, C. (2013), *The Cross and Creation in Christian Liturgy and Art* (London: SPCK).

Kieckhefer, R. (2004), *Theology in Stone: Church Architecture from Byzantium to Berkeley* (Oxford and New York: Oxford University Press).

Seasolz, K. R. (2005), *A Sense of the Sacred: Theological Foundations of Christian Architecture and Art* (New York and London: Continuum).

Stancliffe, D. (2008), *The Lion Companion to Church Architecture* (Oxford: Lion Hudson).

Yates, N. (2008), *Liturgical Space: Christian Worship and Church Buildings in Western Europe 1500–2000* (Aldershot: Ashgate).

Chapter 12

Time

Benjamin Gordon-Taylor

LITURGICAL TIME

There is an insatiable human fascination with time, and the calendar as a means of giving it order and structure has been the subject of much popular interest. The Christian understanding of time is grounded in the Hebrew Scriptures and their interpretative accounts of the intervention of God in human history. Pivotal events in this history, like the exodus, became occasions of regular celebration, not in terms of simple remembering and certainly not in the form of dry historical reenactment. Instead, they were occasions of *dynamic* remembering: the reality of the event celebrated and encountered in the present. The Christian Church has also ordered time in a way that expresses belief in God as Lord of time, and although there have been, and still are, differences of theological emphasis and liturgical expression, the Christian ordering of time is dynamic rather than mechanistic. The liturgical marking of time need not necessarily be seen as the preserve of a particular theological tradition: there is potential for growth, renewal and mission in its creative exploration as tradition has bequeathed and as it continues to evolve in creative tension with contemporary society.

The observance of the Christian year is not merely a pious historical reflection on the life and acts of Jesus Christ, but a celebration of the mystery of God the creator and redeemer in Christ. It is therefore a celebration not of what Christ did or said, but of Christ himself. This mystery is accessible to us through different lenses: each season and festival is a window onto God, a view through a glass darkly, and the celebration of each an aspiration to see God face to face. Thomas Merton wrote that liturgical time is 'humanly insecure, seeking its peace altogether outside the structures of all that is established, visible and familiar, in the shape of a kingdom which is not seen' (Merton, 1976, p. 40).

Beyond human attempts to divide up and organize it, time is already sanctified, because God is Lord of history and creator of all that we experience. For Jews and Christians the meaning of time is found in the self-revelation of the creator God: consequently time is not merely sequential, a 'succession of bare moments', but also 'a powerful thrust home toward its holy source'. This means 'that the liturgy needs time rather than time needs liturgy' (Kavanagh, 1992, p. 24).

Odo Casel, the influential Benedictine liturgist, believed that the liturgical year should be seen not simply as a series of commemorations, 'not a gradual unfolding in the sense that the year of nature develops', but as something which makes present 'a single divine act which demands and finds gradual accustoming on [our] part, though in itself complete'. On each feast and in each season, 'the entire saving mystery' is before us, and 'more concretely on each occasion'. Advent and Lent typify the fact that there is no time of the year in which the entire mystery is not present. For example: 'We celebrate Advent, not by putting ourselves back into the state of unredeemed [humanity], but in the certainty of the Lord who has already appeared to us, for whom we must prepare our souls' (Casel, 1962, pp. 66–8).

Advent is used here as an example of principles that can be applied to the Christian year as a whole. In Casel's understanding, the mystery of God in Christ, even in extended, humanly organized temporal celebration, is one and undivided. It is present in the reality of Christ at all times and in all places as the consequence of Easter and the Ascension. Casel likens the liturgical year to the action of a screw thread: each successive celebration spirals ever upwards. The Church already knows what it contains and that it will come round again, but each celebration of it brings the Church nearer to the *eschaton*, deeper into the mystery of salvation, and it is therefore an experience of grace and renewal: 'just as the sacraments contain and effect what they signify, so the Christian year, in respect of the eternity of grace, is the image and ever-repeated manifestation of the Redeemer-God in our lives.' As the redeeming work of Christ is the primordial mystery, the liturgical year which 'makes it actual and human' is itself 'a derived mystery and a kind of sacrament in the wider sense' (Denis-Boulet, 1960, pp. 120–1).

THE LITURGICAL CALENDAR

The liturgical calendar consists of two cycles: the *temporale* and the *sanctorale*. *Temporale* means the course of **times and seasons** of the year: Advent, Christmas, Epiphany, Lent, Easter, and what several traditions now call 'Ordinary Time', a period when no other season is being observed. The *sanctorale* is the particular choice and sequence of **fixed dates** through the year which celebrate aspects of the mystery of Christ or which commemorate the saints and holy ones recognized by the Church in every age. The calendar is both universal and local: there are seasons and festivals whose observance is celebrated among all the churches with varying emphasis, and others which receive particular emphasis in a given tradition. Within a tradition, there are also universal and local dimensions to the calendar: seasons and occasions marked everywhere and by all, and observances which form part of a much more local selection of commemorations, often reflecting national and regional history and culture.

In the early centuries of the evolution of the calendar a tension emerged between a historical and an eschatological emphasis. This is still present in it today and is of positive and creative value. Another creative tension concerns the *sanctorale* in relation to the *temporale*, and comprises two elements: the cycle of fixed dates in relation to the cycle of moveable seasons, and the life of humanity in relation to the life of heaven.

The first element may seem to suggest that this is a question of reconciling the simultaneous operation of two conflicting systems – it would be entirely and typically human to wish this to happen. However, while it may seem that the seasons have a habit of getting in the way of the observance of saints' days, in fact the seasons should have priority, and in modern processes of liturgical revision such has been the concern to emphasize the primacy of the seasons that the *sanctorale* has been subject to considerable simplification. The liturgical implementation of the Second Vatican Council included a drastic cull of saints, particularly those of dubious reputation or existence, but partly also to avoid the fact that almost every day of the year directed the commemoration of at least one saint, which was rightly deemed to be particularly unhelpful in Advent, Lent and the Easter season. The English Prayer Books had done the same thing in the sixteenth and seventeenth centuries but for different reasons. It was never true that Anglican theology had no interest in calendrical matters, however, and in the Anglican tradition is to be found one of the most eloquent expressions of the nature of liturgical time. A poem by the seventeenth-century English priest John Donne suggests that the attempted reconciliation of the two cycles of season and festival is not the point, and that it is in the very tension that the creative activity of God may best be seen. It happens every so often that the date of the Annunciation of our Lord to the Blessed Virgin Mary (25 March) falls in Holy Week. It happened in 1608, and the result was Donne's poem 'Upon the Annunciation and Passion':

> She sees him man, so like God made in this,
> That of them both a circle emblem is,
> Whose first and last concur; this doubtful day
> Of feast or fast, Christ came, and went away.

For Donne, the point is that the occurrence emphasizes the unity of what Christ achieves, and by implication its presence for the Church in the liturgy. By overlaying the Incarnation with the crucifixion, in merging feast and fast, fixed date and moveable observance, a greater insight is gained into the activity of God in creation and among the people of God – a sacramental activity in which, by the grace of God, outward form points to the hidden mystery of grace and transformation. Therefore, Donne continues,

> This Church, by letting these days join, hath shown
> Death and conception in mankind is one.

This single example from the seventeenth century shows how season and festival are joined in ways far more significant than the superficial incompatibilities of their coexistence. This is no argument for abandoning the transferring of feasts, a technical process which in practice enables a proper focus to be kept on the primary seasons, but there is shown by this one happy collision that the calendar in its temporal and sanctoral aspects has a dynamism which is itself in tension with human systems of order and time. The dynamic character of the calendar results from the fact that God is involved – it is a consequence of the Incarnation, and is vivified by the Passion, resurrection and Ascension.

The second element is the tension in the saints between humanity and the life of heaven. Once more, this is precisely the point, if only because it is in some sense a reflection of the nature of Christ himself. More than this, the saints typify the redeeming work of Christ and the work of the Holy Spirit in men and women throughout history. Christ is the personification of the mystery spoken of in the Letter to the Ephesians:

> he has made known to us in all wisdom and insight the mystery of his will, according to his purpose which he set forth in Christ as a plan for the fulness of time, to unite all things in him, things in heaven and things on earth.
>
> (Ephesians 1.9–10 RSV)

The saints as examples of redeemed humanity are images, a series of lenses through which that single mystery of God in Christ is seen and made present. The historical record is not the only purpose, or even the principal one. The *sanctorale* is

> much more than a mere roll of honour, and its day by day observance is not only a pious recollection of historic events and people . . . It perpetuates the past into the present, and, in one sense, makes all contemporary.
>
> (Cowley, 1960, p. 12)

It is 'sacramental' in this sense of transcending time in that the grace given to the saints is available to the Church of the present. The saints proclaim the possibility of redemption as well as its achievement, and so their 'yearly remembrance', a phrase which recurs in many collects, is an *anamnesis* of a nature akin to that of the Eucharist in that it makes present in reality and newness what Christ did in his holy ones, and so strengthens the Church and gives it hope. The *sanctorale* is therefore sacramental in this sense also: the fruits of martyrdom, for example, become part of the rich outpouring of grace which the sacramental relationship of God and the world entails, and are thus as much 'now' as they were 'then' in historical time. As Cowley further states, 'The Church sees in the saints the reality of the conquest of Christ over sinful human nature and the highest justification of all Christian assertions' (Cowley, 1960, p. 14).

The tensions in the history and the theology of the calendar are thus part of its nature and purpose; they form the basis of an understanding of the liturgical calendar as an aspect of the liturgy which is dynamic and alive, despite its susceptibility to rules and the printed page. Such an understanding is vital. The calendar conveys both the account of God's activity as Lord of history, and the present reality of the presence of Christ in the Church by which it bursts the chains of a rigid and linear, necessarily sequential notion of time. The humanly fashioned tomb could not hold Christ: so humanly conceived time cannot contain his activity.

HALLOWING THE TIME IN THE WEEK AND THE DAY

The Roman civil system of naming days has bequeathed to us the planetary scheme with some later Nordic equivalents, but initially the Christian Church continued the Jewish manner of referring to all other days than the Sabbath by number, save that Sunday became in effect day one, *dies dominica*, the day of the Lord, all other days being numbered from this starting point (Rordorf, 1968, pp. 24ff.). However, the Roman system of *kalends*, *ides* and *nones* (as in 'Beware the ides of March', spoken by the soothsayer in Shakespeare's *Julius Caesar*) was used in liturgical books, and indeed technically survives as a means of identifying the feasts of saints in the *Roman Martyrology*. The avoidance of planetary names probably reflects a desire to prevent obvious pagan associations, particularly in the first four centuries while this debate was being especially engaged in by apologists for both systems of belief. The tensions apparent between secular and ecclesiastical calendars today thus have their roots in the very origins of an organized Christian institution and its interaction with the surrounding culture. However pragmatic the adoption, the pagan associations would have been well known, just as however much we point to 31 October as the eve of All Saints' Day, the association with witches and ghosts will remain. Ironically perhaps it was the vernacular liturgies of the Reformation that gave official admission to the pre-Christian names of days: the Book of Common Prayer has 'Sundays' after Easter and Trinity, 'Monday, Tuesday, Wednesday and Thursday' before Easter, 'Good Friday', and so on. There seems to be no scruple about adopting the pagan names, perhaps because the Roman system was too closely associated with the former liturgy and not easily rendered into English in any case. Four hundred years later, reformed vernacular Roman liturgy began to do exactly the same thing. Therefore the apparent tension of applying pagan names to Christian festivals and holy days has long been a part of the calendar. Indeed, it is often argued that the major Christian festival of Christmas took over a pagan feast of the sun. Is all this, however, merely words, mere cultural history, or is there a deeper significance? A positive interpretation can be found: since Christianity is a religion of divine Incarnation, it should be no surprise if it roots itself in the surrounding culture. This does not have to mean theological compromise, but may instead represent the Christian conviction that God shares the life of humanity. That conviction implies not a barrier against but an engagement with the culture and society in which Christians find themselves. The sacramental action of God is upon the whole of creation, and the activity of God is disclosed not merely in Christian cultic settings but also in what Karl Rahner attractively calls 'the liturgy of the world' (Skelley, 1991), with which the liturgy of the Church is inextricably and deliberately linked.

A tension of a different kind arising from the history of the evolution of the calendar concerns the status of Sunday. The origins of Sunday as the Christian Sabbath are to some extent still a matter of debate: was Sunday observed both in opposition and juxtaposition to the Jewish Sabbath? There is some evidence for a pre-Christian significance of Sunday in some communities, for example Qumran. Then there is the question of Sunday's place in the week – is it the beginning or the end of the Christian week? Josef Jungmann argued that in fact Monday was the beginning, citing as evidence the early-Church designation of Sunday as the eighth day. As Rordorf suggests, this still 'presupposes that Sunday . . . remains the first day of the week.' Furthermore, the existence in older calendars of the liturgical period the *octave*, or period of eight days, supports the notion that for Christians Sunday was both the beginning *and* the end of the week – day one and day eight (Rordorf, 1968, p. 40; Jungmann 1959, pp. 22–3). This has scriptural and theological resonance: God is the Alpha and the Omega, all ends and beginnings are contained in God. Indeed in the Hebrew Scriptures there is the contrast between 'Be still, and know that I am God' and 'let us press on to know the LORD' (Psalm 46.10; Hosea 6.3 RSV). Sunday, therefore, as present celebration of the resurrection, looks both to what has been, what is, and to what will be, all of which is in the hands of God. In the eschatological view, this pull in two directions is surely the humanly experienced preliminary of a state where there are no ends or beginnings. Again the language of the poet and preacher puts it best:

> And into that gate they shall enter, and in that house they shall dwell, where there shall be . . . no darkness nor dazzling, but one equal light . . . no ends nor beginnings, but one equal eternity . . .   (John Donne, Sermon XVI)

Originally, before the evolution of Holy Week, Easter Sunday was the single celebration of the Passion and the resurrection, mirrored by all other Sundays. This 'end' and 'beginning', so to speak, are at the heart of the sacramental character of liturgical time, since it is by the reality and particularity in time of these events that the gospel sacraments of baptism and Eucharist are occasions of participation in and encounter with the crucified and risen Christ: 'The visible presence of our Redeemer passed over into the mysteries' (Leo the Great, Sermon 74). The presence of Christ in historical time and space is thus transformed: the Ascension is understood to be the inauguration of Christ's presence always and everywhere. Therefore time itself is transformed and sanctified by the events of Easter, and itself becomes part of the sacramental economy in which God is encountered and by which all are made ready for the 'equal light' of eternity. The Christian Sunday contains and entails all this.

The liturgical marking of time finds a daily focus in forms of daily liturgical prayer, sometimes called the 'Office', and, in the Roman Catholic tradition, the Divine Office or Liturgy of the Hours. The latter title points to the tradition of dividing the day by 'hours' of prayer, a practice with scriptural roots and which was adopted in the early Church and later evolved in distinct forms in monastic as well as public contexts, but whose public celebration was gradually eroded as an emphasis on monastic and clerical obligation increased. At the Reformation there was a revival of the public character of daily liturgical prayer in the Anglican tradition and in other Reformed communities which, although itself neglected at various times in the subsequent history of those churches, nevertheless survived as a liturgical foundation that has received new life in recent years, and on a broad ecumenical front. Many parishes, pastoral communities and groups of all traditions have rediscovered daily liturgical prayer celebrated in the framework of the liturgical calendar informing the lectionary, and the mood and manner of the celebration.

HALLOWING THE TIME IN WORSHIP AND MISSION

The celebration of the seasons and festivals of the liturgical year has, at least by official intention, always been an integral part of the life of many of the historic and Reformed churches. The degree and manner of actual use of the calendar has reflected the differing strands of ecclesiology, but for many the authorized liturgy of the Church has always assumed the calendar to be of importance to its ordered celebration. The Anglican Book of Common Prayer, for example, is meticulous in setting out the manner in which the calendar and associated lectionary are to be used, and how they are to inform and animate the daily prayer of the people of God around the inseparable tables of word and sacrament. Subsequent revisions of the calendar in its various forms have built on such earlier foundations to reflect in a balanced and imaginative way the historical, theological and pastoral factors that have shaped the liturgical life of the Church. In turn these have brought the opportunity for renewed study of the seasons and feasts of the Christian year, and a fresh consideration of the manner in which the mystery of salvation is encountered in the Christian marking of time.

Each tradition and community will use the calendar according to its own discerned priorities, and each will decide what its pattern of celebration will be, day by day and week by week within the universal structure and guided by the norms of liturgical authority; a renewed appreciation and use of the calendar can, however, enrich existing opportunities for worship and suggest others that may give shape to the vision and enhance the mission to which the Church is called. The seasons, with their recurring themes of death and rebirth, penitence and forgiveness, darkness and light, act as a mirror in which can be glimpsed the redeemed humanity God calls the Church to be. The lives of the saints and holy ones of God down the ages provide further lenses in which are focused both the fragility and the potential of human response, and which offer the hope that broken lives may be remade in God's image. The calendar embeds in the liturgical life of the Church daily reminders of the ultimate goal of every Christian, the vision of God and the joy of eternal life, revealing in human lives the transforming work of God, and alerting the people of God to the action of the Spirit in drawing them closer to the life of heaven of which their worship is a foretaste.

The calendar makes present in the Church and is itself a witness to God's creative and redemptive activity. Christian communities today and those who exercise leadership and other ministries within them make use of the calendar as a vital means of celebrating and sharing the gospel with others. For example, the many catechetical courses now available for new Christians and for all in need of nurture and spiritual growth are frequently offered in the context of the seasons. Thus the Roman Catholic Rite of Christian Initiation of Adults, drawing on early-Church patterns of Christian formation, builds the progress of the candidates into the Lent–Easter cycle and thus declares their exploration and profession of faith to be a function of God's saving work in Christ's death and resurrection.

In one of the resources published in support of the *Common Worship* calendar in the Church of England, Robert Atwell notes that the annual commemoration of the saints

> must have been an extremely moving event in the life of a Christian community. It precipitated within the consciousness of the Church a powerful sense of solidarity, of a belonging in Christ which transcended death. This awareness is something recent generations seem largely to have lost.   (Atwell, 1998, p. iii)

A restored sense of communion with Christ through the remembering and celebration of his holy ones encourages 'prayer in which the whole Church shares, living and departed, commending one another to the mercy of God'

(Atwell, 1998, pp. vi–vii). This assertion may not sit easily with the theological emphases of some communities, but the sense of the continuity and solidarity which the calendar by its very nature encourages can be a valuable framework for prayer and a deepening spirituality which has closeness to Christ and union with God as its goal. As Thomas Merton said, 'In the cycle of the holy year, the Church rhythmically breathes the life-giving atmosphere of the Spirit, and her bloodstream is cleansed of the elements of death. She lives in Christ, and with him praises the Father' (Merton, 1976, p. 33).

VISUAL TIME: LITURGICAL COLOURS

While not a part of the liturgical life of every Christian community, the use of colour in the physical setting and visual character of worship has a long history and contemporary potential as a means of indicating season and festival. Through the Middle Ages increasingly complex schemes of colour evolved, but in the twentieth century the Liturgical Movement inspired an approach to liturgical colours which pointed to a recovery of simplicity and drew on a more consciously psychological interpretation: colours which seemed best suited in the imagination to the tone of the particular celebration, thus drab colours for penitential seasons; white and gold for Easter, Christmas and festivals of the Lord; red for Passiontide, apostles and martyrs; green and sometimes yellow for growth and renewal and Ordinary Time. This is the basis of most use of liturgical colours today, and there has been significant ecumenical convergence. Much Anglican practice, for example, now follows the simplified pattern established in the *Roman Missal* of 1969, although local uses survive, often based on the medieval use of Salisbury, for example blue instead of violet in Advent and Lent, and the continuation of red on the Sundays after Trinity. Some Anglican parishes also retain the custom of rose colour on the Third Sunday of Advent and the Fourth Sunday of Lent, connected with the more joyful tone of the medieval masses for those days. Black as an expression of mourning also survives in use for funerals and requiem Eucharists in some communities, although violet (penitence, forgiveness) and white (resurrection) are more common. Also increasing is the use of 'year round' textiles which are not confined to particular seasons or feasts or tied to particular dominant colours, thus avoiding the need for constant change, and which perhaps allow for greater artistic freedom in the service of the liturgy. It may be argued, though, that this practice lessens the visual emphasis on the observance of the calendar which a full scheme allows.

The discipline of liturgical theology has drawn attention to the context of liturgical celebration and the significance of the visual as well as the spoken as expressions of the inherently performative nature of liturgy. Liturgical colours are one element in this. The *Roman Missal* of 1969 declared that they give 'effective, outward expression to the specific character of the mysteries of the faith being celebrated and, in the course of the year, to a sense of progress in the Christian life' (*General Instruction on the Roman Missal*, 1969, §307). In this sense, then, liturgical colours are an aspect of the common pilgrimage of the Church in response to God's call, and the pilgrimage of the individual towards spiritual growth and maturity. Worship is the corporate and individual response to the mystery of God, and a place of its showing forth in creation. Colour is a factor in the animation of creation, a gift to the senses which assists the human capacity to encounter beauty and see in it the hand of the creator. In this way it has a place in worship, where creation's loving response to the creator is most typically expressed in liturgical time.

Further reading

Adam, A. (1992), 'Liturgical Time (The Liturgical Year)', in A. Adam, *Foundations of Liturgy: An Introduction to Its History and Practice* (Collegeville, MN: Liturgical Press).

Bradshaw, P. F., and Johnson, M. E. (2011), *The Origins of Feasts, Fasts and Seasons in Early Christianity*, Alcuin Club Collections 86 (London: SPCK).

Guiver, G. (2000), *Company of Voices: Daily Prayer and the People of God* (Norwich: Canterbury Press).

Johnson, M. E. (ed.) (2000), *Between Memory and Hope: Readings on the Liturgical Year* (Collegeville, MN: Liturgical Press).

Merton, T. (1976), *Meditations on Liturgy* (London: Mowbray).

Talley, T. (2nd edn, 1991), *The Origins of the Liturgical Year* (Collegeville, MN: Liturgical Press).

Event

Chapter 13

Initiation

Maxwell E. Johnson

'Holy Baptism', according to the 1979 *Book of Common Prayer* (hereafter, *BCP*) of the Episcopal Church in the USA, is 'full initiation by water and the Holy Spirit into Christ's Body the Church' (*BCP*, 1979, p. 298). The study of the rites of Christian initiation constitutes a major field within the discipline known as liturgical studies (see Johnson, 1995, 2001, 2007; Whitaker and Johnson, 2003; Spinks 2006a, 2006b). This chapter seeks to introduce students to the contemporary practice of Christian initiation within the Anglican Communion primarily, with particular attention to its ritual process, biblical themes and images, its relation to the liturgical year, and to modern questions about confirmation and first Communion as well as whether adult or infant initiation should be viewed as the norm for practice, theologically and pastorally.

CHRISTIAN INITIATION AS A RITUAL PROCESS

Rites of initiation in general have often been interpreted according to what many in the anthropological and ritual studies disciplines have identified, since the seminal work of Arnold van Gennep, as 'rites of passage' (van Gennep, 1960). That is, initiation rites, like those of birth, marriage, entrance into adulthood, specific vocations, and even the funeral and other rites surrounding death, are those rites which various communities the world over, since the beginning of time, have celebrated as marking important 'passages' from one level of identity and status in a given community or group to another. Such rites, generally, have an overall three-part structure and take place as a process over a predetermined period of time.

Rites of separation, in which those to be eventually initiated are separated from the community for a time, take place first. This is usually followed by a period of what is called 'liminality' or transition, that is, a period 'betwixt and between' the initiands' former identity and status and their yet-to-be new identity and status. Several different rites, including, for example, instruction in the customs and traditions of the community, may take place during this 'liminal period' of isolation and transition. The final stage is that of the initiation or incorporation itself, in which the initiands now enter completely into the life of the community with a new status and identity as full members of that community. Most often, we are told, this final rite of incorporation includes a sharing in some kind of ritual meal (cf. even graduation receptions, wedding banquets and funeral lunches). Such a process, often quite dramatic and life-threatening in certain aboriginal societies, is commonly viewed in several different cultural contexts as a ritual process of 'rebirth' and/or one of 'death and resurrection'. Those initiated have 'died' to their former way of life and been 'resurrected' or 'reborn' in another. Even the newly married couple has gone through a process of 'dying' to being single so that they might be 'reborn' or 'resurrected' as husband and wife and thus take a new place in society.

While there is nothing specifically Christian about such a ritual process, the Church has made use of something similar to celebrate the initiation of those who, in response to the proclamation of the gospel, the 'good news' of God's salvation in Christ, have been converted, have repented of their sins and sought incorporation into Christ and the Church. The insights of anthropology into what appears to be a rather common human and social process of initiation, then, can be of great help to us in understanding the particular shape of the rites of Christian initiation specifically. Like all human rites of passage, the Christian rites of initiation themselves, especially as the adult catechumenate has been recovered and restored in our own day, came to follow a general pattern consisting of:

1 Entrance to the Catechumenate, a rite of **separation**;
2 The Catechumenate and eventual 'Election' for initiation, a 'liminal' time of **transition** and **preparation**, during which those to be initiated are instructed (catechized) and formed in the teaching and life of the community;
3 The Rites of Initiation (baptism, 'confirmation', and first Communion), rites by which the former catechumens and 'elect' are now incorporated fully into the life of the Christian community;
4 The Period of Mystagogy ('explanation of the mysteries'), a continued process of further incorporation or reintegration into the community by explaining what the 'mysteries' received signify and what their implications are for ongoing life in the community.

And, significantly, these Christian initiation rites are also often interpreted as rites of 'rebirth' (see John 3.5) and 'death, burial, and resurrection' (see Romans 6).

As helpful as the insights of anthropology and ritual studies are for understanding the particular structure or shape of the rites of Christian initiation, however, they tell us very little about the actual content and theological interpretation of those rites. Similarly, Mark Searle liked to say that initiation rites, as they are generally understood, are about initiating people who already belong in some way, by birth, to the community into a new level of membership or status within that same community. Hence, religious rites of 'initiation' are not so much about advancing to a new level of community membership as they are about 'conversion' and 'faith'. They are about entering a new community to which one did not belong before, even by birth, for Christians, in the words of Tertullian in the early third century, are 'made, not born'. The anthropological analogy with the 'rites of passage', therefore, is only partially true in the case of our Christian rites. The ritual process may be similar but the contents, goal and interpretation of that process, as we shall see, are not necessarily the same.

A DIVERSITY OF IMAGES AND INTERPRETATIONS IN THE NEW TESTAMENT

Based on Jesus' baptism by John at the Jordan (Matthew 3.13–17; Mark 1.9–11; Luke 3.21–22; John 1.31–34), possibly on Jesus' own baptismal practice (John 3.22, 26; 4.1), and in general continuity with the overall context of ritual washings and bathing customs within first-century Judaism, new converts to Christianity, at least from the first Christian Pentecost on (Acts 2.38–42), were initiated into Christ and the Church by a ritual process which included some form of 'baptism' with water, a process that eventually would be based in the command of the risen Jesus (Matthew 28.19). The New Testament itself, however, records little detail about this baptismal practice or what additional ceremonies may have been included. While we might assume that some kind of profession of faith in Jesus as Lord was present, we do not know, for example, if any particular 'formula' – e.g. 'I baptize you in the name of the Father and of the Son and of the Holy Spirit' from the dominical command for baptism in Matthew 28.19, or 'in the name of Jesus' (Acts 3.6) – was employed. Nor do we do know precisely how baptisms were regularly conferred (by immersion, complete submersion or pouring), whether infants were ever candidates for baptism during the earliest period, what kind of preparation may have preceded adult baptism, whether anointings were already part of the process, or if occasional references to the apostolic conferral of the post-baptismal gift of the Holy Spirit (Acts 8; 19) were regular features of baptismal practice in some early communities or exceptional cases in particular situations.

Whatever the particular rites employed in the Christian initiation of new converts in the primitive communities may have been, it is clear from the New Testament that the meaning of initiation itself was understood in a variety of ways. These include: forgiveness of sins and the gift of the Holy Spirit (Acts 2.38); new birth through water and the Holy Spirit (John 3.5; Titus 3.5–7); putting off the 'old nature' and 'putting on the new', that is, 'being clothed in the righteousness of Christ' (Galatians 3.27; Colossians 3.9–10); initiation into the 'one body' of the Christian community (1 Corinthians 12.13; see also Acts 2.42); washing, sanctification and justification in Christ and the Holy Spirit (1 Corinthians 6.11); enlightenment (Hebrews 6.4; 10.32; 1 Peter 2.9); being 'anointed' and/or 'sealed' by the Holy Spirit (2 Corinthians 1.21–22; 1 John 2.20, 27); being 'sealed' or 'marked' as belonging to God and God's people (2 Corinthians 1.21–22; Ephesians 1.13–14; 4.30; Revelation 7.3); and being joined to Christ through participation in his death, burial and resurrection (Romans 6.3–11; Colossians 2.12–15).

Paul Bradshaw has noted that 'this variation in baptismal theology encourages the supposition that the ritual itself may also have varied considerably from place to place' (2002b, p. 61). And, if not already present in some places already, these theological interpretations will certainly give rise to specific ritual practices later on. Literal anointings with oil, for example, will develop in all early Christian liturgical traditions to express ritually the gift, anointing and seal of the Holy Spirit in initiation. Putting off the old nature and being clothed with the new nature of Christ (Galatians 3.27) will eventually be expressed by pre-baptismal strippings of clothes and post-baptismal clothings in new white garments. Whether connected to an anointing or not, the mark of God's ownership of the newly initiated will come to be signified by various signings or consignations with the cross. Enlightenment will be expressed by the use of baptismal candles or tapers. And the baptismal font and waters will come to be interpreted as either or both womb (John 3.5) and tomb (Romans 6), grave and mother – or both. Such a theology will give rise architecturally to how fonts themselves will come be shaped: tomb-like appearance; eight-sided reflecting the entrance into the eighth day or first day of the new creation; quatrolobe to suggest the shape of the cross; six-sided to suggest the Passion; and circular to suggest a womb. Given the rich variety of New Testament interpretations of Christian initiation, it was only inevitable that the rites themselves would evolve in this way. That is, a rich biblical theology such as this would seem to call for an equally rich liturgical expression and practice.

Of all these New Testament interpretations, however, two will stand out with particular emphasis in the evolving life of the Church: Christian initiation as new birth through water and the Holy Spirit (John 3.5ff. and Titus 3.5); and Christian initiation as being united with Christ in his death, burial and resurrection (Romans 6.3–11). The first of these finds its foundation in Jesus' own baptism by John in the Jordan – if not in Pentecost itself – and the second in the ultimate completion of that baptism in his death on the cross. Liturgical scholars have sometimes asserted that the contrast between these images is Johannine ('birth') and Pauline ('death and burial'). But this is more apparent than real. Baptismal regeneration, new birth and adoption images are also Pauline. That is, in addition to Titus 3.5, the baptismal theology of Galatians, for example, is especially that of adoption in Christ, becoming in the Son a child of God, brought about by the work of the Holy Spirit who cries out 'Abba! Father!' in the baptized (Galatians 4.1–7). Further, while these two interpretations need not be mutually exclusive, each one by itself will serve as the dominant interpretation of Christian initiation within specific liturgical traditions. Not surprisingly, then, it is around these two primary interpretations that all the other New Testament images and metaphors as particular ceremonies will eventually tend to cluster as either pre- or post-baptismal rites.

FEASTS AND SEASONS AND THE CELEBRATION OF CHRISTIAN INITIATION

In our own day, the churches of the Anglican Communion, like the Roman Catholic and Lutheran churches and others, have reclaimed the theological priority of Romans 6 as their theology of Christian initiation as well as the centrality of Easter as the baptismal feast par excellence, with the result that what is called the Paschal Mystery of Christ's dying and rising is commonly viewed as the foundational paradigm for ongoing life in Christ. However, if for good theological reasons we may have centred our attention here, the biblical and liturgical baptismal tradition of the Church is much richer than this and invites us to consider other times and occasions for its celebration. My graduate students know that I like to say, 'We have tended to place all of our baptismal eggs in the Easter basket today.' But surely, without minimizing the importance or significance of Easter baptism in the least, other occasions like the Epiphany (or, more regularly, the Sunday after the Epiphany), where the baptism of Jesus is celebrated, Pentecost or All Saints', suggest themselves as most fitting and suitable occasions for the celebration of baptism itself, just as other feasts of Mary and the saints might also be quite appropriate (see Johnson, 2001). In fact, it is a mark of the contemporary Anglican and Lutheran traditions to emphasize this diversity of options. As, for example, the 1979 *BCP* of the Episcopal Church states:

> Holy Baptism is especially appropriate at the Easter Vigil, on the Day of Pentecost, on All Saints' Day or the Sunday after All Saints' Day, and on the Feast of the Baptism of our Lord (the First Sunday after the Epiphany).
>
> (*BCP*, 1979, p. 312)

With these four feasts as the four primary occasions for both baptismal vigils and the corporate and public celebration of baptism throughout the liturgical year, parish catechetical programmes (especially for the pre-baptismal preparation of parents, godparents and sponsors) might also be easily structured in the autumn, winter and spring in close proximity to these festal occasions. In those places where the sheer number of infant baptismal candidates makes waiting for one of these major feasts problematic, certainly other feasts on the calendar suggest themselves as suitable baptismal occasions as well, with the result that, in addition to these four central feasts, other regular occasions in relationship to the liturgical year might be highlighted. The words of Tertullian are still true in this context:

The Passover [i.e. Easter] provides the day of most solemnity for baptism, for then was accomplished our Lord's passion, and *into it we are baptized* . . . After that, Pentecost is a most auspicious period for arranging baptisms, for during it our Lord's resurrection was several times made known among the disciples, and the grace of the Holy Spirit first given . . . For all that, every day is a Lord's day: any hour, any season, is suitable for baptism. If there is any difference of solemnity, it makes no difference to the grace.

(*De Baptismo* 19, Whitaker and Johnson, 2003, p. 10, emphasis mine)

But if Tertullian was correct that 'every day is a Lord's day: any hour, any season, is suitable for baptism', and that 'if there is any difference of solemnity, it makes no difference to the grace', the fact remains that it is precisely this 'difference of solemnity' associated with various feasts on the calendar that provides us with the very models of 'grace' that baptism sacramentally signifies and effects. Christian initiation is always participation in the death, burial and resurrection of Christ, and baptism is our common grave and tomb. But how better to underscore and highlight that than actual baptism at the Easter Vigil, after a Lent oriented towards baptismal–catechumenal preparation and/or renewal? Christian initiation is always new birth and adoption through water and the Holy Spirit (John 3.5; Titus 3.5). But how better to emphasize and bring this to light than by the celebration of baptism on the feast of Jesus' own baptism, where our attention is directed to the divine declaration of Jesus' and our own baptismal identity conceived and given birth in the womb of the life-giving font, and where the Spirit descends to empower us for life and mission? Indeed, attention to this might even help us come to celebrate the Advent season with new understanding and insight. Baptism is always the great sacrament and 'seal' of the Holy Spirit. But how better to restore this much-needed emphasis that Christian baptism *is* Spirit baptism than by celebrating baptism on Pentecost itself, where the Apostles themselves are 'baptized' in the Holy Spirit and this 'new birth' of the Church is marked by the baptism of three thousand converts? And baptism is always initiation or incorporation into Christ and his body, the Church. But what better way to renew the ecclesiological dimension of baptism than to celebrate baptism on All Saints' Day, when the very nature and communion of the Church, both militant and triumphant, is already one of the major emphases in our liturgical celebration? Yes, Tertullian was correct in saying that 'If there is any difference of solemnity, it makes no difference to the grace.' But sacramental validity, or the 'grace' of baptism, is not really the issue as we seek to do our baptismal catechesis and mystagogy in the best ways possible. Because the very 'difference of solemnity' provides for us abundantly rich and various baptismal models and images for our celebration, understanding and lifelong appropriation of the meanings of baptism, we might say, instead, that the 'difference of solemnity' makes all the difference.

CONFIRMATION AND THE EUCHARIST AS THE CULMINATION OF CHRISTIAN INITIATION

If 'Holy Baptism is full initiation by water and the Holy Spirit into Christ's Body the Church', what, then, do we make of confirmation? Ever since the sixteenth-century Protestant and Catholic Reformations, the rites and meaning of confirmation among Anglicans have been matters of some debate, culminating in the famous and opposed positions of Gregory Dix (Dix, 1946), who argued for its New Testament origins, and Geoffrey Lampe (Lampe, 1967), who argued instead for its much later development and even questionable theology in separating the 'Seal' of the Spirit from baptism itself. Adherents of both positions can be found in contemporary Anglicanism.

Recent Anglican rites of Christian initiation, however, have tended to restore to baptism either those classic 'confirmation' elements of post-baptismal hand-laying prayer for the sevenfold gifts of the Holy Spirit and its accompanying 'signing' of the forehead with the cross (including optional use of chrism in some churches), or, as in the case of the Church of England's *Common Worship* (*Common Worship: Christian Initiation*, 2006, p. 71), a post-baptismal prayer with the signing with the cross (and the optional use of oil) containing explicit mention of God's 'anointing Spirit'. In *Common Worship* this prayer is viewed as being so important that if omitted at baptism the bishop is to supply it at confirmation before the laying on of hands. Hence, one might say that what was traditionally known as confirmation is simply again now part of the rites of baptism. Here it is interesting to note that what contemporary initiation rites have incorporated in this way bears a remarkable similarity to what Thomas Cranmer already anticipated in his 1549 Book of Common Prayer by changing the then existing 'christic' post-baptismal anointing prayer to an explicit 'unction of the Holy Spirit':

> Almighty God, the Father of our Lord Jesus Christ, who hath regenerated thee by water and the Holy Ghost, and hath given unto thee remission of all thy sins; he vouchsafe to anoint thee *with the unction of his Holy Spirit*, and bring thee to the inheritance of everlasting life. Amen.
>
> (Fisher, 1970, p. 94, emphasis mine)

Nevertheless, 'confirmation' by bishops remains a characteristic rite within the Anglican Communion. Such a rite, however, is increasingly seen today not as part of the sacramental initiation process but rather, in a manner consistent with several sixteenth-century Protestant traditions, as an affirmation, renewal or the personal owning of one's previous baptismal vows and promises after an extended period of catechetical instruction, often occurring during adolescence. Together with this, other rites, modelled on confirmation, have been developed for various pastoral situations like reception into full Communion, corporate renewal of baptismal vows (e.g. at the Easter Vigil), or personal reaffirmation of baptismal vows adapted to various circumstances or crisis moments in someone's life.

What has been the most radical shift in the Anglican world, as well as in the ecumenical liturgical world in general, has been the severing of the ties between confirmation and first Communion. That is, together with the renewal of the Eucharist throughout the churches today, there has been an increased focus on the Eucharist itself as the very culmination of the initiation process. And if 'full Christian initiation' is accomplished for all ages by baptism, especially now with explicit post-baptismal rites associated with the Holy Spirit, the age for the first reception of Holy Communion has been drastically lowered to include even baptized infants in some churches of the Anglican Communion, as it was for the first twelve centuries of the Christian West (see Fisher, 1965), and as it remains so in the Christian East. While some (e.g. *CW*, 2000, pp. 188ff.) have a special rite of admission to first Communion at a time after preliminary catechesis on Communion, others are quite willing to postpone catechesis on the Eucharist until after reception has taken place. In several Episcopal dioceses of the USA, in fact, infant and early childhood Communion reception is becoming something of a norm.

INFANT OR ADULT INITIATION?

The modern recovery and restoration of the adult catechumenate and adult initiation as a ritual process leading from initial conversion to Christ through catechetical and liturgical formation (often during Lent) and culminating in the rites of baptism, perhaps confirmation, and Eucharist (often at the Easter Vigil) is seen by many today as constituting a theological and liturgical 'norm' for celebration and interpretation (e.g. Kavanagh, 1978). Some, in light also of new theological interpretations of original sin as having less to do with the Augustinian notion of the inheritance of guilt and sin and as related more to the social or collective nature of fallen human life into which one is born and in which one is socialized, have argued that infants be enrolled in a type of catechumenate leading to their full initiation only at age seven or later after sufficient catechesis. As a result, the narrative of the fall of Adam and Eve into sin in Genesis 3 has been rescued from its almost biological use as a 'proof text' for the reproductive transmission of sin and restored as a paradigm for the universal human condition of sin, a condition overcome by the death and resurrection of Jesus Christ and celebrated in the rites of Christian initiation. And with this the perceived necessity of *quam primum* ('as soon as possible after birth') baptism based on fear of the consequences of original sin is slowly disappearing.

Others, recognizing the 'norm' of the process and ritual sequence of initiation in the adult form, contend that if infants of active Christian parents are to be baptized at all, then, as we saw above, they are to be initiated fully, including the reception of first Communion at their baptism. It was Roman Catholic liturgical scholar Mark Searle who best summed up the rationale for restoring the fullness of Christian initiation of young children, when he said that:

> At a time when the Church is so intent on rescuing the humane values of Christianity and is concerned to do greater justice to the role of the family . . . and a time when the role of the nonrational and pre-rational dimensions of the life of faith is being recovered, perhaps infant initiation ought to be seen less as a problem to be grappled with than as an opportunity to be grasped. Far from barring children from the font, the chrism, and the altar, the Church should welcome their participation in these sacraments as a reminder both of the catholicity of the Church and of the fact that, no matter how informed or committed we might be as adults, when we take part in the sacramental liturgies of the Church we are taking part in more than we know.
>
> (Searle, 1987, pp. 408–9)

It is important to note, however, that such recovery and restoration has not come about because of sacramental romanticism, or from any attempt at a liturgical repristination of a supposed, normative 'Golden Age' of the Church of the first few centuries. Far from it. Rather, such a move is coming about, ultimately, because of the recovery of the theology of initiation itself, because of the rootedness of all Christian initiation and life in the very graciousness of God, the God who through both word and sacrament always acts first, always acts in love prior to our action, leading us by the Holy Spirit to the response of faith, hope and love within the community of grace. Indeed, what could be more counter-cultural, more against the prevailing tide of modern individualism, and still more anti-Pelagian and grace-filled than doing something so apparently foolish as to celebrate God's salvific activity, God's choice, God's adoption of children, into God's reign as it is known and celebrated in the faith community through the initiation of infants? As Eugene Maly put it:

> Through infant Baptism we *initiate* a person into a faith-community long before he or she can choose whether to belong. And through infant Baptism we also *celebrate* a person's salvation long before he or she consciously experiences the need to be saved or can take any responsibility for turning self toward God. Something about this flies in the face of very basic notions in our culture about individual freedom and the importance of personal choice – in short, our insistence on individualism. We want to believe that we choose God (rather than that God chooses us). We want to believe that we can and should save ourselves (rather than that we are saved) . . . [B]iblical faith challenges our basic human temptation to individualism. Infant Baptism is . . . one way we have institutionalized our conviction that community is central to Christian life, to God's plan of salvation.　　　　　　　　　　　　　　　　　　(Maly, 1981, p. 95)

CONCLUSION

Although this chapter has concentrated on various topics or themes with regard to Christian initiation within the Anglican Communion, all that has been said certainly applies to similar developments in Roman Catholicism and among other churches including the Lutheran, which, at least in the USA, was fostered both directly and indirectly by work of scholars in the Episcopal Church. Indeed, the modern ecumenical movement has been a strong catalyst for liturgical renewal. Still today a similar approach to Christian initiation has vast ecumenical implications for the churches as together we come to realize more fully what our common baptism signifies for our life together in Christ. As Gordon Lathrop asks in his book, *Holy People*:

> If Baptism constitutes the assembly that is the church, ought not the Christians in a given locality enact that truth? Can we not do much of the process of Baptism together? Could a renewed catechumenate be undertaken by many or even all of the Christian assemblies in a given local place? Could we be present at each other's baptisms? Could we do baptisms on the great feasts and do them side by side? Could we even consider constructing a single font for the local churches in our towns and cities?   (Lathrop, 1999, pp. 146–7)

May such questions continue to shape our approach to Christian initiation in the future.

Further reading

Johnson, M. E. (ed.) (1995), *Living Water, Sealing Spirit: Readings on Christian Initiation* (Collegeville, MN: Liturgical Press).

Johnson, M. E. (2001), *Images of Baptism* (Chicago, IL: Liturgy Training Publications).

Johnson, M. E. (rev. edn, 2007), *The Rites of Christian Initiation: Their Evolution and Interpretation* (Collegeville, MN: Liturgical Press).

Myers, R. A. (1997), *Continuing the Reformation: Re-Visioning Baptism in the Episcopal Church* (New York: Church Publishing).

Spinks, B. D. (2006a), *Early and Medieval Rituals and Theologies of Baptism: From the New Testament to the Council of Trent* (Aldershot and Burlington, VT: Ashgate).

Spinks, B. D. (2006b), *Reformation and Modern Rituals and Theologies of Baptism: From Luther to Contemporary Practices* (Aldershot and Burlington, VT: Ashgate).

Whitaker, E. C., and Johnson, M. E. (eds) (rev. edn, 2003), *Documents of the Baptismal Liturgy*, Alcuin Club Collections 79 (London: SPCK).

Chapter 14

Eucharist

Gordon Jeanes

'They beheld God, and they ate and drank' (Exodus 24.11).

Meals are an integral part of Jewish and Christian religion, especially of the former. For Christians the religious meal has been monopolized by the Eucharist, and the meal element of that service has been minimized physically, in sharp contrast to the symbolic importance laid on the bread and wine. But, if we are to make sense of what the Eucharist is, we need to start with those meals recounted in the New Testament.

It is natural to begin with the Last Supper, but it needs to be seen in the context of meals that formed an important part of Jesus' ministry: 'Why does he eat with tax-collectors and sinners?' (Mark 2.16). In welcoming these people to eat and drink with him, Jesus was gathering around him those whom he was calling into the kingdom of heaven. Often he compared the kingdom to a feast: the marriage feast (Matthew 22.1–14), or a feast of reconciliation and homecoming (Luke 15). To eat and drink with Jesus is to repent and embrace the kingdom. The miraculous feedings likewise looked to the banquet of the kingdom: in John (6.15) the crowds recognized the messianic connection and tried to make Jesus their king.

From these meals and the miracles and parables associated with them, we can turn to the Last Supper when Jesus gave thanks over the bread and wine, speaking of them as his body and blood, foretold his sacrificial death and commanded the disciples to 'do this' in memory of him. The Gospels (except for John) present the Last Supper as a Passover meal and certainly it was held at Passover time. Christ's Passion was from the beginning imbued with the symbolism of the season (1 Corinthians 5.7–8), the Passover themes of God's redemption of Israel and the continual prayer for the coming of the kingdom, though it was now framed by his rejection and betrayal by Israel and his own disciples.

The resurrection appearances are often connected with food. Both Luke and John include meetings with the risen Christ in which he provides the disciples with food and makes himself known to them in the breaking of the bread (Luke 24.13–35; John 21.1–14). Rowan Williams presents these meals as Christ extending forgiveness and restoration even in the judgement of betrayal (Williams, 1982, p. 109). The resurrection – and the Eucharist – offers to us transformation and restoration as a community together. And so the first Christians 'broke bread' together even daily (Acts 2. 41–47). These meals are a continuation of those to which Jesus summoned sinners, only now they are a meeting with the crucified-and-risen Christ. It is not for nothing that very early on the celebration of the Eucharist was settled on Sunday, the day of resurrection.

HISTORY OF EUCHARISTIC WORSHIP

A couple of generations ago, much effort was put into researching the history of the Eucharist in the early centuries, often with the ecumenical hope that we could achieve a 'return to the sources' which would somehow surmount the differences between modern denominations and traditions. More recently, however, that endeavour has lost its lustre, partly because what evidence we have gives no clear picture of any one original eucharistic practice, and also because the ecumenical agenda has moved from a search for uniformity to an acceptance of diversity. To a large extent, historical research has mirrored ecumenical fashion. But the extent of historical uncertainty is seen even in the diversity of Jewish prayer forms in Jesus' time before the destruction of the temple in AD 70 and the reconstitution of Jewish society under the rabbis. It is by no means certain what forms Jesus and the apostles would have used, and what influenced the liturgical tradition of the first Christian generations. But what we see is a diminution of the meal element and the growth in importance of the central prayer (perhaps based on something like the Jewish meal blessing, the *birkath ha-mazon*) or Eucharistic Prayer.

After the first generations of Christianity, three periods in history have had particular influence on the development of the Eucharist in the modern day. First, the fourth and fifth centuries saw the establishment of the classic texts of the eucharistic prayers, such as the Roman Canon in the Latin West and the Liturgies of Basil and John Chrysostom in the Greek East: these are with us today with little change from that time. These prayers are marked by a strong emphasis on sacrifice; indeed in the Roman Canon the theme is pervasive. The state establishment of Christianity reinforced and extended the respectability and wealth it already enjoyed in some areas of the Roman Empire, and its worship was marked by increased ceremonial but also by limited participation on the part of many: those attending who were not yet baptized and so would leave early, and also a growing reluctance by the baptized to receive Communion frequently for fear of incurring guilt. In the Middle Ages worship patterns were by no means static, but for our purposes the Reformation in the sixteenth and seventeenth centuries is important for the rise of conflicting understandings of the Eucharist and for the many different rites which resulted. This was a time in which worship was consciously shaped by religious controversy and theological precision. Even the Roman Catholic Church, which held tenaciously to traditional teaching, engaged in radical reform of its liturgy to expunge superstition and abuses. The twentieth century, our third important period, was one in which there was again radical reform, but pastoral rather than theological. The Liturgical Movement emphasized the corporate nature of worship, that it is an action by the whole people of God and not something performed on their behalf by the clergy. Active participation is achieved both through lay people leading parts such as readings, intercessions and the preparation of the table, and also through the whole congregation sharing in music, in the Peace, and in frequent Communion, something which was not the case in general a century ago. The ecumenical movement has been a major influence and by appeal to the early centuries as described above has led to shared patterns of worship, partly overcoming the divisions of later years.

THEMES IN EUCHARISTIC THEOLOGY

The Eucharist can be discussed in many ways: as memorial, thanksgiving, sacrifice, eschatological banquet, Communion meal, liberation and so on, and such themes will recur in this chapter. But it is worth discussing three themes in more detail: memorial or remembrance, sacrifice or offering, and transignification or presence, because these have undergone considerable theological development.

Memorial/Remembrance

Jesus commanded us to 'do this' in remembrance of him, and remembrance is a key concept in the Eucharist, but what does it involve? In order to understand the meaning of remembrance, scholars have often investigated the Greek word *anamnesis* and its Hebrew equivalent *zikkaron*, and how they were used in Judaism at the time of Jesus. There have been suggestions that the idea was that God should remember Jesus the Messiah, but broadly it is understood that Christians are the ones bidden to remember. It is often said (and also has been denied) that *anamnesis* means, more than mere remembrance, an effectual making present and effective. But what this remembrance entails derives more from the immediate context than from the dictionary or other uses of the word: we remember Jesus not just as a historical figure, or for his betrayal, death and resurrection, but also his living presence today and the coming of his kingdom. It is, after all, rather difficult to remember Jesus' death without calling to mind his resurrection. Therefore remembrance is often expressed as celebration, proclamation, encounter, transformation; for remembrance is never a merely passive or neutral mental process.

Sacrifice/Offering

Along with the *anamnesis* is the Church's response to Christ's sacrifice. This often uses the language of offering or sacrifice. Differences between denominations on offering sometimes derive from fear of historical abuses (or from projections onto other traditions' uses) but all are agreed fundamentally that there is no propitiatory sacrifice but that of Christ once for all. Any notion of offering entails participation in that one sacrifice or is our self-offering in response to it. Thus the ecumenical document *Baptism, Eucharist and Ministry* (World Council of Churches, 1982, para. 8) states:

> The Eucharist is the sacrament of the unique sacrifice of Christ, who ever lives to make intercession for us. It is the memorial of all that God has done for the salvation of the world. What it was God's will to accomplish in the incarnation, life, death, resurrection and ascension of Christ, God does not repeat. These events are unique and can neither be repeated nor prolonged. In the memorial of the Eucharist, however, the Church offers its intercessions in communion with Christ, our great High Priest.

The Roman Catholic mass identifies strongly with Christ's offering of himself, liturgically linking it to a strong sense of remembrance as Christ's death and resurrection present and effective here with us now. Calvinist tradition makes a connection with his eternal intercession at the right hand of God the Father (a keyword, **pleading**, is often used in this context). Lutherans and evangelical Anglicans are among those most guarded in their use of the language of offering. Historically the English Prayer Book tradition *remembers* the sacrifice of Christ and in response to that the worshippers offer to God their sacrifice of praise and thanksgiving along with a self-offering in their unworthiness (Romans 12.1). In that line of thought any offering of the bread and wine is treated with great suspicion. But more needs to be said about the rationale of 'offering': that any bringing to God of the bread and wine can best be seen as part of our unworthy offering of ourselves. Rowan Williams writes:

> The Christian Eucharist provides a central interpretative model . . . our food and drink is given up into the hands of Jesus so that we become his guests and receive our life from him. The elements are shifted from one context of meaning to another, from being our possession to being gifts given and received back (and in spite of a proper caution about speaking too loosely of the elements as 'offered' to God in the Eucharist, we still need to say that the moment of *relinquishing what is ours* is crucial in the eucharistic process).
>
> (Williams, 1982, p. 111)

Transignification/Presence

The various traditions have differing approaches to the idea of the presence of Christ but none deny his presence. For some the emphasis is on identifying the consecrated bread and wine with the body and blood of Christ; others stress the presence of Christ more with the worshippers than with the elements. In the words of the Anglican–Roman Catholic International Commission (ARCIC):

> In the mystery of the Eucharist we discern not one but two complementary movements within an indissoluble unity: Christ giving his body and blood, and the communicants feeding upon them in their hearts by faith. Some traditions have placed a special emphasis on the association of Christ's presence with the consecrated elements; others have emphasized Christ's presence in the heart of the believer through reception by faith. In the past, acute difficulties have arisen when one or other of these emphases has become almost exclusive. In the opinion of the Commission neither emphasis is incompatible with eucharistic faith, provided that the complementary movement emphasized by the other position is not denied. Eucharistic doctrine must hold together these two movements since in the Eucharist, the sacrament of the New Covenant, Christ gives himself to his people so that they may receive him through faith.
> (Eucharistic Doctrine: Elucidations (1979), para. 7; ARCIC, 1982, p. 22)

The commission rightly speaks of the presence of Christ as active: Christ *giving* his body and blood. The presence of Christ cannot be restricted or reduced to passive objects; but within the gathering of his people Christ makes himself known in the breaking of the bread and gives himself bodily to bodily beings so that we might be remade more fully as his body. Christ's self-giving to us is perceived and received by faith, but is not the result of our faith.

THE EUCHARISTIC LITURGY

Names for the service

The service goes under different names: Eucharist, Holy Communion, Lord's Supper, Mass, Liturgy; but thanksgiving is regarded as the essential theme whatever else may also be expressed, following on Jesus himself giving thanks to the Father at the Last Supper. Hence a common preference today for 'Eucharist' (from the Greek for 'thanksgiving', *eucharistia*) for the service as a whole and 'Eucharistic Prayer' for the central Prayer of Thanksgiving (in the US Episcopal Church, 'The Great Thanksgiving'), however technical the word may seem to the outsider or even the ordinary churchgoer. In the Church of England, both in popular language and in the official title in the service books, priority goes to 'Holy Communion'.

Liturgy of Word and Sacrament

There are some ways in which the Eucharist has enjoyed a classic 'shape' since the early centuries. While the first generation may have experienced it essentially as a meal, from some early point it became the common custom, at least on Sundays, to preface it with readings from Scripture, preaching and intercessions, and that basic structure has remained up to the present day, often identified as the Liturgies of Word and Sacrament. Physically in a church building these two parts may involve two different foci: the lectern for reading Scripture and the altar or holy table for the sacrament. But they are normally presided over by the same priest or minister, who again may have a physical focus in the presider's chair. Other elements have grown over time, and songs, psalms and hymns are often included, especially in certain areas (sometimes known as 'soft spots'): the beginning of the service, the preparation of the table, and the Communion and dismissal rites.

Gathering rites; the Liturgy of the Word

The beginning of the service, gathering the people together and preparing them for worship, can be quite lengthy and involved. Penitential material is included either at the beginning of the service (more usual today) as a preparation for worship as a whole, or later, either to prepare for the reception of Communion or in response to the Liturgy of the Word. This includes not just readings from Scripture but also normally a sermon and intercessions. The creed is usually recited as a statement of the Christian faith of which the day's readings are only part.

Intercession

The Eucharist brings, to the reality of the world as we experience it, the world as it is called to be in the will of God under the kingship of Christ. The most obvious point at which this is expressed is the intercessions; but the prayers of penitence should identify in the light of God's grace our human failings and offer his healing; and prayer for the Church and the world is included often in the Eucharistic Prayer, placing them in God's hands for they belong in God's future. But the Peace and the Communion also belong to this proposal of the kingdom: when harmony overcomes division and inequality, and when we all alike and together receive grace and life from Christ who extends healing to the sick and welcomes sinners to his table. And both the Peace and Communion (as every aspect of the Eucharist) extend beyond any one gathering: they embrace Christians throughout the world and in every age from Christ to the coming of his kingdom.

Liturgy of the Sacrament

In the Church of England's *Common Worship* the Peace comes as the first item in 'The Liturgy of the Sacrament', thereby defining it as preparatory to this part of the service in response to Jesus' command in Matthew 5.23–24 to be reconciled to our neighbour before we come to the altar. Where the confession and absolution come after the intercessions, they are concluded by the Peace. The Roman Catholic Church has the Peace immediately before Communion, but its rationale is much the same as in the Church of England. In the early Church the Peace was seen more as concluding the prayers, claiming Christ's promise that when we are one in his name he will grant our requests. This is a classic example of one practice with different rationales. Whatever its theoretical rationale, the Peace, borrowed from the Church of South India where it was introduced to overcome caste divisions, reflects the importance of the Church as the whole body of Christ.

Within the Liturgy of the Sacrament the structure has been analysed in various ways, but it is important to understand that such an approach is analytical: the scholar observing the activity of the community and projecting a pattern on it, and this by its very nature is somewhat artificial. A very influential pattern was that proposed by Gregory Dix who spoke about the 'shape' of the Eucharist as made up of four actions traceable to the Gospel accounts of Jesus at the Last Supper and the miraculous feedings: taking the bread and wine, giving thanks to God, breaking the bread, and sharing the bread and wine in Communion. This analysis was then fed back into liturgical reform in the late twentieth century where the Eucharist was consciously constructed around the four actions. More recently the fourfold structure has been treated with some reserve: for example, some liturgists would speak of the twofold structure of giving thanks and sharing in Communion, to which the other two actions are practical preliminaries.

The purely practical business of bringing the bread and the wine to the table can be accompanied by much ceremonial. The Eucharist is to be celebrated with wheat bread and wine made from grapes. In that simple description there are many potential questions. The symbolism is generally taken to reflect both basic foodstuffs and the element of celebration, the product both of nature and of human labour, and this is reflected in prayers sometimes used at the preparation of the table. What is to be done in cultures that use other foodstuffs and in which wheat and grapes are not part of life? Most Anglican provinces stay faithful to the historical link with the materials that Jesus himself used. The wine is required (in the Church of England at any rate) to be the fermented juice of the grape; some other churches where alcohol is frowned on may use various substitutes. Bread may be leavened or unleavened. But the symbolism also speaks of broken bread and a shared cup, shared by all so that we clearly belong to one another as parts of the one body of Christ and his life broken and shared. Individual wafers or cups obscure 'discerning the body'.

The Eucharistic Prayer

We need to ask first, what is the central aim of prayer in the sacrament? In most traditions there is a central Prayer of Thanksgiving or Eucharistic Prayer (in Eastern liturgies it is often called the Anaphora or 'offering', but the role of thanksgiving is still central). What do we give thanks for? In some traditional prayers such as the Roman Canon (the first Eucharistic Prayer in the contemporary *Missal*) or the Church of England 1662 Prayer Book, interest is almost exclusively on the redemptive work of Christ; but Eastern Orthodoxy has preserved from antiquity, and has offered as an example for contemporary worship, the broader vista of all of God's work in creation and redemption, including the story of the Old Testament and his work today through the Holy Spirit in the Church and the world and looking to the coming of his kingdom. This gives a Trinitarian approach to the prayer as a whole, with a threefold pattern of creation–redemption–sanctification, though it is important that the work of each divine Person be seen as the work of the one triune God. The Eastern Orthodox shape is often adopted in twentieth-century Western prayers, as will be seen in the table on p. 143, and in addition its greater emphasis on the role of the Holy Spirit has been borrowed in Western-shape prayers.

But the Eucharistic Prayer can be analysed in different ways, and one important contemporary approach is to see it overall as a movement from thanksgiving to supplication, in which the emphasis on praise of God for creation and redemption looks to its final completion in the kingdom (see division in table opposite). Other prayers do not fit such a pattern. The 1662 Book of Common Prayer had the Preface and Sanctus totally separate, then the 'Prayer of Consecration', ending with the words of institution, followed immediately by the Communion, and left other elements to the post-Communion prayer.

Dialogue, Preface, Sanctus

The prayer begins with the opening dialogue, inviting the congregation to join in the thanksgiving. Culminating in the hymn of praise, the Sanctus ('Holy, holy holy'), there is a strong emphasis on joining earth to heaven. The first section of thanksgiving leading up to the Sanctus, called the Preface, may follow two different patterns. The traditional Western approach was to make the content topical to the occasion, so that the whole story of redemption is told in the circuit of the year. In the Middle Ages and in the Reformation liturgies including 1662, this section was treated as a separate prayer from what followed. The Eastern Orthodox Preface has an unchanging account of creation and redemption, extending beyond the Sanctus to a section covering the ministry of Christ and the account of the Last Supper. Modern Anglican prayers may follow either pattern, or indeed a combination of the two with a varying section inserted into a longer unchanging narrative.

The Sanctus seems to have become general in the Eucharistic Prayer from about the fourth or fifth centuries, and operates as a focus of the element of praise to God, joining in the universal worship by all creation. In 'Western' eucharistic prayers it concludes the section of praise and thanksgiving.

Elements in both 'Eastern' and 'Western' shape eucharistic prayers	'Western shape' (e.g. Roman Missal *Prayer 2*; Common Worship *Prayer B*)	'Eastern shape' (e.g. Common Worship *Prayer F; ECUSA Prayer D*)
Dialogue		
Preface: thanksgiving	Changing in whole or part or thematic	Unchanging, emphasis on creation and Old Testament dispensation
Sanctus (Benedictus)		
After the Sanctus	Prayer for consecration of elements (epiclesis of Holy Spirit) denominationally determined	Continuation of thanksgiving with emphasis on work of Christ
Words of institution	Often seen as consecratory	Part of the historical narrative but often prominently proclaimed
Anamnesis, picking up the command of Jesus 'to do this in remembrance of me'		
Offering	Denominationally determined	Denominationally determined
Epiclesis	Invoking the Holy Spirit on the congregation for fruitful Communion	Prayer for consecration of the elements and for communicants
Intercession	Often very brief or absent	Can be extensive
Doxology, Amen		

Thanksgiving

Supplication

The words of institution

The narrative of the Last Supper is all but universal in celebrations today; indeed its inclusion is so taken for granted that many have supposed it has always been there, and popular and novelistic accounts of early Christianity treat it as the one sure element of worship. However, it was probably introduced gradually over several hundred years; and its central position in contemporary worship is due above all to popular devotion, while theologically it may fulfil different roles in various traditions. The one constant is more literary than theological (in that this can be done in various ways): to link what we do today with what Jesus did then and to pick up the fulfilment of his command to do this in remembrance of him. In the Reformed tradition the custom has been to use the Supper narrative as a 'warrant', reciting it either as a preliminary to the sacramental action as a whole or immediately before Communion. 'Eastern' prayers have it as the conclusion and focus of the thanksgiving section within the Eucharistic Prayer. In the Roman Catholic, Anglican and Lutheran traditions the words of institution (also within the Eucharistic Prayer) have often played an important role in the notion of consecration. Grammatically the narrative is simply that – a narration of a past event; but the medieval Catholic tradition fostered a tradition from at least the time of Ambrose of Milan (died AD 397) in which the consecration was regarded as effected by the priest repeating the very words of Christ. Dramatically this is a strong and direct image, often accompanied by elaborate ceremonial, and has led to a notion of consecration being by simple repetition of the narrative. Today that idea is generally avoided and modern rites are more likely to emphasize the whole prayer as what consecrates the elements, and the Holy Spirit is seen as involved. But 'Western' prayers have the words of institution preceded by a petition for consecration as if to reinforce it; while 'Eastern' prayers include the supper narrative clearly in the section of thanksgiving and have the petition for consecration after.

Anamnesis, Offering

The whole Eucharistic Prayer has remembrance as its theme (see above) but the term *anamnesis* is also used specifically for the section of the prayer that follows the words of institution, picking up Christ's command to remember him. In 'Eastern' eucharistic prayers the anamnesis marks the move from thanksgiving to supplication. Many prayers then go on to describe a particular response, very often in terms of offering to God the eucharistic sacrifice (see above for denominational differences).

Epiclesis

At this point in 'Eastern' prayers, or before the words of institution in 'Western' prayers, there is generally a prayer for consecration, often called the *epiclesis* (invocation) because it includes an invocation of the Holy Spirit. Theologically there is no need for a petition for 'consecration'. It has often been stated as a liturgical principle that by the whole Eucharistic Prayer we are joined with Christ in giving thanks to the Father, and through this whole act of worship meet him in the breaking of the bread. Nevertheless it is general to include a petition of this kind in the Thanksgiving. The precise wording used reflects denominational markers: Roman Catholics and Orthodox ask that the bread and wine may 'become for us' the body and blood of Christ; Anglicans, fearing any suggestion of material change, prefer 'be' instead of 'become', thus implying symbolic representation. Some Anglicans adopt what could be seen as a minimalist understanding of consecration as setting something apart from a worldly to a spiritual use, which indeed may well apply to buildings and objects; but in the Eucharist this must be seen in the context of a divine institution rather than a human action. The petition for consecration is always linked to the recipients: there is no idea of consecration without communion.

In many Reformation churches the prayer is directed more to the worshippers than to the elements and this part of the prayer is sometimes called 'invocation' rather than 'consecration' (whether or not the Holy Spirit is specifically invoked at this point). The distinctions between consecration and invocation are not always clear in practice. The 1662 Prayer Book has a prayer for the communicants that 'receiving these thy creatures of bread and wine . . . may be partakers of his most blessed Body and Blood'. Grammatically that is an invocation, but the prayer (which is entitled 'the Prayer of Consecration') then directs the priest to recite the words of institution while repeating the actions of Christ at the Last Supper in taking the bread and cup and laying hands on them when reciting 'This is my Body' and 'This is my Blood' so the emphasis is clearly on the elements. In *Common Worship*, Prayer E is deliberately ambiguous: 'Send your Holy Spirit, that broken bread and wine outpoured may be for us the body and blood of your dear Son.'

An epiclesis after the words of institution flows naturally into prayer for the congregation; when the petition for consecration is before the words of institution, there is often a second epiclesis later when the Spirit is invoked on the congregation. The petition for the consecration of the elements and for the congregation is joined with the vision of the whole of creation made perfect in God's kingdom. Sometimes this part of the prayer includes specific intercession. The vision is all-embracing, and culminates in the doxology where God is all in all.

Communion

At one level Communion, the congregation receiving the bread and wine, is the purpose of the service. In practice there is widespread variation. In Orthodox churches Communion is usually received only rarely, and, while it has become more common in Roman Catholic churches, in Anglican and other churches, which formerly presupposed that only communicants should attend the service, the number of non-communicants, both children and adults, has grown enormously in recent years.

But Communion occupies a devotional centre stage such that its practice and logic has always been at the heart of eucharistic understanding. From St Paul, who could use the breaking and sharing of the bread as the defining symbol of the Church, to the modern Liturgical Movement with its rediscovery of the Eucharist as the core of Christian worship, the notion of the Church as the body of Christ has found its theological and social reality in this act. Communion is not just between the individual and Christ: it is also between Christians in a congregation and with other Christians throughout the world and in every age.

An interesting mark of the differing approaches to the eucharistic presence can be found in the practical problems around Communion: what is to be done if the bread or wine runs out, and what is done with any that remains afterwards? In the former situation, churches of the Reformation which have a low emphasis on the consecration of the bread and wine, the Eucharistic Prayer having a prayer of invocation on the worshippers, extra bread and wine can simply be added without ceremony or prayer. At the other extreme in the Roman Catholic Church there is no provision for when the consecrated bread or wine run out. In practice there is normally sufficient reserved from another mass, but in instances when that has failed Communion simply stops; and it is considered sufficient that the people have attended the service prayerfully. The Anglican tradition is the only Western church which regards both Communion as integral to the celebration and consecration as an important feature, and so makes provision for a brief prayer to be said over any extra bread and wine used for Communion. The 1662 Prayer Book stipulated simply that the relevant words of institution be recited by the priest over the additional bread or wine. Likewise with the disposal of consecrated bread and wine the practice of different churches indicates their eucharistic theology: Roman Catholic and Anglican churches require that which is not kept for future Communion to be consumed. In other churches which do not have a strong understanding of consecration the bread and wine can be put back in the vestry or used at home; many ministers, however, hold that it is wrong to use domestically what has been set aside for a holy use, and the practice of reverently consuming the remains is common.

An important part, easily overlooked, is the post-Communion section and dismissal with blessing. In traditions where Communion is commonly received only on major festivals, ceremonies such as the blessing have had an important devotional place and indeed in the Western Church the dismissal gave its name to the whole service, as the Mass. The post-Communion prayers look beyond the service to the life of the body of Christ in the world and the unity of what happens in church, what Christians do in their lives, and the time when all are gathered in the kingdom of God.

The Eucharist lies at the centre of Christian worship and theology. As this survey demonstrates, the student has to ask not simply what might be pastorally appropriate but also what is theologically important both in understanding the Bible and the Christian tradition and in embodying one's denomination's or tradition's insights.

Further reading

Bradshaw, P., and Johnson, M. E. (2012), *The Eucharistic Liturgies: Their Evolution and Interpretation* (London: SPCK/Collegeville, MN: Liturgical Press).

Cocksworth, C. J. (1993), *Evangelical Eucharistic Thought in the Church of England* (Cambridge: Cambridge University Press).

Gerrish, B. A. (1993), *Grace and Gratitude: The Eucharistic Theology of John Calvin* (Edinburgh: T&T Clark).

Kereszty, R. A. (ed.) (2003), *Rediscovering the Eucharist: Ecumenical Conversations* (New York: Paulist Press).

Stevenson, K. (2002), *Do This: The Shape, Style and Meaning of the Eucharist* (Norwich: Canterbury Press).

Wybrew, H. (2013, reissue of 1st edn), *The Orthodox Liturgy* (London: SPCK).

Chapter 15

Service of the Word

James Steven

Services of the word are generally understood to be gatherings for worship marked by readings from the Bible, prayers and often (though not always) preaching. Study of this liturgical phenomenon can take various forms. An historical approach reveals huge variety in the way that Christians have gathered in this way. This includes daily prayer in the monastic tradition, the eighteenth-century Methodist Preaching Service, twentieth-century evangelistic conventions, Evensong according to the Book of Common Prayer, and the Liturgy of the Word in the Eucharist, often referred to as 'ante-Communion'. An approach focusing on the liturgical elements that normally constitute a service of the word will highlight the practices of Bible reading (lectionary), prayers of intercession and preaching. A study of the architectural space of gathering will offer an interpretation of how pulpit, lectern and congregation relate. Finally, attention also can be given to the ecclesial and theological perspective that affirms that the service of the word is the Church's celebration of the Bible as holy Scripture, the writings that form the authoritative witness to God's salvation through Israel and in Christ, and by which the Spirit of God calls the Church into being.

The aim of this chapter is to draw attention to the liturgical use of the Bible that services of the word manifest and to explore how theological readings of the shape of the service inform an understanding of receiving the Bible as the 'word of Christ'. However, no contemporary discussion of services of the word would be complete without recognition of recent liturgical revision. In 1993 the Church of England authorized *A Service of the Word* which has subsequently been included in the *Common Worship* Sunday services book. A similar order appeared in the Church of Ireland's 2004 Book of Common Prayer and also in the 1999 *Methodist Worship Book*, under the 'Guidance for Ordering a Morning, Afternoon or Evening Service'. These three orders present a word-based service as a liturgical structure accompanied by rubrics and guidelines on liturgical content. The Church of England's order serves as an interesting case study in the evolution of liturgical thinking, the background to which has been well summarized elsewhere (Bradshaw, 2001). *A Service of the Word* is the result of a number of factors: the desire to respond to the pastoral needs of the communities served by the Church, the continuing popularity of word-based liturgy and the willingness of the Church to authorize experiment with local liturgies. This chapter will raise some of the important issues for leaders of liturgy in working with this kind of service of the word.

THE BIBLE IN WORSHIP

'Let the word of Christ dwell in you richly; teach and admonish one another in all wisdom; and with gratitude in your hearts sing psalms, hymns, and spiritual songs to God' (Colossians 3.16).

This apostolic directive is one way of imagining the place of the Bible in worship: the word of Christ inhabits the prayers, praises and teaching of the Church. Among liturgical scholars, Roman Catholics have been at the forefront of reinvigorating Christian thinking and practice in relation to the place of the Bible in liturgy. Among them, Louis-Marie Chauvet argues that liturgy is the Bible's home, its natural habitat: 'the Bible is in the liturgical assembly as a fish in water' (Chauvet, 2001, p. 127). This insight is by no means particular to Catholics; the recognition of the deeply embedded place of the Bible in worship is also an Anglican conviction. For example, Jeremy Taylor, the seventeenth-century Anglican bishop, defends the legitimacy of the Book of Common Prayer on this basis: 'Very much of our liturgy is in the very words of Scripture. The Psalms and Lessons and all the Hymns, save one [the Gloria], are nothing else but Scripture' (Taylor, 1839, p. 292).

In considering the liturgical function of the Bible within services of the word, we will comment upon lectionary and psalms.

Lectionary

When Christians refer to the Bible as sacred Scripture, they draw attention to its liturgical character and in particular the tradition of public reading in the liturgical assembly. Inherited from the Jewish synagogue tradition, this formed an important part of early Christian practice (1 Timothy 4.13). Maintaining this practice, the King James Version of the Bible, which endured as the standard biblical text for most English-speaking Protestant churches until the late twentieth century, states simply but significantly on its frontispiece that it is 'appointed to be read in churches'.

When faced with the question of what portions of the Bible should be read on any particular occasion, again inheriting Jewish practice, the Church looks to its lectionary. The three-year *Revised Common Lectionary*, the fruit of liturgical revision in the Roman Catholic Church following Vatican II, has become the standard Sunday lectionary among a variety of other denominations. The lectionary integrates two patterns of Bible reading common in historic Christian worship: sequential reading where passages of the Bible are read continuously (often called *lectio continua*) and thematic reading where the chosen Bible passages typically cluster around a seasonal celebration (often called *lectio selecta*). Historically, these approaches defined a demarcation between Protestant and Catholic approaches to Bible reading. The *Westminster Directory of Worship* (1645), a seminal document for Reformed worship, requires that the Bible be read 'chapter by chapter' on each successive Sunday:

> How large a portion shall be read at once, is left to the wisdom of the Minister; but it is convenient, that ordinarily one Chapter of each Testament be read at every meeting; and sometimes more, where the Chapters be short, or the coherence of matter requireth it.
>
> It is requisite that all the Canonical Books be read over in order, that the people may be better acquainted with the whole Body of the Scriptures; And ordinarily, where the Reading in either Testament endeth on one Lord's day, it is to begin the next.　　　　　　　　　　　　　　　　(Breward, 1980, p. 11)

By contrast, Roman Catholic lectionary practice has traditionally been governed by the calendar of seasons and saints, and readings cluster around the festival theme. Working with a distinction in the calendar of Seasonal and Ordinary Time, the *Revised Common Lectionary* provides a hybrid approach, allocating sequential reading to Sundays in Ordinary Time and themed reading to Sundays that celebrate the major seasons of the Christian calendar.

The juxtaposition of Bible readings deserves consideration. The practice of including both an Old Testament and New Testament reading (in a eucharistic context a gospel reading would also be included) is a witness to the central yet richly textured golden thread of Scripture, the story of God's grace revealed in Jesus Christ. As Augustine of Hippo remarked, echoing a conviction held among Christian theologians, 'In the Old Testament the New is concealed, and in the New the Old is revealed' (*De Catechizandis Rudibus*, IV, 8). Herein lies both the symbolic and homiletic value of including readings from both Testaments.

The relationship between Bible reading and sermon is equally important to delineate. Common practice in contemporary evangelicalism, and its nineteenth-century predecessor of revivalism, is for the reading to be subsumed into the sermon as part of the unitary act of preaching. However, even traditions with a similarly high view of preaching, such as the Reformed tradition, have generally insisted upon Bible reading and sermon being separate liturgical acts; the *Westminster Directory for Worship*, for example, assumes that reading and sermon are distinct elements in a Reformed order of service. The coexistence of these distinct liturgical elements highlights the nuanced relationship between Bible and Church. The reading witnesses to the primacy of Scripture as it 'containeth all things necessary to salvation' (Article VI, Articles of Religion in 1662 Book of Common Prayer). Considered as such, the reading is the primary proclaimed word to which preaching, a derivative activity, forms the first response to the spoken word. However, the sermon plays a crucial role in maintaining the long-standing practice of interpretation, exhortation and instruction that helps the Church receive and celebrate the life-giving 'word of Christ' (Luke 4.16–22).

When only one Bible reading is chosen there is the opportunity for a longer portion of Scripture to be read. One of the unintended, though inevitable, consequences of the traditional lectionary approach to public Bible reading has been a conditioning of the listener to a standardized length of reading, which may interrupt the flow and trajectory of an ongoing story or, in the case of the New Testament letters, a developing argument. The common practice of an extended reading of the Passion narrative on Palm Sunday points to the wisdom of this way of receiving the Bible liturgically and *A Service of the Word* entertains the possibility of just one reading. The opportunities are endless: Genesis, for example, is full of story cycles, ranging from shorter accounts (such as the reconciliation of Jacob and Esau) through to more substantial events (the story of the flood) and then to the very long story of Joseph and his brothers. Old Testament books such as Jonah and Ruth could be read comfortably at one sitting. The Gospels could be treated similarly (the Sermon on the Mount or the Johannine Farewell Discourse), along with major incidents in Acts (such as the conversion of Cornelius and its impact) and the letters (where either whole letters or sections of letters could be read). The practice of single readings in services invites the development of suitably different kinds of reading and listening habits and extends the range of receiving the Bible in worship.

The Psalms

The Psalms provide an obvious example of how the Bible inhabits liturgy. Since its beginnings, Christian worship has drawn generously on the Jewish psalms as a language of prayer (see Gelston, 2008). This is a tradition that is maintained in lectionaries by a psalm being appointed as a companion to other readings and in hymnody by the continual reappropriation of the Psalms for congregational singing. Despite this legacy, however, recent trends have threatened the once unchallenged position of psalms in Christian worship.

While the reasons for this change are complex, ranging from shifts in musical repertoire to the habit of dropping the set lectionary psalm on account of time saving, services of the word provide an opportunity to reclaim the Psalms as a normative and constituent feature of Christian worship. The Psalms supply a rich resource for integrating the life of faith within worship. Such is their breadth of scope that they can be used as calls to worship, praise, invitation to confession, confession, absolution, intercessions, lament and blessing. The presence of the psalm in the liturgy is an interrogation of all Christian prayer and singing: how does it enable the word of Christ to dwell within us richly?

LITURGICAL SHAPE AND ECUMENISM

Recent ecumenical discussion has focused upon the importance of the liturgical shape as a means of encouraging mutual understanding among Christian traditions. In 1995 the Faith and Order Committee of the World Council of Churches recommended that churches focus upon the fundamental eucharistic fourfold pattern (*ordo*) of Gathering, Word-Service, Table-Service and Dismissal (Best and Heller, 1998). This has influenced the way *A Service of the Word* has been understood as a fourfold shape of Gathering, Ministry of the Word, Prayer and then Dismissal.

The advantage of this focus upon shape is that it identifies arenas of liturgical activity that have their own distinct character and hence a self-organizing liturgical rationale. It also highlights that these arenas are what they are in relation to each other; there is a flow of activity that unfolds, facilitating prayer. *A Service of the Word* draws attention to the need for leaders to understand worship and its shape: 'It is important that those who prepare and take part in *A Service of the Word* should have a clear understanding of the nature of worship and how the component parts of this service work together' (*CW*, 2000, p. 21).

Attention has been given to the way in which this fourfold shape reflects a Christian understanding of prayer. David Stancliffe (2003), for example, interprets the sequence by correlating each stage in relation to the phases of Christ's Incarnation. Following Stancliffe's lead, *A Service of the Word* could be understood in the following way:

1 The Gathering corresponds to the advent of God's coming kingdom, with its waiting and preparation for God's coming and the expectation of his call. Gathering for worship is an opportunity to renew Christian identity as being dependent upon the call of Jesus and to find in him the wisdom and love of God.
2 The second phase of Jesus' ministry is his teaching, launched in dramatic style at his home synagogue in Nazareth, continued in the Galilean region and for which he became known as an authoritative teacher, prophet and sage. In attending to Scripture through reading, proclamation and faith, we encounter the living Word that both judges and recreates us.
3 The third phase of the ministry of Jesus is his Passion, his suffering at the hands of the religious and political authorities. Interpreted as a priestly act of service, following the example of the letter to the Hebrews, his passion becomes both the pattern and the possibility of our prayer. As the North American liturgist Don Saliers puts it,

Prayers for others in the context of Christian liturgy show a fundamental christological orientation: as Christ had compassion, so must we; as he encountered the brokenness of the world, so must we; as he loved even in the face of death, so must we.   (Saliers, 1994, p. 132)

4 The final phase of Jesus' ministry is his resurrection and Ascension, which together mark his enthronement and an authorization of the Church for the continuation of his mission in the world. Death has been defeated and through the gift of the Spirit the Church is empowered to be his body in the world. The concluding actions in the liturgy reflect this confidence mingled with prayerful dependence as we are commissioned for life in the world.

LITURGICAL SHAPE: EUCHARISTIC ECHOES

Historically oriented introductions to the Liturgy of the Word will tend to discuss its origins in terms of its constituent role within early forms of Eucharist, drawing upon the Jewish synagogue tradition of the reading of Scripture, preaching and prayers, all of which precede the eucharistic celebration. This tradition is reflected in the provision of the order 'A Service of the Word with a Celebration of Holy Communion' in *Common Worship* (2000, p. 25).

This historical anchoring of the service of the word within the Eucharist has important implications for its present role within the worship of the Church. Conceptually it challenges the separation of word and sacrament that has been a common feature of the way in which post-Reformation worship has evolved. This, in part, is due to a dualism whereby word and sacrament are two distinct forms of activity, each with their own spheres of theological logic. This fuels, and has itself been formed by, ingrained hierarchical views of liturgical practice: a catholic approach treats eucharistic worship as a higher form than word-based worship, and an evangelical approach prioritizes the word-based worship over eucharistic. The Reformers themselves were not so prone to such fragmentation in outlook since they saw both word and sacrament as unified by the action of God in Christ, the Word. This unity of action was typically presented in the distinction Reformers made between the spoken word of the gospel preached and the visible word of the sacraments.

Furthermore, the language of eucharistic action can be used to illuminate the dynamics of services of the word. This is not new, as the nineteenth-century hymn 'Break Thou the Bread of Life' illustrates, with its prayer that Jesus would bless the sacred page as he had blessed loaves for feeding the multitude in Galilee. Services of the word can be interpreted within the fourfold eucharistic dynamic of taking, thanksgiving, breaking and distributing. 'Taking' Scripture draws attention to the same kind of care that would be taken over preparing the bread and wine for Eucharist: the choice of reading, readers who are suitably prepared and who can be heard, and a congregation which is attentive. 'Giving thanks' places the reading of Scripture within a larger context of celebrating God's salvation, its story and its transformative power, and so prayer and praise that recall the purpose of Scripture, its role in salvation and some kind of request for enlightenment would be most appropriate. The 'breaking' of Scripture, making it available, is the function of the sermon. The preacher's voice is the first public voice to indicate how we might receive the word 'today', and begins the process by which the word is taken and digested. While the sermon could well still be included when we consider the distribution, there is a more fundamental and far-reaching end in view, of distributing the word to the world as the listeners take the word, and put it into practice in everyday life, a challenge that the prayers and a concluding blessing are well suited to support and nurture.

LITURGICAL LEADERSHIP

As the notes accompanying the Church of England's *A Service of the Word* state, the service is 'authorised as an alternative to Morning Prayer and Evening Prayer. It provides a structure for Sunday services, for daily prayer and for services of an occasional nature' (*CW*, 2000, p. 26). However, it is relatively easy to pass over the order for *A Service of the Word* (it occupies just one page in the *Common Worship* Sunday service, nestling inconspicuously near the beginning of an 850-page book), and, for those liturgical leaders who are used to beginning their planning and preparation with a full liturgical text, the skeletal framework of the order can appear genuinely disconcerting.

The rationale of *A Service of the Word* is only fully appreciated with its companion publication *New Patterns for Worship* (*NPW*, 2002). Like its predecessor, *Patterns for Worship* (1995), *NPW* contains a rich and broad range of commended liturgy for use with *A Service of the Word*. *NPW* differs from the other *Common Worship* liturgies in two ways. First, it is organized as a directory of resources so that those who are planning worship can find and compare liturgical texts for use in a service. Second, *NPW* is designed as a training manual for those who plan and lead worship. With each resource section, for example, there is discussion of the principles and practice of worship. Four fictional churches provide examples of how worship might be conducted, scenarios that both spark the imagination and expose poor practice. Discussion questions are offered for Parochial Church Councils and associated worship planning groups. Sample service orders give an indication of the variety of contexts within which *A Service of the Word* can be used, elaborated further in the practical *Using Common Worship* guide by Tim Stratford (Stratford, 2002).

As the fascinating study by Stephen Burns on *A Service of the Word* and *NPW* illustrates (Burns, 2006), this kind of service structure, stripped of detailed liturgical text, exposes primary questions that are integral to the task of liturgical leadership. These include understanding the rationale for the service structure and its implications for planning, recognizing which liturgical texts to use, and appreciating how these texts can be best employed; in many ways *A Service of the Word* forms an apprenticeship in liturgical leadership, a means of developing skills and wisdom for this significant ministry.

One of the specific demands of leadership is finding a healthy balance in managing the tension between what could become contradictory impulses; for example, encouraging an imaginative appropriation of liturgical resources while maintaining ecclesial identity through attention to the disciplines of the Church's common prayer. In *A Service of the Word* the use of authorized texts (chosen primarily on account of their doctrinal sensitivity: confessions, creeds and affirmations of faith and collects), together with liturgical structure, serve as guarantors of common prayer in the Church. Framing the same issue pastorally, leaders need to negotiate the delicate balance between variety in liturgical options and continuity, developing liturgy that becomes established and meaningful only through regular repetition. This issue becomes very important in the light of the increased availability of liturgy from other worshipping traditions. Perhaps never before has there been such opportunity for the local church to explore the fruits of the Church universal through ecumenical sharing and significant technological advance in everyday media.

Liturgical leadership will also need to address the contradictory place of the Bible in society, an irony generated by the simultaneous growth of technological advance and secularism. On the one hand, the present age is one of unprecedented availability of Bible translations and paraphrases of the Bible in printed and digital forms. On the other hand, the knowledge and grasp of the Bible's contents and purpose even among churchgoers (never mind the rest of society) shows every sign of being in decline. *A Service of the Word* represents a strategy for recovering a biblical literacy whereby Christians grow to know not only what the Bible contains but also its formative wisdom for Christian living and worship.

There are pointers in *NPW* to the ways in which both Bible reading and the Psalms can be arranged and prayed imaginatively. For instance, during Ordinary Time 'after due consultation with the Parochial Church Council, the minister may, from time to time, depart from the lectionary provision for pastoral reasons or preaching or teaching purposes' (*NPW*, p. 540). To help local leadership in their choice of alternative readings, *NPW* provides what it calls 'modular' lectionary material. Nearly 50 sample modules are offered, each with a controlling reading that sets the theme, with supporting readings and psalm. Most modules focus on a biblical book or character and some explore a theme, such as 'Feasts in the Gospels' or 'Women in the Messianic Line'. *NPW* also highlights different ways in which a congregation could be helped to pray a psalm, either with music or by various forms of responsive speech (*NPW*, pp. 125–39, §D).

Attending to the symbolic dimensions of worship is another way a liturgical leader can imaginatively celebrate the role of the Bible in liturgy. Even something as simple as the location of a Bible within the space for worship will communicate an understanding of how the Bible and people relate to one another. The coaching notes of *NPW* state that 'action' is among the four major liturgical ingredients, along with 'word', 'prayer' and 'praise' (2002, p. 15). *NPW* gives examples of procession, dance, music, silence, together with candles and lighting, all of which are to be considered carefully as a means of contributing to the unfolding drama of encountering the word of Christ.

CONCLUSION

This overview has offered a conceptually varied reading of the significance of services of the word for the worship of the Church. Alongside an appreciation of the liturgical and theological dynamics of such liturgy, recent revision, as *A Service of the Word* illustrates, highlights opportunities for developing liturgical leadership. Perhaps it would not be too ambitious to suggest that the tradition of services of the word provides both compass and feast for the Church. As compass, the liturgy is a means by which the Church's life gains its bearings from the ultimate measure of God's intentions for the world, revealed through the witness of the Bible. As feast, the liturgy nourishes the Church in the word of Christ, a table evoked by the voice of Wisdom in Proverbs:

> 'You that are simple, turn in here!' To those without sense she says, 'Come, eat of my bread and drink of the wine I have mixed. Lay aside immaturity, and live, and walk in the way of insight.'
> (Proverbs 9.4–6)

Further reading

Best, T. F., and Heller, D. (eds) (1998), *Eucharistic Worship in Ecumenical Contexts: The Lima Liturgy – and Beyond* (Geneva: WCC).

Breward, I. (1980), *The Westminster Directory: Being a Directory for the Publique Worship of God in the Three Kingdomes* (Bramcote: Grove Books).

Chauvet, L.-M. (1992), 'What Makes the Liturgy Biblical? – Texts', *Studia Liturgica* 22.2, pp. 121–33.

Saliers, D. E. (1994), *Worship as Theology: Foretaste of Glory Divine* (Nashville, TN: Abingdon Press).

Taylor, J. (1839), *The Whole Works of the Right Rev Jeremy Taylor D.D., Lord Bishop of Down, Connor and Dromore: Volume VII – Containing Episcopacy Asserted, an Apology for Authorised and Set Forms of Liturgy and a Discourse on the Liberty of Prophesying* (London: Longman, Orme, Brown, Green and Longmans, et al.).

Chapter 16

Healing and reconciliation

David J. Kennedy

INTRODUCTION

The Christian tradition is realistic about human sickness and mortality and the fact of human sinfulness. The Christian gospel, however, celebrates and anticipates the ultimate reintegration of our disordered, flawed and mortal human nature in the hope and experience of new and eternal life through Christ. Rites of healing and reconciliation express this realism and hope. Healing rites include individual and corporate prayer for healing, often accompanied by anointing with olive oil, the laying on of hands and reception of the Eucharist. Such prayer can be offered as part of a dedicated rite (a 'healing service'), as part of regular ministry in church in the context of the celebration of the Eucharist or services of the word, or in ministry in private homes, hospitals, hospices and care homes. Rites of reconciliation, also called rites of penance, are concerned with confession of sins and the gift of absolution. Such rites may be corporate, but are more commonly celebrated in a private context with individual confession of sin to a priest or minister.

RENEWING OUR BAPTISMAL STATUS

Contemporary reflection on sacramental theology interprets both healing and reconciliation in a baptismal context. This arises from the Church's understanding of the concept of salvation. Salvation is essentially the entering into a right relationship with God through Jesus Christ, in which human beings find forgiveness and experience fullness of life, through the indwelling gift of the Holy Spirit. Baptism celebrates and proclaims the gift of salvation. For St Paul, baptism stands at the intersection of two worlds, the 'old' world characterized by sin, corruption and death, and the 'new' world, characterized by newness of life (Romans 6.5–11), as we are joined to Christ's saving death and resurrection, and so live no longer under the dominion of sin and death. In the life of the Christian, the old age that is passing away and the new age that is being brought to birth run in parallel; as Paul states in 2 Corinthians 4.16, 'though our outer nature is wasting away, our inner nature is being renewed day by day.' Healing and reconciliation are part of the outworking of salvation in the context of a fallen yet redeemed human nature, and a hope of a renewed humanity in the midst of our frail bodies of flesh and blood.

There is a close linguistic relationship between the biblical concepts of salvation, wholeness, healing and peace. For example, in the New Testament, the Greek words for 'heal' and 'save' are used almost interchangeably (Mark 5.23, 28, 34; Matthew 9.21–22). Similarly, the services of reconciliation, corporate and individual, can be regarded as a theological and liturgical outworking of the premise in the Nicene Creed: 'We believe in one baptism for the forgiveness of sins.' What is bestowed once and fundamentally in baptism is renewed through confession and absolution as we are restored to our baptismal status.

This anchoring of the sacramental acts of healing and reconciliation in the gospel sacrament of baptism not only helps to set historic divisions over the number of the sacraments in a new theological context, but also places the prayer and desire for wholeness and forgiveness in the wider salvific framework to which baptism witnesses, where salvation is both present gift and eschatological hope.

HEALING AND WHOLENESS

Christian rites of healing are careful to set the Church's ministry in a broad context. The role of the medical professions should always be honoured and acknowledged as part of God's loving wisdom bestowed on humanity, while the frequent use of the concept of 'wholeness' emphasizes the breadth of this ministry with its physical, emotional, social and spiritual aspects. Wholeness and healing are understood as part of the continuing ministry of the risen Christ, whose Incarnation both identified with our human weakness and inaugurated the renewal of our human condition. The Christ, who in his acts of healing and deliverance demonstrated the in-breaking of God's kingdom, a present experience of the promises of the age to come, continues his healing and reconciling work, by the power of the Holy Spirit and through the ministry of the Church. 'Wholeness', therefore, embraces the desire not only to be physically healthy, but also to experience emotional well-being, to be restored to a right relationship with God and our neighbour, and to be delivered from the powers of evil. This accords with the biblical word *shalom* or 'peace', which in Hebrew thought expresses the desire for harmony with God, with our neighbour and with the created order. This broad and multidimensional understanding of wholeness, however, also recognizes the 'already' and the 'not yet' aspects of salvation; we continue to experience the realities of a sinful, alienated and divided world, our human mortality, and the effects of injustice and social oppression.

We must also beware of a simplistic link between sickness and sin. Jesus' words in John 9.3, for example, repudiate a direct association of disability and sin, in contradistinction to the commonly held beliefs of his time. And yet the sheer complexity of our human nature often means that the realities of sin, individual and corporate, are part of our dis-ease, our falling short of full health. Indeed, the reception of forgiveness and the grace of forgiving others may enable and assist our growth in wholeness. For that reason, the various liturgical celebrations include prayers of penitence.

The broader issues of spiritual conflict are also often recognized in liturgical rites. While this needs careful handling in the light of contemporary popular and sometimes sensationalist understandings, the reality of spiritual forces of wickedness and evil is part of the Christian tradition, impacting on both individuals and the social order. Many churches provide prayers for situations of personal disturbance or unrest, while most churches set out clear procedures for the ministry of deliverance and exorcism.

SACRAMENTAL SIGNS

Christian rites for healing normally include two distinctive ceremonies: the laying on of hands, and anointing.

The laying on of hands

While the laying on of hands is not invariably mentioned in the account of Jesus' healing ministry, nevertheless, it does appear in a significant number of passages: at Capernaum (Luke 4.40); in response to the request by Jairus (Mark 5.23; Matthew 9.18); at the healings at Nazareth (Mark 6.5), of the man who was deaf and unable to speak (Mark 7.32), of the blind man at Bethsaida (Mark 8.23, 25), and of the woman who was bent over (Luke 13.13). In other healings there is also physical contact, especially in the healing of blind people (Matthew 20.34; John 9.6) and the touching of the leper (Mark 1.41; Matthew 8.3; Luke 5.13). The laying on of hands is also present in the Acts of the Apostles (9.12, 17; 28.8).

This strong biblical testimony underlies the liturgical practice of the Church. For example, the specimen prayer in the Church of England rite specifically mentions Christ's *touch*, emphasizing that this is his ministry exercised through the Church:

> In the name of God and trusting in his might alone,
> receive Christ's healing touch to make you whole.

> May Christ bring you wholeness
> of body, mind, and spirit,

> deliver you from every evil,
> and give you his peace. **Amen**.
> (*Common Worship: Pastoral Services* (*CWPS*),
> 2005, pp. 21, 33, 93)

The Roman Catholic rites for the Anointing of the Sick include the laying on of hands, with the following petition:

> Give life and health to our brother/sister *N*, on whom we lay our hands in your name: **Lord, have mercy**.
> *In silence, the priest lays his hands on the head of the sick person.*
> (*Pastoral Care of the Sick* (*PCOTS*), 1982, §121, 122, 138, 139)

The Methodist Church (Great Britain) provides three specimen texts for use at either the laying on of hands or anointing:

> *Either*   Father,
>   send your Spirit of life and health on your servant, *N*; in the Name of Christ. **Amen**.
> *Or,*   *N*, the grace of Christ brings you wholeness and gives you peace. **Amen**.
> *Or,*   May the Spirit of the living God,
>   present with us now,
>   heal you of all that harms you,
>   in body, mind, or spirit;
>   in the Name of Jesus Christ. **Amen**.
> (*The Methodist Worship Book* (*TMWB*), 1999, p. 413)

The Methodist texts reflect the New Testament emphasis that healing is ministered in the *name* of Jesus (Mark 16.17, 18; Acts 3.6, 16; 4.10, 12).

These forms of prayer are broad in their scope, embracing all aspects of our human condition, body, mind and spirit, while the use of the words 'wholeness' and 'peace' reflect the biblical word *shalom* (see above). It is common for the laying on of hands to be administered, sometimes at more than one 'station', by teams including both ordained and lay ministers. Prayer and the laying on of hands may also be received vicariously.

Anointing

Oil has long been associated with healing; for example, Isaiah 1.6 cites the use of oil for the softening of wounds and, in the parable, the Good Samaritan pours oil and wine onto the wounds of the stricken man (Luke 10.34). A more symbolic and spiritual role is, however, suggested in Mark 6.13, where the

Twelve 'anointed with oil many who were sick and cured them', and in James 5.14–15:

> Are any among you sick? They should call for the elders of the church and have them pray over them, anointing them with oil in the name of the Lord. The prayer of faith will save the sick, and the Lord will raise them up; and anyone who has committed sins will be forgiven.

While there is no specific reference in the New Testament to Jesus anointing the sick, apostolic practice is understood against the background of Jesus' fulfilment of the messianic hopes of Israel (see especially Luke 4.18–21); Jesus, anointed by the Spirit, brings in the blessings associated with the messianic age, including his authority to heal. In James 5, the close association of anointing with prayer is evident. It is this apostolic practice that underlies the Church's ministry.

While for many centuries the anointing was administered as part of the Church's healing ministry, from the late eighth century onwards anointing became associated with final preparation for death, forming, with penance and administration of the *viaticum* (last Communion), the 'last rites' and so was designated as 'extreme unction'. From the twelfth century, it was counted as one of the seven sacraments. The Roman *Ritual* of 1614 prescribed anointing of the eyes, ears, nostrils, mouth, hands and feet, each of them related to sins associated with each part of the body. Anointing was therefore understood as a means of preparation for death rather than as a sign of healing grace. Most Reformed traditions rejected anointing as a full sacrament of the gospel on the basis that there was no formal 'institution' by Christ. While Cranmer retained an optional rite of anointing in the 1549 Prayer Book, this was deleted in 1552 and not restored in 1662.

In twentieth-century liturgical renewal, anointing, while remaining an important aspect of ministry before death, has been restored to its biblical dignity as a sign of life and healing and as part of the Church's regular ministry to the sick. In Catholic theology, it is still understood as one of the seven sacraments; in Reformed theology, it is normally understood as a sacramental ministry. The reference in James to the 'elders of the church' (*presbuterous*) has led some churches to designate anointing as a priestly or presbyteral ministry. This is certainly true of the Roman Catholic tradition, while Canon B37 of the Church of England states:

> If any such person so desires, the priest may lay hands upon him and anoint him with oil on the forehead with the sign of the Cross . . . and using pure olive oil consecrated by the bishop of the diocese or otherwise by the priest himself.

In the Methodist rite, while there is a prayer for the blessing of the oil, it is not explicitly stated that a presbyter says it, or in the context of the Eucharist, the presiding minister (although that may be implied), while the rubrics simply refer to 'those exercising this ministry' (*TMWB*, 1999, p. 413); it is certainly not restricted to ordained ministers.

The Roman Catholic and Church of England rites also include texts for the blessing of the oil for healing. In the Roman Catholic rite, 'the oil for the sick is ordinarily blessed by the bishop on Holy Thursday' (*PCOTS*, 1982, §21), though a priest in cases of necessity may bless it. In Anglican practice, many priests will use oil consecrated at the diocesan Blessing of the Oils (normally on Maundy Thursday or during Holy Week), but provision is made for priests to bless it. In the Church of England rite 'A Celebration of Wholeness and Healing', normally to be used for a diocesan or deanery occasion, the notes state the desirability for the oil to be consecrated during the rite, as its theological significance is set out in a prayer of blessing (*CWPS*, 2005, p. 25, note 5). The renewed emphasis on anointing for healing in the Roman Catholic rite is illustrated by the prayer for the blessing of the oil:

> Bless this oil + and sanctify it for our use.
> Make this oil a remedy for all who are anointed with it;
> heal them in body, in soul, and in spirit,
> and deliver them from every affliction.
>
> (*PCOTS*, 1982, §123)

The Methodist text prays that those who receive this ministry may 'be made whole by the power of the Holy Spirit' (*TMWB*, 1999, p. 409), while the Church of England formula says,

> may they be made whole in body, mind and spirit,
> restored in your image, renewed in your love,
> and serve you as sons and daughters in your kingdom.
>
> (*CWPS*, 2005, p. 33)

At the administration of the oil, the Roman Catholic rite includes a two-stage anointing, first of the forehead:

> Through this holy anointing
> may the Lord in his love and mercy help you
> with the grace of the Holy Spirit. **Amen.**

and then of the hands,

> May the Lord who frees you from sin
> save you and raise you up. **Amen.**
>
> (*PCOTS*, 1982, §124)

It then gives a series of additional prayers for general use, *in extremis*, advanced age, before surgery, and for a child and young person. In the Church of England rite, in contrast to the laying on of hands, the formula for anointing is a prescribed text:

> *N*, I anoint you in the name of God who gives you life.
> Receive Christ's forgiveness, his healing and his love.
>
> May the Father of our Lord Jesus Christ
> grant you the riches of his grace,
> his wholeness and his peace. **Amen**.
>
> (*CWPS*, 2005, pp. 21, 34)

The phrase, 'the riches of his grace' recalls the prayer after baptism celebrating the work of the anointing Spirit. While the Holy Spirit is not specifically mentioned here, nevertheless the sacramental act of anointing can be seen as both the action of Christ and the Holy Spirit, who first anointed Jesus at his baptism as the fulfilment of the promises of Isaiah 61.1–3 (see Luke 4.18–21). Anointing is administered by making the sign of the cross on the forehead and in some circumstances on the hands as well.

The Eucharist

The provision for the celebration or distribution of the Eucharist is prominent in the various healing rites. The Methodist service for healing and wholeness states in the Introduction, 'The most appropriate setting for this service is Holy Communion, where the risen Christ is present in the sacrament to heal and renew our lives' (*TMWB*, 1999, p. 407). This recognizes that Communion itself witnesses to the grace and spiritual life flowing from the cross, as we eat and drink to our souls' health, and receive 'remission of our sins and all other benefits of his passion'. The Church of England rite makes provision for the laying on of hands and/or anointing to be administered in the context of the Eucharist in church at a corporate celebration or in private houses or in hospital, with a full celebration or administration of Communion with elements consecrated previously. The efficacy of 'spiritual Communion' is recognized for those unable to receive the sacrament physically.

Reconciliation

Rites of Reconciliation designate liturgical rites that mediate and celebrate the forgiveness of sins. The contemporary Roman Catholic rite is called the Rite of Penance; in other traditions, 'reconciliation' or 'the reconciliation of a penitent' is often used. This is because reconciliation is a biblical word (Matthew 5.24; Romans 5.10, 11; 2 Corinthians 5.18–20; Ephesians 2.16; Colossians 1.20), stressing

God's prevenient action, and witnessing to the conviction that God has, in Christ, reconciled the whole world to himself through the Incarnation, death and resurrection of Jesus Christ. Christ's identification with us in our human frailty and his sacrificial death to atone for the sins of the world means that the proclamation of the forgiveness of sins has been a central Christian conviction from the first. The Church's authority to minister forgiveness finds primary expression in baptism. Baptism is administered once 'for the forgiveness of sins', but after baptism Christians continue their conflict with sin, and so, through repentance, confession and contrition, are recalled and restored to their baptismal status. This restoration is also characteristic of a community that seeks to give and receive forgiveness both within its own life and in the way the Church offers to the wider community in which it is set the very gift it has itself received. In all this the Church recognizes the continuing reality of human sin, but also seeks to deal with it through the call to repentance, and in the role of confession and absolution in its corporate life.

In the gospel tradition, one of the most radical aspects of Jesus' ministry was his claim to bestow the forgiveness of sins (Mark 2.5; Matthew 9.2; Luke 5.20). For pious Jews, this was blasphemous as it seemingly abrogated the divine prerogative. It also challenged the temple cult where the sacrificial system was regarded as the divinely instituted means of restoring the community to holiness. As with other aspects of Jesus' ministry, this authority both to forgive and to retain sins was entrusted to Peter (Matthew 16.19), to the Church (Matthew 18.18) and to the apostles (John 20.23). In Luke 24.47, the risen Christ charged his apostles that 'repentance and forgiveness of sins' are to be proclaimed 'in his name'. As the last text makes clear, there was from the first a close connection between repentance, which carries the idea of 'turning right round', and forgiveness. Repentance includes a sense of contrition and amendment of life, recognizing that human sin separates us from both God and our neighbour.

In Christian tradition, forgiveness has been understood to be mediated in a variety of forms, both individual and corporate. In the Roman Catholic tradition, forgiveness is bestowed through the sacrament of Penance. While the contemporary Rite of Penance includes an order for general confession and absolution, this is seldom used; the norm remains individual auricular confession to a priest. In the Anglican tradition, while general confession and absolution are a regular part of corporate worship, there is also provision for individual confession and absolution where the adage 'All may, none must, some should' is often cited. While individual auricular confession has not been a historic part of Methodist piety, *The Methodist Worship Book* (1999) includes 'A Service of Repentance and Reconciliation' for individual penitents. The Methodist rite does not state explicitly that confession must be made to an ordained minister.

This embracing of *individual* auricular confession and absolution by a wide variety of Christian traditions has arisen from an increasing recognition that for some Christians issues of sin, guilt and a burdened conscience need to be explored and ministered to as part of a confidential and personal pastoral encounter. This has been strengthened by the growth of spiritual accompaniment and pastoral counselling in the life of the Church and by insights from psychology and other social sciences. For others, going to confession is an aspect of a 'rule of life', or as part of personal preparation for the celebration of a major festival, particularly in the preparatory seasons of Lent and Advent.

THE RECONCILIATION OF A PENITENT

Historically, rites of reconciliation have included four core components:

- confession of sin;
- act of contrition;
- act of penance;
- absolution.

These four elements were variously, though not unanimously, regarded as the *res* or 'inward reality' of the sacrament by medieval theologians. They are normally found in contemporary rites and, while they still constitute the heart of the sacramental action, they are often preceded by words of welcome and a brief sharing of the Word, and followed by an act of praise or thanksgiving and dismissal.

For the **confession**, the priest or minister invites the penitent to confess his or her sins; this may be done in the penitent's own words or in a given form of prayer, perhaps incorporating an extempore expression of particular sins. The Methodist rite gives a simple form:

> I confess to almighty God,
> before you and all the company of heaven,
> that I have sinned through my own fault
> in what I have thought, said, and done,
> and in what I have failed to do.
> In particular I confess . . .
>
> These are the sins which I remember.
> I ask God's forgiveness for them and for all my sins.
> (*TMWB*, 1999, p. 424)

In response, counsel or guidance may be given.

Contrition is an expression of true sorrow and remorse for sin, showing repentance and the firm desire to walk in newness of life (Romans 6.4). It articulates a deliberate turning away from sin with the intention of falling into sin no more. The Church of England rite gives a specimen text:

> My God, for love of you
> I desire to hate and forsake all sins
> by which I have ever displeased you;
> and I resolve by the help of your grace
> to commit them no more;
> and to avoid all opportunities of sin.
> Help me to do this,
> through Jesus Christ our Lord. Amen.
> (*Common Worship: Christian Initiation*
> *(CWCI)*, 2006, p. 277, 284)

The **Act of Penance** is intended as a remedy for sin and an expression of the fruits of repentance. The example of Zacchaeus, who made actual restitution for his sin (Luke 19.8), is often cited and in some cases an actual restitution (for example, for theft) may be undertaken. Alternatively, the penitent may undertake some recommended spiritual exercises as a token of repentance, such as Bible reading or saying prayers. Such acts of penance are intended as a help towards walking in newness of life, not as a means of 'earning forgiveness' and certainly are not to be regarded as a form of punishment.

Absolution is the formal declaration by the priest or minister of the forgiveness of sins. In pronouncing absolution, the priest lays hands on or stretches hands over the penitent, and may make the sign of the cross over the penitent or on the penitent's forehead. The Book of Common Prayer, in the Rite for the Visitation of the Sick, retained the traditional medieval form of the prayer:

> Our Lord Jesus Christ, who hath left power to his Church to absolve all sinners who truly repent and believe in him, of his great mercy forgive thee thine offences: And by his authority committed to me, I absolve thee from all thy sins, In the Name of the Father, and of the Son, and of the Holy Ghost. Amen.

This also finds expression in the contemporary Roman rite:

> . . . through the ministry of the Church
> may God give you pardon and peace,
> and I absolve you from your sins
> in the name of the Father, and of the Son, +
> and of the Holy Spirit. **Amen.**
> (*Rite of Penance*, 1975, §46)

The Book of Common Prayer text is retained among other texts in the contemporary Church of England rite (*CWCI*, 2006, p. 288). The formula *ego te absolvo*, 'I absolve you from your sins', has been criticized by some, notably evangelicals, on the grounds that it could be held to prejudice the divine prerogative. However, the text is careful first to ask that Christ 'of his great mercy forgive you your offences'. 'I absolve you' is thus an expression of the authority given to priests to pronounce absolution in the name of God. The other five absolution texts avoid such a formula (*CWCI*, 2006, pp. 288, 289), as does the Methodist text, 'I declare that your sins are forgiven' (*TMWB*, 1999, p. 425).

Even in a 'private', individual, context, reconciliation remains a corporate action of the Church, because sin affects the unity of Christ's body, and the intention of this ministry is to restore penitent sinners to their baptismal status and in some cases to active discipleship perhaps after a period of exclusion from reception of Communion. For this reason, in contemporary theology reconciliation with the Church is regarded as the *res* of the sacramental action.

'The seal of the confession' remains an important aspect of this ministry, requiring the absolute keeping of confidences, including after death. Most churches issue guidelines on issues around abuse or other serious crimes, or behaviour that may threaten the priest's/minister's or other people's well-being, and advise on the traditional right to withhold absolution.

Further reading

Atkinson, D. (2011), *The Church's Healing Ministry: Practical and Pastoral Reflections* (Norwich: Canterbury Press).

Dallen, J. (1986), *The Reconciling Community: The Rite of Penance* (New York: Pueblo).

Dudley, M., and Rowell, G. (eds) (1990), *Confession and Absolution* (London: SPCK).

Dudley, M., and Rowell, G. (eds) (1993), *The Oil of Gladness: Anointing in the Christian Tradition* (London: SPCK).

Headley, C., and Nichols, B. (2006a), 'Wholeness and Healing', in P. Bradshaw (ed.), *A Companion to Common Worship*, vol. 2, Alcuin Club Collections 81 (London: SPCK), pp. 142–67.

Headley, C., and Nichols, B. (2006b), 'Reconciliation and Restoration', in P. Bradshaw (ed.), *A Companion to Common Worship*, vol. 2, Alcuin Club Collections 81 (London: SPCK), pp. 168–79.

Lloyd, T., and Tovey, P. (2004), *Celebrating Forgiveness: An Original Text Drafted by Michael Vasey*, Alcuin/GROW Joint Liturgical Studies 58 (Cambridge: Grove Books).

Chapter 17

Marriage

Trevor Lloyd

Is marriage Christian? Not necessarily. Rather, some kind of pair-bonding ritual is something which is intrinsic to society, found in different cultures across the world and over the centuries. The main elements of the marriage ritual do not seem to change very much. What do you need in order to have a marriage? You need two people who agree to commit themselves to one another, and the ratification of that brings with it an element of celebration, joy, thanksgiving, blessing, call it what you will. All the other elements in the ritual gather around these two bases, which are what Kenneth Stevenson calls the 'deep structures' of the rite: consent and blessing.

A glance at history and Scripture bears this out and pinpoints the dilemma for the Church in relation to contemporary culture. Look at the readings from the Old Testament suggested for the Marriage Service in contemporary service books such as *Common Worship*, the Roman Catholic *Rite of Marriage*, the *Methodist Service Book* or *A Prayer Book for Australia*, and you will find what initially looks like a kaleidoscopic jumble of stories.

Genesis 1.26–28, 31 reminds us that God created us male and female, with at least a hint that the image of God is reflected in the male–female mix and not just in man. And then he blesses them and tells them to be fruitful: blessing and fertility continue to be a linked theme through the rest of the biblical story.

Genesis 24.48–51, 58–67 takes us to the story of Isaac and Rebecca. Here we find family negotiations, gifts of gold and silver jewellery, garments and costly ornaments for both Rebecca and her brother, the betrothal question 'Will you go with this man?' and consent, followed by a familial blessing for fecundity: 'May you . . . become thousands of myriads; may your offspring gain possession of the gates of their foes.' She puts a veil on before meeting Isaac, and only at the end, when he has taken her into his tent, do we hear 'he loved her'. There is a strong sense of God's intentions being met in the search and the negotiations.

Blessing is again the main theme of various selections from chapters 7 and 8 of the apocryphal book of Tobit, with the sense of divine guidance and protection: Tobit gets Sarah out of bed when her parents have finished installing them in the specially prepared bridal chamber (where her seven previous partners have died on their wedding night) so they can both pray for protection and blessing: 'Grant that she and I may find mercy and that we may grow old together.' But there are other elements here too – a joyful, tearful feast at the betrothal, which is marked by a written and sealed contract, and festivities for 14 days after the consummation of the marriage.

There is no clear pattern here, but it is not simply a kaleidoscopic jumble. Put the stories in the readings together with other scattered references to marriage and you begin to get some common elements: betrothal, or a contract or consent to marry, backed by a bride-price, blessings, a veil, a procession from the bride's house to the bridegroom's, prayer over the nuptial bed, a feast going on for several days. But such a list does not necessarily indicate any liturgical content, or even a Judaeo-Christian theological background. A marriage in pagan Rome, preceded by a legal marriage contract between the parents, features the veiling of the woman, a procession to the man's house, the payment of the bride-price, the putting of the ring on the bride's finger indicating ownership, offerings to the gods by the bride's parents, a feast with speeches, the bridegroom carrying the bride over the threshold, the specially prepared bedchamber, the 'blessing' of the bed with water by the bride in the hope of fertility. Some of this sounds familiar. There are common elements, some of which are given a varied amount of religious interpretation in different religions or cultures. It is this commonality which enables the Church – if it is wise and mission-focused rather than self-centred – to reach out and provide a service to those who might otherwise have nothing to do with it.

But does this then mean that marriage is a 'creation ordinance', something which is shared with all humankind simply in virtue of being human? Not necessarily. Again, look at the readings suggested by contemporary servicebooks. There are hints in the Old Testament of something which is made gloriously explicit in the New.

The Song of Solomon (e.g. 2.8–16 and 8.6–7) is a beautiful, emotive and graphic poem about a man searching for the woman, finding her but then their drifting apart and coming together again. Its accounts of the chase, the beauty of the body and the emotional ups and downs are very contemporary, but at a deeper level describe the mystery of God seeking for his people, and his rejection when they go away from him. This is the explicit theme of the book of Hosea, and one of the marriage readings – Jeremiah 31.31–32a, 33–34a – talks about the need for a new covenant and a new heart. This covenantal parallel between the relationship of the two partners in a marriage and the relationship of Christ to his Church is the mystery unveiled in Ephesians 5.21–33 and is at the heart of any Christian view of marriage. The fact that the mystery is unveiled in the midst of a very down-to earth set of instructions for husbands and wives underlines the earthiness of God's otherness. Jesus did the same in the parables, and in revealing his glory in the miracle at the wedding at Cana (John 2.1–11). The penetrative unity between Christ and the Church gives a greater depth to the meaning of being one flesh and measures the extent of love by his sacrifice on the cross. The marriage readings about love from the New Testament are inseparable from this view and measurement of love. Romans 8.31–39 focuses on the love of Christ; 1 Corinthians 13, with its practical descriptions of the activity of love, is built around the fact that love lasts for eternity; Ephesians 3.14–21 is a prayer that we might know the enormity of the love of Christ.

The problem for the Church in simply seeing marriage as a 'creation ordinance', to which the Church adds various Christian elements, is that that approach ignores the Christian revolution. For those who are Christians are a new creation, and the whole scene has changed. No longer is it necessary to procreate in order to achieve immortality. In 1 Corinthians 7, arguably the most important passage on the marriage relationship in the New Testament, though rarely used as a marriage reading because it is too explicit, sex and its frequency is not directly linked to procreation. It is only recently that phrases like 'the delight and tenderness of sexual union' have replaced the Cranmerian 'for the procreation of children . . . and to avoid fornication' in the Marriage Service Preface. For those living under the law, under the old covenant, sin and therefore death were a major threat to marriage, hence to society. For those living under the new covenant, the governing principle of forgiveness and new, eternal, life provides a radically different motivation. At the heart of the marriage relationship is a self-giving love modelled on that of Christ. It is this love that sustains the marriage. It is because of this model that marriage is monogamous – he only has one bride – and indissoluble, for life. Divorce, on this model, no longer makes sense, and we have returned to the Genesis 1 situation, before sin and the fall: it is because the two have 'become one flesh' that Jesus says the words used at the first climax (see below) of our service: 'What God has joined together, let no one separate.' But the problem, as always, is living out in practice, in an environment still dogged by sin, those new covenant principles. That is why, in the lists of New Testament readings in the marriage service, we have texts not only about the love of Christ but also practical instruction for husbands and wives.

This brief review of the evidence leads us to an interim conclusion, a caveat and a fundamental question. The interim conclusion is that there are clearly shared elements in the establishment of any human relationship of deep and loving commitment, but that Christian marriage is radically different because of the union of the partners with the Godhead, 'in Christ'. The caveat is that it is difficult to read back a liturgical structure or evidence of a text into either the Old Testament stories or the New Testament theological undergirding and stimulation of the relationship. It would be too easy to see something that looks close to what the Church has done since medieval times and assume that there is a linear development, when we simply do not have the evidence. One of the reasons for this is that for centuries the process of getting married was simply a domestic ritual, often with very little in the way of customary texts. Which leads us to the question, or rather, some linked questions: should the Church be involved in this business at all? Why can it not be left to the local family level, where decisions about who can get married to whom need not be a matter of international debate? Should the Church concentrate on producing a marriage service for Christians, rather than foisting something called 'Christian marriage' on a public who do not know what that means? Or should the Church be offering something which everyone can use – or a service designed for the faithless? The Anglican Church in Canada has opted for the latter, with its 2001 rite 'Celebration and blessing of a marriage between a Christian and a person of another faith tradition' which omits all distinctively Christian content. The Roman Catholic *Rite of Marriage* is clearly intended for the faithful and involves Communion: the standard rite is the Nuptial Mass. The Church of England's *Common Worship* Marriage Service is designed for everyone, but with a lot of optional extra richness, including Holy Communion. The Church of England's website joyfully invites anyone who wishes to do so to get married in church, an approach very different from most of the other provinces in the Communion, who would see the service as a rite for the use of Christians, recognized as such by their baptism. There are clear missiological and historical reasons why the Church of England service is different, and they affect the style, language and content of the service. The answer to our fundamental question is going to determine the nature of the liturgical provision.

To explore this we need to go back to our brief historical review. Both pagan and Jewish marriage rites were domestic in character. They were public because of the processions – and noise – but they happened in the home rather than the temple or synagogue, and were under the control of the leaders of the families rather than the local priest. The same domestic pattern continued when Christians were married. This is probably why there is very little evidence about marriage liturgy until the fourth century. And when bishops do begin to write about marriage, it is sometimes difficult to tell whether they are writing about the husband–wife relationship or about a marriage liturgy. But there is evidence of a growing tension between the domestic and the ecclesial, with the betrothal remaining domestic, and the blessing, solemnization or marriage (which might be some time after the betrothal) gradually taking place in church with a priest rather than the head of the household now responsible for the blessing. It was only when the social order had broken down in the West in the eighth century that the Church found it necessary to recognize the matrimonial consent and the conditions attaching to it. To prevent clandestine marriages, both the betrothal and marriage rites were now to take place at the doors of the church. So began a long history of the Church's involvement in the legal aspects of marriage: from the eleventh century until 1857 in England the Church ran the courts dealing with marriage and divorce. From the twelfth century onwards, the rite consisted of an enquiry by the minister about consent, the giving away of the bride, the reading of the scrip of the dowry, the blessing of the ring and putting it on the hand of the bride, the giving of some pieces of gold or silver by the bridegroom and the wedding blessing. All this was at the door and if there was to be a wedding Mass it was only then that the party entered the church. The Mass (of the Holy Trinity) involved some further symbolism including the veil.

The major change of the Reformation to this rite was allowing consent and promises to take place in the body of the church, and marking the beginning of the second part by the procession to the sanctuary. It is worth noting that Cranmer's service, the main vehicle for all weddings in England and Wales for 450 years, has no readings, and no prayer until after the exchange of rings, in the blessing immediately before the declaration of the marriage. It is the familiar historic structure of the consents followed by a blessing, seen down the centuries, the same kind of pattern available to believer and non-believer alike. For many, it is no more than the local British pair-bonding ritual. As such, it is an essential part of the structure of British society. Fewer people are now getting married: the total number of marriages is about the same as in 1895, when the population of England and Wales was 30 million compared to 56 million now, and the number of women getting married per thousand of unmarried women has fallen from around 50 in the 1970s to fewer than 20 today.[1] Despite this, marriage is still a major building-block of society. It contributes in many different ways through its networks, supportive family relationships, patterns of childcare and personal growth and development, joys as well as stresses and sadnesses. The importance of marriage in the community is recognized in modern marriage services in a number of ways. The Preface at the beginning of the service says marriage 'is given as the foundation of family life in which children are [born and] nurtured' and says that 'it enriches society and strengthens community.' In most services now the friends and relatives are invited to show their support with a question such as 'Will you, the families and friends of *N* and *N*, support and uphold them in their marriage now and in the years to come?'

This community aspect of marriage is one of the key elements in what the Church has to offer to everyone, part of its gift to society, part of its mission. It is the church door part of the rite, the legal and public aspect of the marriage. Some

---

1 These are 2009 figures from the Office for National Statistics. Available from: <http://www.ons. gov.uk/ons/rel/vsob1/marriages-in-england-and-wales—provisional-/2009/marriages-summary. html>. However, the provisional 2010 figures show a small upturn in the marriage rate, the specific reasons for which are discussed in 'Marriages in England and Wales' (provisional) 2010, released 29 February 2012 at <http://www.ons.gov.uk/ons/rel/vsob1/marriages-in-england-and-wales—provisional-/2010/index.html>.

would argue that this could just as well be done by the secular authorities, that the Church has no business in getting involved and should only be providing the celebratory and blessing parts of the service for those who are Christians. On the contrary, the public promises are an integral part of the rite, and need the context of the reading of the word of God and prayer. As the Introduction to the *Common Worship* service says, 'It is based upon a solemn, public and life-long covenant between a man and a woman, declared and celebrated in the presence of God and before witnesses.' God, as creator, started the whole thing off, and does not just arrive on the scene later to give it a blessing. Understanding marriage as a gift of God in Trinitarian creation is crucial to understanding what is going on spiritually. This should pervade and inform all parts of the rite, not just the blessing and Eucharist. Relationship is at the heart of the triune God, and that relationship is echoed in domestic rites, at the church door and in the sanctuary.

So we have now two main parts to the structure – the consents and the blessing of the couple, and three elements which are spiritual threads through the whole rite – community, Trinity and the concept of marriage as gift. The Church has so much more to offer than enabling or presiding over a traditional pair-bonding ritual and ensuring all is legal, decent and in order. If the couple making their promises are swept up into a vision of the covenant God makes with his people, then their betrothal rite – as in the case of the anointing ceremony in the Coptic Church – might have some understanding of betrothal as vocation; a call not just to commitment to one another, but to serve God in the estate of matrimony. The images and visions of marriage in the Scripture readings, and the allusions to Scripture in the prayers, should enable some of the joy of love in all its forms, *eros*, *philia* and *agape*, to take hold of the couple and of the congregation.

If this enhanced vision of marriage is part of the Church's gift to society, it is only possible because it is God who gives marriage. Both marriage as a construct, and this particular marriage of these two people, are made by God, part of his dealings with his people, one of his many gifts demonstrating his love for us. The consummation of this is the gift of Jesus Christ, his death and resurrection and the door he holds open for us to heaven, his invitation to the marriage supper of the Lamb. This view of marriage as a gift is both eschatological – what we do has eternal effects – and charismatic. It involves recognizing the call of God's Holy Spirit in bringing these two people together, and calling down the presence and blessing of the Spirit on the couple, with thanksgiving for the love that has brought them to this point. This 'added value' of the Church's involvement in marriage makes God's activity explicit and exalts marriage from being a legal formula enacted in the context of reading Scripture and singing psalms, to being a mystery, an earthly part of a greater eternal celebration, prefigured for Christians in the Eucharist. As St Paul says in the Ephesians reading (Ephesians 5.32), 'This is a great mystery, and I am applying it to Christ and the Church.' The couple are lifted up into the relational activity of the Trinity.

But is this real? There are always problems with mountain-top experiences and starry-eyed people smitten with love and the Spirit at the same time, when down at the bottom of the mountain there are dirty nappies, unwashed dishes, problems with the relatives, no money and a real struggle to live out any of the expectations and commitments made earlier. So the service needs to include indicators that the message of the Incarnation is that God knows about all this, that God's grace is there to help, that admission of guilt and acceptance of forgiveness are part of our life together in Christ.

So how does this theological vision and inherited historical pattern work in today's marriage service? Kenneth Stevenson makes the point that the 'deep structures' of a rite tend to act as focal points around which other elements gather. They can also be the focus for other elements in the rite which spin off to have a separate life of their own, resulting in a multi-event or staged rite, taking us through a series of stages. If the 'deep structures' here are the consents and the blessing, what are the other elements we should expect to see gather around them?

There are some things that are preliminary to the consents, some of which could be done as domestic rituals such as a modern form of betrothal, engagement party or shower, or prayer before leaving on the morning of the wedding itself. Other preliminary things are part of the public and community nature of the event, involving gathering witnesses together and providing for banns or a licence. And if people are to give their consent, it is as well that they – and those present – know what they are giving their consent to. This does not normally involve the public reading of any prenuptial agreement, but focuses on the Preface, which sets out what the Church's understanding of and hope for marriage is. This is one of the oldest things in the service, and we find Chaucer itemizing similar concerns in the *Canterbury Tales* as long ago as 1387. The preface has to set the scene both theologically ('Marriage is a gift of God in creation . . . made holy by God') as well as in terms of personal expectations (sexual union, companionship, children) and the expectations of society (more about strengthening community nowadays than setting up a new home). But perhaps the first thing we need to do when we get to church, as on other occasions, is to greet one another and to say a prayer. So the approach to the consents sorts itself out.

The mutual consents are the key legal moment of the ceremony. The 'I will' establishes the contract, and denotes a freely made commitment of the will in the present tense, not a promise to do something in the future. Legally, it could be very brief, but the form of words for the consents and the promises used in most churches today has a long pedigree; even in the Latin Sarum Rite before the Reformation these words were in English, with the priest charged to ascertain that the couple were indeed free to marry.

Around the consents cluster various other items, of which the question to the congregation is the latest addition, together with – if Communion is to follow in the *Common Worship* rite – the confession and absolution, though why it is only those that are having Communion who need to be forgiven is a mystery. This part of the service is now generally set within the context of the ministry of the word, so readings and sermon are part of this cluster. The earliest additional rite here is the giving or exchanging of rings (the latter arriving only slowly from the eleventh-century Byzantine custom, via Spain and Germany). The prayer for blessing the rings can sometimes take on some of the character of the nuptial blessing, and indeed Cranmer used some of the elaborate Sarum prayer at this point for one of his post-marriage blessing prayers. The joining of hands and the declaration of the marriage end the first part of the rite, and it is probably at this point, in English law, that the registration of the marriage should take place, as it is required as soon as possible after the couple are married.

The second part of the rite focuses on the marriage blessing. Even in Cranmer's service, the sequence of prayers after the marriage covers the traditional themes: the creation of man and woman, mention of Adam and Eve, Abraham and Sarah (and Isaac and Rebecca in the ring prayer earlier), God's consecration of marriage as signifying the relationship between Christ and the Church, love and faithfulness, being 'fruitful in procreation', and at the last inheriting the everlasting kingdom. The longer nuptial blessings emerging in Protestant churches in the twentieth century cover similar areas, usually in a more coherent order, and with the addition of the Holy Spirit and the eschatological sign of the joy of feasting around God's table in heaven. Examples may be seen in the Prayer Book of the Episcopal Church in America, a wonderful responsive one ('May he bless your herds and flocks') in the Anglican Church of Kenya, several options in *A New Zealand Prayer Book* and in the Church of England's *Common Worship*, as well as a eucharistic-prayer-style thanksgiving and blessing in the Church of Scotland's *Book of Common Order*.

The major item attaching to the nuptial blessing is the Holy Communion itself. For Cranmer in 1549 and 1552 this was mandatory: 'the newe married persons the same daye of their marriage *must* receive the holy communion.' The 'if it is convenient' was added in 1662, but there is not much evidence of it happening. It is still the expectation in the Roman Catholic Church that the Marriage Rite will take place within the Mass, but that is not mandatory. It is there in the *Common Worship* rite, with a fully eucharistic option provided, and the possibility of restoring the nuptial blessing to its historical position at the end of the Eucharistic Prayer. This provides a single climax to the rite, avoiding the double climax which happens if the nuptial blessing is in the earlier place. Putting the marriage rite within the Eucharist emphasizes the concept of grace, the extraordinary gift of God in the Incarnation and crucifixion, setting this particular marriage within that eternal context.

Other items which gather around the nuptial blessing include a number of symbols which may rightly vary according to local culture and understanding – the veiling of the bride in the Western Church and the crowning of both bride and bridegroom in the East, both attested in the fourth century. Another ancient one is the holding of a canopy over the couple during the blessing (from the Jewish custom, a reminder taking us back to the bedchamber prayers). Other symbols include the lighting of a candle together and drinking from a common cup of wine (arguably a better symbol as it leaves not a burned-out candle-end but a warm internal glow).

More distant ancillary material at this end of the nuptial blessing cluster includes some rites which might be considered for inclusion as part of a set of staged rites – a blessing in the Eucharist after return from honeymoon, blessing of a new home, and various opportunities for thanksgiving for marriage, which might be at an anniversary, or when a number of couples together reaffirm their vows, or after a time of separation or difficulty in marriage. These could be domestic rites or take place in church, and there are English texts in existence for all of these. Then there are rites which might not necessarily be regarded as part of such a sequence, such as the blessing of a civil marriage, the blessing of new rings, and the ritual recognition of a separation or divorce. Nor is gay and lesbian marriage part of this sequence, but part of a different order of debate, which is both about the willingness of the churches to accept such marriages and also about the suitability of the traditional texts, with their theological background, for such a rite. Again, texts for all these exist, and there is no doubt that such an industry, somewhat akin to the greetings card industry, could go on inventing more. And some of these might be useful pastoral and missiological opportunities for maintaining contact with people who have been married in church.

This brings us back to the fundamental question noted earlier about whether the Church should be involved in the marriage business and whether it ought to focus only on a rite exclusively for the baptized. One interesting side issue points to an area of debate which impacts on this. Who is the minister of this rite? The Church of England, perhaps curiously, nowhere formally holds to the Roman Catholic view that the couple are the ministers of the rite. A prior qualification to be a minister of an ecclesial rite is baptism, which puts those entering mixed-faith or no-faith marriages in the difficult position of committing perjury or going elsewhere. The Church of England's traditionally open stance on this, dating from the time when it was responsible for all marriages, is that, while God, the couple and witnesses are all involved, the minister must be in holy orders. It is the minister who declares that God has joined the couple together, says the nuptial blessing and signs the register. This position is even clearer if marriage is set within Holy Communion, with one person presiding over the whole rite. The Church of England seems pretty clear, at least, that it is offering God's great gift of marriage to everyone. This would seem to be totally in tune both with the historic contexts for marriage which we have reviewed and with the basic theological concept of marriage as gift, and not just law.

Further reading

Kasper, W. (1993), *The Theology of Marriage* (New York: Crossroad).

Lawler, M. (1993), *Marriage and Sacrament: A Theology of Christian Marriage* (Collegeville, MN: Liturgical Press).

Stevenson, K. (1982), *Nuptial Blessing: A Study of Christian Marriage Rites*, Alcuin Club Collections 64 (London: SPCK).

Stevenson, K. (1987), *To Join Together: The Rite of Marriage* (New York: Pueblo).

Stevenson, K. (ed.) (2011), *Anglican Marriage Rites: A Symposium*, Alcuin/GROW Joint Liturgical Studies 71 (Norwich: SCM-Canterbury Press).

Chapter 18

Death and dying

Lizette Larson-Miller

INTO YOUR HANDS I COMMEND MY SPIRIT . . .

Christians do not have a monopoly on dying and death. All human beings die, care for the dying and for the body of the deceased; and mourning is a universal human experience. But, as evidenced throughout Christian history, the common experiences of suffering, of dying, of death and of mourning have been interpreted differently by Christians, distinguishing them from their neighbours both culturally and religiously. The ways in which Christians understand, articulate, ritualize and hand on the meaning of dying in Christ, as well as the theology of life after death, are created and expressed in the rituals and liturgies of the Church.

In this chapter, we will look first at the process of dying through the lens of liturgical theology and ritual practice. Dying in the Lord is not theologically isolated from life in Christ nor is it neatly separated ritually from rites with the sick and rites for healing, as well as liturgies for the dead; it is part of a ritual process, and, therefore, embedded in a theological continuum that roots itself in both Christian anthropology and Trinitarian theology. Second, the focus on the death of a Christian is, in a similar way, neither theologically nor liturgically separated from other aspects of Christian life, beliefs which have found new life in both the renewed links between baptismal and funeral liturgies in the past 50 years of modern liturgical reforms, and the eschatological trajectory of Christian life overall.

Within the Church of England, particularly in the past decade as the multiple volumes of *Common Worship* have emerged, an almost dizzying array of 'how to' volumes have also been produced which give a clear overview of these ritual relationships, as well as a map of how the Book of Common Prayer, *Common Worship: Pastoral Services*, *The Promise of His Glory* and other volumes provide elements of liturgies related to the dying and the dead. In other member churches of the Anglican Communion, supplements to local versions of the Book of Common Prayer have also been published, such as the second and third volumes of *Enriching Our Worship* (*EOW*) in the USA. It is important to know the multiple resources, their official or commended status in one's own worshipping community, the best of the secondary writings on the subjects and, above all, the reasons why the Church felt new liturgies were necessary. To that end, this overview is primarily an introduction to those theological shifts or expansions which made necessary these augmented liturgical resources. While this is not a volume on the history of liturgy, these theological shifts in relation to dying and death must have some rooting in history because they are the inheritance of different threads of ritualized expressions of Christian faith.

DYING IN THE LORD

The historical development, theological reflection and ritual practices surrounding the death of a Christian meet individual and communal faith in particularly intense ways. When we enter into the dying process ourselves, or accompany the dying of others, we come face to face with the unavoidable importance of what we believe about life after death, about the ongoing engagement of God in our lives and in our death, and what it is that we are doing in ritual activities. Medical experts on a parallel and increasingly intertwined path with the Church's engagement have often been more explicit about these moments of truth.

> The confrontation with death lays bare the spiritual core of the human condition . . . confronted with the mystery of life – and death – we reflexively try to make some meaning of our experience in the world, strengthen our relationships with others, and feel part of something larger and more enduring than ourselves. (Byock, 2012, p. 291)

This is not to suggest that the Church has the answers to the great mystery of death, but faith is unavoidable in what we say and do in the rituals of dying.

As with the rites for the sick which include prayer, laying on of hands, anointing and more, ministry to the dying is not just 'to' the dying, it is 'with' the dying. The dying minister to us also; to accompany them on this journey is to be a recipient of sacramental ministrations; it is to stand on holy ground, to come face to face with our own mortality and our faith in 'sure and certain hope of the resurrection'. Whether we are engaged with the official rites of the Church or private devotional practices, it is important to remember that Anglicanism in particular has inherited elements of Reformed Protestantism and traditional Catholicism in its ritual (and therefore theological) practices. To ask why that matters is to ask, 'For what are we preparing?' or 'What is a good death?' Is the sole focus of ministering to the dying to offer them comfort, medically through the alleviation of pain and spiritually through an affective companionship? Is it to prepare their souls to face judgement immediately on their death, or to assure them of their place in heaven regardless of how they have lived their life? Is it to do ritual things and say ritual words to offer comfort to the family and friends surrounding the dying person? Is it to 'save' the dying person from having to confront death by encouraging medical intervention at all costs as well as continually offering prayers for physical healing? All these approaches are verifiably in operation at the beginning of the twenty-first century; some are historical inheritances, while some are far more influenced by contemporary culture than theology.

If one painted ministry with the dying in large historical sweeps throughout Christian history, certain overarching approaches could be detected. The early-Church confidence in the resurrection, in the saving conformity of each individual Christian to Christ from baptism through death and beyond, and the corporate nature of salvation as a communal action would dominate. These theologically informed approaches were ritually expressed in the chanting of the Passion Gospels as a Christian lay dying, in the commending of the dead to God with confident prayers that God would forgive any remaining sins, in the chanting of psalms and antiphons focused on the journey to God, in the giving of *viaticum*, the last Communion, the food for the journey, and in the numerous literary and artistic references to the *refrigeria*, the antechamber of heaven, where Christians awaited the final resurrection in a place of refreshment, light and peaceful rest.

As Christianity took root in different cultures and locations, these understandings of dying and their related ritual expressions shifted, or expanded to include these and newer rituals. Above all, however, by the second millennium of Christianity the lack of confidence in one's ability to do enough to die in a state of grace radically changed rites for the dying and the dead. The shifts in the rites for individual confession, with absolution prior to the doing of penance, meant that the possibility that penance for sins might need to continue into the next life changed the Christian rituals that accompany the dying. Together with the developing articulation of the teaching of purgatory, replacing the antechamber of heaven with the antechamber of hell, dying was not so much a conforming to the person of Christ through baptism and suffering as it was an intense series of intercessions praying to be saved from evil powers and the harsh and deserved judgement of God. By the twelfth century, *viaticum* as the primary ecclesial ritual act was replaced by additional sacramental means of repentance, now both in confession proper and in anointing of the dying moved to the extreme last position (extreme unction), as another rite focused on the forgiveness of sins. These last rites of confession, Communion and anointing were surrounded by a vast assortment of rites ecclesial and domestic. Many of these practices were rooted in a combination of the social economy of gift exchange, shifting atonement theories and ecclesial power struggles, such that salvation often seemed more a matter of economic transaction than confident faith in a merciful God.

In the various Protestant reformations which had public impact by the fifteenth century and for centuries to follow, the abuses of this approach resulted in a number of changes to the rituals and liturgies accompanying the dying. In England, the emphasis on the individual had already added a sense of familial responsibility in such practices as the church reminding the dying to make a will for family members, and for the dying to express reconciliation with the living. But from the more Reformed end of Protestantism, the abuses connected to prayers for the dead and payment for release from purgatory resulted in a reaction that was theologically founded on the belief that an individual was judged immediately at death, and, therefore, no prayers for the dead could possibly have any impact because of that reality. While this shift changed funeral liturgies, it also had an effect on prayers with the dying, resulting in a newfound urgency for confession of sins and profession of faith in preparation for the moment of dying – now even more weighted as a moment of eternal reckoning.

Even in the ecclesial compromise of the 1662 Prayer Book, this latter strand is still evident, particularly in the 'Visitation of the Sick' for when someone is 'very sick'. There the chastisement is seen as a purification in this life, 'therefore, taking your sickness, which is thus profitable for you' as an aide to prompting both confession of proper faith and preparation for judgement:

And forasmuch as after this life there is an account to be given unto the righteous Judge, by whom all must be judged without respect of persons, I require you to examine yourself and your estate, both toward God and man; so that, accusing and condemning yourself for your own faults, you find mercy at our heavenly Father's hand for Christ's sake, and not be accused and condemned in that fearful judgement.

The sick person is asked to consent to believing the 'Articles of the Faith' summarized in the creed before being examined of sins, verbalizing repentance, making right relationships with family members and beyond, remembering the poor with alms, and, if necessary, making a 'special confession of his sins' followed by absolution. This and other prayers are followed by 'The Communion of the Sick' with an exhortation to be diligent in receiving Communion throughout one's life in preparation for death, followed by permission to celebrate Holy Communion in the home of the sick person if he or she is not able to come to church. The rubrics for this home Communion include the exception to the reception of Communion when the sick person is physically unable, assuring the benefits of Communion 'to his soul's health, although he do not receive the Sacrament with his mouth'.

In addition to these formal rites in the 1662 Book of Common Prayer, we know many other rituals were taking place. Drawing on the Prayer Book's wealth of prayers, domestic piety and additional handbooks for priests, the ministry of presence, comfort, material assistance, exhortation and practical preparations were aided by the reality that most people, outside extraordinary events and war, died at home, so that the living were familiar with death and the dead were ideally surrounded by the living.

One cannot jump from 'The Order for the Visitation of the Sick' in the 1662 Prayer Book to *Common Worship: Pastoral Services* without stepping out of the Church to acknowledge momentous cultural changes around dying and death. The first major change is a result of the end of Christendom in cultures with deep roots in Christianity. Because of this, the UK, the USA and other countries have moved from the perception of a homogeneous understanding of dying and death to a multiplicity of understandings, including what may be the largest group, those people with no reflected understanding of death and dying beyond the immediacy of daily life. Dying was for centuries of Christianity a spiritual passage that became, by the late eighteenth century, a physical or natural process 'overseen by doctors' in many industrialized countries (Walter, 1994, p. 12). Then, perhaps by equal degrees, death became individualized and isolated as 'modern' societies embraced Ernest Becker's classic understanding of the denial of death (Becker, 1973). The lack of experience with the dying, the lack of a spiritual framework in which to understand dying, and the unwillingness to accept dying have ended, for many people, any sense of death as a natural part of the life cycle.

However, many writers on modern dying acknowledge a shift in the last decade with regard to public willingness to acknowledge death. In the USA, much of this reality lesson is tied up with the experiences of the terrorist attacks of September 11, 2001. In other places, it may be widespread diseases such as HIV/AIDS, the ageing of a population, or global awareness of war and violence.

> In only a decade we have moved from a society in which many members refused to contemplate their mortality or were denied the opportunity to do so, to one in which a substantial proportion of middle-aged and elderly know that they or a close kin have a life-threatening disease which may not kill them for years but in whose shadow they must in the meantime live.
>
> (Walter, 1994, p. 50)

The second contributing factor to shifting perceptions of dying is the rebirth of the hospice. This modern return to an ancient practice is a contribution shaped by members of the Church of England. In the 1950s and 1960s, Cicely Saunders and her establishment of St Christopher's Hospice in London brought attention to the reality of death and the return of the concept of a good death. The many benefits of the emerging hospice movement include compassionate and humane engagement with the dying, a critique of the medical industry trained to extend physical life at all costs, and care of the whole person including their spiritual needs at the end of life. Since Saunders' groundbreaking work, the modern hospice movement has spread internationally and changed contemporary health-care, giving rise to the medical field of palliative care. In addition, the movement has resisted the cultural trend to remove the dying from our midst, by engaging family and friends, as well as medical staff, chaplains and caretakers, in a communal effort to accompany the dying.

The third factor is that, in spite of the tremendous growth of the hospice movement, death happens most frequently in a hospital, often with mechanical devices that perpetuate physical life but restrict the fundamental sacramental encounters which mark the Church's ministry to the dying. Hospital deaths, if not specifically in a hospital-based hospice, perpetuate the isolation of the dying, especially if it is of an elderly person already absent from community for an extended period. In many cases, therefore, the isolation is not only of the person dying, but that of family members, especially children and youth, who are isolated from death, and from being part of the ministering community.

Last, another important shift in rites with the dying returns us to the Church with an ecclesial shift in the broadest sense. As with all the changes in liturgy in the past 50 years, the ecumenical Liturgical Movement of the nineteenth and twentieth centuries, and its return to the early Church as a more normative theological and liturgical source, has impacted on the rites for dying as well as for the dead. The movement, along with the crucial cultural and medical shifts noted above, has influenced the shape of liturgy in *Common Worship*. To look at a few of the differences between the 1662 Prayer Book and *Common Worship* is to immerse ourselves in the field of liturgical theology – the study of theology and culture which changes liturgy, and liturgical practices which change theology – the hands-on work of liturgical scholars.

The first difference to be found in the liturgies of *Common Worship* is the literal separation of rites for the dying from rites for the sick, the latter under the category of 'Wholeness and Healing', the former under 'Funeral'. This shift from the 1662 Prayer Book, as well as other Anglican versions of the Book of Common Prayer, is striking in that it finds a middle ground between the medieval diminishing of healing rites in favour of dying rites (generally grouped under 'extreme unction') and returns anointing of the sick to a form far more familiar to the early Church tradition. The 'Ministry at the Time of Death' follows a medieval outline of 'last rites', with a suggested reconciliation section first, the laying on of hands and anointing second, and the reception of Holy Communion last. Here is the return to the early Church *viaticum*, both in the allowance (here and in the rites for the sick) of Communion from the reserved sacrament as food for the journey, and in the restoration of Communion to its ultimate ritual position as the sacrament of the dying.

While the reception of Communion is present in the 1662 book as an additional rite, in *Common Worship* it is a more integrated and essential action. The reality mentioned above, however, that many people today die in a hospital setting, means that the reception of Communion may not be physically possible. In many ways this returns us to the central sacramental action of the Middle Ages, the anointing, which often functions as the primary ritual action when a person cannot receive Communion. As with the anointing of the sick, the threefold heart of this rite – prayer, laying on of hands and anointing with oil – is present in the same way. To put it slightly differently, this is prayer in three forms: verbal, by touch and by oil.

One of the challenges in the US Episcopal Church has been the overuse of anointing of the sick, to the extent that it has become almost trivialized in many parish communities. *Enriching Our Worship 2* addressed this concern by reiterating the occasional nature of this sacramental rite as well as the theological reality that healing is not the end in itself: 'healing is not merely the alleviation of affliction, but testimony to the wholeness and salvation God intends for us' (*EOW 2*, 2005, p. 16). One unintended consequence of the use of anointing for minor needs is that its use with the dying loses its multivalent symbolic power. *Common Worship* assists in this by joining the laying on of hands and anointing to different words when used with the dying, juxtaposing the three forms of prayer (verbal, by touch and by oil) in ways that communicate a different trajectory. The emphasis in the prayer language restores the ancient Christian images of light and peace and everlasting life associated with the *refrigeria*, as well as retaining the language of deliverance from evil drawn from many New Testament passages. The anointing language has similar differences, but most importantly in the optional text associated with the anointing of the dying. This prayer picks up on the images of the older stratum of extreme unction in spiritual healing (forgiveness of sins): 'of his great mercy may he forgive you your sins and release you from suffering. May he deliver you from all evil, preserve you in all goodness and bring you to everlasting life; through Jesus Christ our Lord' (*CWPS*, 2005, p. 226). The echoes of absolution are not accidental, particularly as this is the rite that takes ritual precedence in the eyes of the gathered family members and friends. Here is one of the many choices that these flexible and adaptable rites offer the minister. When those gathered around want the minister to 'do something', it is most often the anointing, this last anointing now with specific texts, that would meet that criteria, as opposed to the ancient practice of *viaticum*, which the dying person is often not able to receive.

The first of the three ecclesial rites in the ministration to the dying, reconciliation, follows the traditional pattern of hearing the word of God, and responding to that with prayer, confession and absolution. Here the absolution carries not only the pronouncement of God's forgiveness and the Church's absolution, but also a tangible expression of the Church's shift from healing ministry to palliative spirituality and the encouragement to a good death. The preparatory note states this quite clearly: 'the person should be helped to be aware that the time of death is approaching.'

These three rites, the 'last rites' of reconciliation, anointing and Communion, are joined to two ancient prayers for the dying, the *proficiscere* and the *commendatio*, which carry in liturgical language much of the meaning of Christian dying. The first prayer is historically addressed to the soul of the dying Christian ('Depart, O Christian soul from this world') and shows up in liturgical manuscripts in the eighth century, with elements dating several centuries before that. The prayer sends the Christian on his or her journey; indeed, medieval manuscripts often entitled the rites for the dying and the dead simply as 'the migration of the soul'. Through the centuries it has taken longer forms, listing all the saints and angels and biblical figures who accompany the dying, as well as more compact summaries. The second prayer in *Common Worship* reflects best these summary versions:

N, go forth upon your journey from this world,
in the name of God the Father almighty who created you;
in the name of Jesus Christ who suffered death for you;
in the name of the Holy Spirit who strengthens you;
in communion with the blessed saints, and aided by angels and archangels,
and all the armies of the heavenly host.
May your portion this day be in peace, and your dwelling the heavenly
Jerusalem.   (*CWPS*, 2005, p. 229)

The use of this prayer requires great pastoral sensitivity, including an appreciation of the psychological power of these words as it gives permission for the dying person to die, to let go, not to hang on for the sake of family members. The prayer was officially suppressed with the 1549 Prayer Book and continued to be so into the 1662 book because it implied again that prayer for the dying, or perhaps the already dead, could have an effect. In a wonderful biography of the prayer, John Lampard traces its disappearance and its reintroduction in recent years in very public ways, using the prayer text as theological reflection (Lampard, 2005, p. xxi).

The second traditional prayer, 'returned' to the rites for the dying in *Common Worship*, is the commendation proper:

Into your hands, O merciful Saviour, we commend your servant *N*.
Acknowledge, we pray, a sheep of your own fold, a lamb of your own flock,
a sinner of your own redeeming.
Enfold *him/her* in the arms of your mercy
in the blessed rest of everlasting peace
and in the glorious company of the saints in light.   (*CWPS*, 2005, p. 230)

This prayer begins to appear in liturgical manuscripts earlier than the previous prayer, appointed for both the moment of death and the end of funeral liturgies, and again captures the early-Church images of what was believed to await the

Christian as well as the strong sense of journey, of sending the Christian forth to be received by others 'on the other end'.

This brief overview of the liturgy for the dying in contemporary Anglicanism highlights both what has changed and why those changes have come about, as catalysts for change from within the Church amid theological and historical scholarship, and from cultural shifts and attitudes towards dying, have pushed liturgy to reflect as well as create and sustain hope in the resurrection. Turning to liturgies for the dead will reveal a pattern of similar shifts, dependent on the same historical developments and responding to contemporary society's multiple concerns about care for the human body and care for the earth.

I AM THE RESURRECTION AND THE LIFE

Why do we do funerals? Who are they for? What do they actually accomplish? The answer to those questions and the theological influences to the answers are very much tied up in the variable history of prayer for the dead and assumptions about the ongoing relationship between the living and the dead. But aside from that often contentious issue in Christianity, the sequence of rites that make up the contemporary funeral liturgy, or 'The Order of the Burial of the Dead' as it is entitled in the 1662 Prayer Book, are charged with doing several different things. The Liturgical Commission of the Church of England listed five essential actions (as they reflected in 1964 on the 1662 Book of Common Prayer and experimental materials prior to *Common Worship*):

> To secure the reverent disposal of the corpse;
> To commend the deceased to the care of our heavenly Father;
> To proclaim the glory of our risen life in Christ here and hereafter;
> To remind us of the awful certainty of our own coming death and judgement;
> To make plain the eternal unity of Christian people, living and departed, in the risen and ascended Christ. (Lloyd, 2000, p. 22)

These five points help to answer and remind us that the funeral is not for one thing alone, but for several. It is for the deceased – to be commended; it is for the mourners – to be comforted; it is, like all liturgy, the praise and worship of God; it has some practical dimensions, inclusive of reverently disposing of the physical remains of the dead. These multiple purposes of funerals are assisted by the return in *Common Worship* of an older, pre-Reformation pattern of a series of rituals, outwardly expressing the movement of the deceased from life to new life, the movement of the mourners through the many stages of grieving, the movement of the community in reshaping itself around the absence of the missing member, the movements of solidarity with Christ no matter what appears to divide us, the movement of restatement and recommitment to a reality of eternal life.

While acknowledging that, in contemporary life, families and friends are often separated by distance, that taking time off for funerals is not always possible, and that the inescapable reminder of mortality is unsettling to many, the funeral liturgies stand firm in expressing 'sure and certain hope in the resurrection', resisting the cultural pressure for 'celebrations of life', which look back at the life of the deceased person rather than forward to life to come. The adaptation of a centuries-old pattern of vigil, funeral and committal forms the primary structure of most funerals in contemporary liturgical churches, whether Roman Catholic, Anglican or Lutheran.

Each of these three primary liturgical stages has its own character and focus: the vigil (or wake) is a primary time of comfort for those who mourn, of telling stories of the deceased, of keeping watch with the dead in continuity with the women who watched at the tomb of Jesus, of making 'plain the eternal unity of Christian people, living and departed' as the Liturgical Commission described it.

The funeral liturgy proper, with the pre-Reformation Western pattern of a eucharistic liturgy restored as an option, shifts the attention of the living from the story of the deceased to the story of the resurrected Christ and the deceased within that story. In other words, the focus moves to the incorporation of the dead into the larger story of the resurrection, the Liturgical Commission's third point ('to proclaim the glory of our risen life with Christ here and hereafter') as well as the continuance of a primary theme in the 1662 Burial Service in the reminder of preparation and judgement at every death ('to remind us of the awful certainty of our own coming death and judgement'). Particularly in the context of Holy Communion, the funeral liturgy proclaims that this is a foretaste of the heavenly banquet celebrated in the communion of saints, of the whole Church, living and dead, one of the most tangible ways of communion in love that transcends death. The funeral liturgy has two additional parts, with the reception of the body at the door at the beginning, and the commendation at the end. The reception of the body brings the Christian and the community full circle, by linking the funeral liturgy to baptism. As the coffin is sprinkled with water, we are reminded of the apostle Paul's teaching on the links between baptism and death, as well as the symbol of the pall, the baptismal garment, placed on the deceased one last time. Similarly, the symbolism of the door, the liminal space, reminds us of the journey that the dead are making, as well as the journey we are all on, outwardly expressed in the funeral procession. At the end, the commendation again focuses on the coffin, commending the dead to God, and entrusting them to God's mercy. These two extra rituals, at the beginning and at the end, along with the third liturgy, the committal, give expression to the fundamental Christian theology of the Incarnation and the human body as temple of the Holy Spirit. It is hard to avoid the body in a funeral liturgy, especially if these various rites are done prior to cremation. That is intentional – Christians are not only spirit, but spirit and body, made in the image of God and professing a resurrection of the body in the creeds. God became flesh, and, in much of historical theology, the image of God become human in order that humans might become divine has influenced the reverent care of the body. Historically the coffin, the body, is incensed at this point, as sign and symbol of the sanctity of the body that was baptized and communicated with the Eucharist, putting on Christ and taking in Christ, to die and rise with Christ.

The third liturgy, the committal, brings us to the first point of the English Liturgical Commission: 'to secure the reverent disposal of the corpse'. Christians in the UK have been leaders in being the first to allow and then encourage cremations. Many Christian churches still forbid cremation, or have reluctantly allowed cremation, stating clearly their preference for burial as the pattern established by Christ himself. And while denial of death may have been a factor in choosing cremation over burial for some, increasingly the relative cost of cremation versus burial and a growing concern for ecology and care for the earth are influencing others to opt for cremation. In the UK, Douglas Davies has written and reflected on cremation extensively, as has Richard Rutherford in the USA. Certainly cremation raises ritual questions. Where does the liturgy happen (in church first or in the crematorium)? Who leads the service? What about the ongoing relationship between the physical remains of the dead and the living if the ashes are scattered? But cremation also raises theological questions, particularly with regard to our theology of the resurrection of the body, the focus on the soul, rather than the body, in so much Christian discourse regarding death, and the model of Christ's own burial. Other issues include the emotional impact of a body in a coffin as ultimately helpful in assisting the living through the stages of grief, and the reality that most liturgical language is still very much focused on the burial of the body.

Just as the rites with the dying bring the Church into ministerial partnership with the world of medicine and medical experts, rites with the dead bring the Church into partnership with funeral homes, crematoria and an ever-expanding number of entrepreneurs of death. Within the official rites of the 1662 Prayer Book and *Common Worship*, there is very little directed to cremation itself, aside from the burial of the ashes following the funeral. Specific canons for the Church of England are given in Canon Law B 38:3–7 but more widely known to many in the Church of England is the 2001 ecumenical publication, *Funeral Services of the Christian Churches in England*, for funerals at cemeteries and crematoria. These are often, in reality, the briefest of services with a minimum of the dialogical character of so much liturgical action, and so, just as with the partnership between Church and medical experts with regard to the dying, the partnership with funeral homes and crematoria must be both a dialogue of mutual respect and a clarity that the Church has much to offer to the funeral sequence. The funeral liturgies of *Common Worship*, as well as the American counterpart in *Enriching Our Worship 3*, are clear about reclaiming their primary role as context and shaper of the rituals surrounding the dying and the dead.

The liturgies for the dead and for those who mourn the dead have many more elements than the three primary liturgies used as theological starting points above. Most notable are the various memorial services and the rituals for remembering the anniversaries of the dead including the materials inviting Anglicans to commemorate all the faithful departed found in *The Promise of His Glory*. How will these resources, and more to the point, these practices, change official, public and private perceptions of prayer with and for the dead? How will the annual celebrations answer the needs of many people for expressions of ongoing relationship?

This overview of two sets of liturgies, for the dying and for the dead, has used the development, structure, words and actions of the liturgy as a way to reflect theologically on liturgical practice as well as on how liturgy forms our beliefs regarding Christian death. But all of this is only a very small beginning to the study of meaning-making rituals and practices.

Further reading

Bradshaw, P. (ed.) (2006), *A Companion to Common Worship*, vol. 2, Alcuin Club Collections 81 (London: SPCK).

Byock, I. (2012), *The Best Care Possible: A Physician's Quest to Transform Care through the End of Life* (New York: Avery).

Davies, J. D. (1990), *Cremation Today and Tomorrow* (Bramcote: Grove Books).

Lampard, J. S. (2005), *Go Forth, Christian Soul: The Biography of a Prayer* (Peterborough: Epworth).

Lloyd, T. (2000), *Dying and Death Step by Step: A Funerals Flowchart* (Cambridge: Grove).

Rutherford, R. (2001) *Honoring the Dead: Catholics and Cremation Today* (Collegeville, MN: Liturgical Press).

Walter, T. (1994), *The Revival of Death* (London and New York: Routledge).

Dimensions

Chapter 19

Ethics

Siobhán Garrigan

It is inspiring to notice how liturgy has helped to change for the better both individual lives and corporate projects. The cadences of great African-American preaching resounded through the speeches that shaped the civil rights movement. Rice cakes blessed, broken and shared in thanksgiving by political prisoners in China sustained their struggles for freedom. And the poetry of the Book of Common Prayer kept Terry Waite sane and hopeful through years of captivity as a hostage, just as it, or the recitation of the Rosary, still regularly restores so many people from so many desolations. There is a great diversity of worship practices in Christianity and, as with these few instances, many of them can be seen to undergird public and private ethical struggles throughout the world.

However, it is also worrying to notice how liturgy has failed to change, and might even have aided, some of the world's great unethical situations and some individuals' unethical choices or actions. In both overall shape (*ordo*) and specific detail (such as the ancient prayers of the Church, or the words or tunes of hymns), the worship of most German Christians during the Third Reich was remarkably similar to that of many Christians today. The un-ethical, in the form of discrimination, oppression and even genocide, has been supported – or at least not challenged – by Christian liturgy throughout history. And all manner of causes, from slavery to homophobia, have been justified (and, alternately, fought against) from within these selfsame rites.

There is evidently, then, no automatically effective link between Christian worship and Christian ethics. This is not just because there is no single view of Christian ethics, or their content. (Although that is certainly true; the question of how to live a good life, a Christian life, being almost as varied in its answers as the Christians who struggle with it.) It is also because the relationship between worship and ethics, or liturgy and life, has been a controversial one for at least 2,760 years.

The prophet Amos preached against the early inhabitants of Israel, telling them they had their priorities all wrong:

I hate, I despise your festivals, and I take no delight in your solemn assemblies. Even though you offer me your burnt-offerings and grain-offerings, I will not accept them; and the offerings of well-being of your fatted animals I will not look upon. Take away from me the noise of your songs; I will not listen to the melody of your harps. But let justice roll down like waters, and righteousness like an ever-flowing stream. (Amos 5.21–24)

A similar message – that what God wants is acts of justice, not edifices of worship – was still being given by the prophet Jeremiah in Jerusalem two centuries later:

Do not trust in these deceptive words: 'This is the temple of the LORD, the temple of the LORD, the temple of the LORD.' For if you truly amend your ways and your doings, if you truly act justly one with another, if you do not oppress the alien, the orphan, and the widow, or shed innocent blood in this place, and if you do not go after other gods to your own hurt, then I will dwell with you in this place . . . (Jeremiah 7.4–7)

It is not difficult to recognize in these ancient texts warnings against the same sort of hypocrisy to which we are prone today: 'You troop off to church in your Sunday best, but how does that help half the world who are living in poverty, children dying for want of clean water, or the degradation of the environment?' It is very clear, now as then, that living faithfully to God involves a commitment to constantly practising certain forms of justice and mercy, and that these are more important than merely going to church.

Those forms of justice and mercy are multiple and varied. Some have a more outward effect, others a more inner one; most, if not all, require a bit of both, a turning of the heart and also a consequent action. Some are automatic, obvious (e.g. feed the hungry person; visit the prisoner; be more patient with your children); others are ambiguous and extremely complex but nonetheless essential to a Christian's ethics (e.g. given that poverty is at least in part institutionally produced, is it better to dismantle capitalism or to reform it?). Christians disagree, inevitably, on nearly every ethical question, from how money should be spent to who should be allowed to marry whom. As John Henry Newman said of both liturgy and life, if there are no disagreements, it is not Christianity.

But what all Christians have in common is that their actions are supposed to speak louder than their words. That 1970s hymn was right to sing, 'And they'll know we are Christians by our love', and not – to update Amos – by the quality of our icons, the fervour of our praise songs or the piety of our prayers.

To read some introductions to Christianity, you would think that all you need is worship. Worship does indeed matter greatly to Christianity, but it matters as orientation to faith and sustenance in faith, and not as the life of faith itself. Worship thus serves a dual purpose with regard to ethics: it prompts, and it consolidates. (It does this, one hopes, by itself embodying Christian ethics, and more will be said about this later.) Consequently, it can make a vital contribution to the formation, in an ongoing sense, of the Christian. But the actions that make up the 'ethics' of a distinctively Christian life, the actual, daily practices that articulate how one loves – caring, healing, teaching, prophesying, forgiving, self-sacrificing, serving – these happen mostly elsewhere.

Different worshipping traditions in different times have understood their relationship to ethics in very different ways. For some Christians, worship is where they gain instruction and inspiration for specific actions and campaigns. For others, worship is an experience of awe in the face of transcendent mystery, where little or nothing 'political' is ever mentioned. (Which is not to say it is unconcerned with ethics. On the contrary; it may just have a more aesthetic understanding of the relationship between liturgy and ethics.) But in no situation is it acceptable to merely worship: what matters is what you bring to the table, to be re-presented, redeemed and, ultimately, given thanks for. All you did that week. But also what you go forth to do in the next week. Every Christian act of worship starts with a gathering-in but it also ends with a sending-forth. It is a sending-forth to serve, a specific aid and command to do God's work in the world, and a blessing for participation in that precise work. It is not a generalized goodbye or farewell.

Noting the importance of paying attention to the relationship between Sunday's service, the week that was, and the week that will be, Karl Rahner at the Second Vatican Council questioned the supposedly 'parenetic' character of worship. This referred to a long-held belief that by truly and faithfully celebrating the divine liturgy, the ethical ordering of society would inevitably follow; the one would 'exhort' the other. Rahner, perhaps in light of having lived through the Holocaust as a German Christian, queried the basis of this belief, proposing that getting liturgy right does not necessarily result in getting life right. Indeed, he argued that if you do not get life right, then you cannot get liturgy right. Get life right first, he said, because only then can what you bring to the table, to prayer, to confession, be a 'sacrifice of praise'; that is, a gift capable of receiving the transformation offered by God's action in liturgy.

What Rahner was bringing to light was the symbiotic nature of the relationship between liturgy and ethics. This stemmed from the conviction, which was central to his theology, that love of God (the ultimate ethics) and love of neighbour are one and the same thing. According to Rahner, our everyday lives are all that we offer to God, and the Eucharist is not a magical additional thing: it is the weekly, communal thanksgiving for the ordinary, the place we remember God's redemption not in some esoteric realm but at the very heart of this ordinary life. And because God's presence is, for Rahner, as closely bound up in our quotidian lives as in our worship, he calls the ordinary the 'liturgy of the world' (see O'Meara, 2007, p. 101).

Accordingly, Christians need to be committed to a slew of attitudes and actions in daily life in order to 'get life right'; if they are not, their sacrifice in worship is hollow no matter how they might, technically, 'get liturgy right'. At the same time though, worship can provide the hope, encouragement, counsel and example that Christians need in order to cultivate and hold to these necessary commitments.

There are two main schools of thought about how worship accomplishes this. The first considers the ways in which matters of ethical concern are proclaimed, preached, sung and prayed about in worship, and it is to these considerations that we now turn our attention. The second articulates the ways in which liturgy may itself be thought of *as* ethics, and we will come to that towards the end of this chapter.

Much of what Christians do in worship stems from the example, the teaching and the commands of Jesus. Liturgically, Jesus gave us a prayer and a way of praying, foot-washing and thanksgiving, storytelling and a meal. Moreover, his trusted friends gave us baptism, laying-on of hands, anointing and many other such ritualized improvisations from the cultural worlds in which their lives were embedded. Jesus also preached – rabbinically, in parables – and so did his followers; just look at Paul. It is therefore not good enough to say that preaching is somehow secondary (to the Eucharist or whatever else might be thought the 'real' focus of worship), because it is the point where explicit connections are made between Scripture, tradition and today's world. Dietrich Bonhoeffer, another German Christian pastor who protested against the Nazi regime (and was eventually executed by it), worked from the premise (attributed to Karl Barth) that, for worship to treat ethics appropriately, you need to preach with the Bible in one hand and the newspaper in the other. God's word, in this view, has been broken open not just for all time, but for this time, in this place, and preaching is the primary way Christians have been given to receive that word.

The art of preaching – and of supporting the preacher – is not always well practised. One recent attempt to revitalize it has focused explicitly on the connection between liturgy and ethics, advocating the practice of 'prophetic preaching'. Leonora Tubbs Tisdale describes this way of preaching, like that of the Hebrew prophets and of Jesus, as clearly and directly challenging the status quo, countering its materialist and unjust vision of human- and bio-spheres with a re-presentation of God's vision for Creation. Prophetic witness, she writes, may be 'more about "afflicting the comfortable" than "comforting the afflicted"' (Tisdale, 2010, p. 14) but the prophetic preacher's task is not only to criticize. It is also to 'energize', so that the congregation leave worship having been given hope and encouragement for the work of actually changing the present social order. 'For in the end the task of prophetic witness and ministry does not ultimately belong to the pastor; it belongs to the whole community of faith' (Tisdale, 2010, p. 14).

Nor does the task of prophetic witness and ministry belong only to the preaching, although preaching is key to it. The prayers, hymns, visual imagery and other arts all play a part in 'bringing home' the gospel in such a way that it speaks to the ethical demands of our own day. The great hymn writers of the eighteenth and nineteenth centuries knew that, as my song-leading colleague Patrick Evans now teaches, the theology that is deepest within us is that which we have sung – not that which we have read, or heard. Singing is an integrating bodily act, and it is well known that singing with others also creates bonds between people. Singing to, for or of God reinforces our theologies as pretty much nothing else can. Hymnody and spiritual songs therefore have a very powerful role in shaping our ethical commitments, and it is for this reason that the choice of hymns and sung responses is given great attention in worship planning: singing is the point in the service where the congregation will bodily and intellectually integrate their ethical and theological commitments.

One significant development in liturgy in the English-speaking world has been the introduction of 'global hymnody' from the worldwide church. By singing the songs of praise, prayer and lament of Christians from traditions, countries and cultures other than our own, we enter into the theologies of their words and tunes and, by doing so, we enter more fully into the catholicity we profess in the creed. Moreover, by singing with those people who live in other parts of the world, especially the places that our wealthy countries have made poor, we have an opportunity to enter into greater solidarity with them, to reorient the boundaries of 'our world' and, ultimately, to readjust our ethical commitments towards others.

In all the above ways in which ethics are figured out in worship – through the ministries of praying, preaching and singing – the actual words used matter a lot, not just because of what they alert us to, or by how they persuade us (criticizing and encouraging), but also by whether they are themselves ethical. Words can wound, or mislead, or otherwise harm, and this is perhaps an even more acute concern for the words used in worship for prayers, songs and translations of Scripture than for preaching. We live in an age whose ethical obsession is the pelvic zone, but the ethical concerns that have most occupied Christianity down the years are different. They are works of mercy, commitment to poor people, and – perhaps most overlooked in our own day, with its political spin and anonymous Internet communications – the need to not harm through one's speech.

This brings us to a consideration of the ways in which worship can itself be ethical, or ought to 'model' ethics, in addition to being a site in which the Christian community figures its ethics out through activities like those just mentioned: proclamation, preaching, singing and prayer.

The ethical issue most mentioned in the Bible is neither sex nor money, but tongue-wagging: gossip, flattery, lying, suggestion, distortion and all other forms of careless, manipulative or malicious speech. This is perhaps why speech – the words we choose and the ways we deliver them – is such an important issue in Christian worship in our times. How we name God, each other, aspects of the material world, everything – it all matters. Words matter because of accuracy, and it is for this reason Janet Walton, among others, argues that naming God only ever with masculine nouns and pronouns is unethical.

> Precision in naming speeds a process of truth telling and faithful relationships. It is an act of justice . . . Not even names we have used for thousands of years can possibly convey the total reality of God. To believe otherwise is idolatrous.
> (Walton, 2000, pp. 34, 36)

Words also matter for the same reason that Wycliffe's great labour to translate the Bible into the vernacular was an ethical issue in his day: people need to be able to apprehend the word of God in words capable of conveying it, words they can fully understand and, in turn, use. And words matter because they help us rehearse avoiding the very sin that the biblical writers knew to be one of the easiest to fall into, the most pernicious, and the most destructive of the possibility of relationship, or of communion. All the words in worship matter, ethically, therefore. They are 'illocutionary': they put in place the reality they bespeak, and that, for Christian worship, has to be a glimpse of the reign of God.

At the same time, it is important not to mistake words as mattering more than embodied acts, because our bodies, their senses and intuitions, their capabilities and disabilities, and the material world with which they continuously interact play an equally vital ethical role in worship. Lest we move too quickly from recognizing embodiment in liturgy to more abstract ideas of incarnation and sacramentality, it must be remembered that these bodily and materially ethical aspects of worship are usually very plain, very human. That is why they work as carriers of God's word. So, for example, we can forget that potentially the most radically ethical thing we do when we worship is simply to get together in the first place. Gordon Lathrop reminds us that the Greek word for church, *ekklesia*, originally meant 'assembly' (Lathrop, 2006). The fact of assembling, of coming together, in the name of one who eschews all earthly powers and preaches love and mercy through non-violence and an overturning of worldly boundaries is a counter-cultural act in itself. Remembering that the Church is, by definition, an 'assembly' of bodies oriented to something very different from the government or the media's plans for them is a striking ritual embodiment of Christian ethics.

What you say and do once you are gathered also needs attention if it is to build on this ethical beginning. Because of worries that the actual ethical teachings of the gospel might be communicated too vaguely, Christian assemblies often try to be very clear about communicating their commitments in worship. The hymns and prayers, banners and artwork, tunes and smells, can all be orchestrated to bring home a particular message. For example, there is a cyclical recurrence of a fashion for 'theme Masses', whereby a service of Holy Communion is celebrated in such a way that a particular theme, such as, say, ecological awareness, a campaign to end poverty, homelessness or the plight of political prisoner, is highlighted throughout the service.

As with all worship, people react to such services in different ways. I am of the opinion that the Eucharist already has a theme, and it is already social justice, so I can be a bit grumpy about services like this. However, an episode of the TV comedy series *Father Ted* points out the limits of such grumpiness. Father Ted receives a call to say there is a bomb and, pressed by Father Dougal as to what they should do in response, all Ted can come up with is to say Mass, repeatedly. They do not telephone the bomb squad, or clear the area, or take any other action to offset the negative effects of the information they have received. Sometimes, obviously, it is not enough to just say Mass as usual and trust its powerful, poetic, multidimensional reinstatement of freedom from all oppression and damnation. Sometimes, you need to explicitly address a particular matter.

For Louis-Marie Chauvet, meditating on Thomas Aquinas's understanding of liturgy, the sacraments are dynamic prolongations of the Incarnation and, because of this, they are intrinsically linked to particular matters, to history (even more so, he argues, than Thomas elucidated). The celebration of the sacraments is, therefore, the (primary, not optional) means by which we participate in God's presence here in our earthly lives. It accomplishes this partially, as Thomas and others have had it, by cultivating within us a set of dispositions (affections and virtues) over time, which condition any and all actions we subsequently take. But, according to Chauvet, it also accomplishes this by being the place where we enter into the sacramental living out of Scripture, where we inhabit Scripture and let it inhabit us (see Brunk, 2007). For want of a more contemporary metaphor, liturgy in this view is not the glue between supposedly sacred and secular realms, but the lifeblood of an inseparable union between liturgy and life. Such a view reinforces an idea of liturgy as one with life, as itself 'ethics', and not just as something that helps us to work them out.

One scholar whose work is especially helpful in understanding this quite abstract view of liturgy is Don Saliers. In particular, he describes worship as a 'deliberate rehearsal' (with a phrase he credits to Stanley Hauerwas), a description that has helped many Christians to grasp the ways in which worship is constantly and profoundly shaping their ethics without necessarily saying anything explicitly about particular ethical matters. According to Saliers, 'When liturgy is regarded primarily as a means to moral exhortation or ethical motivation, it loses its essential character as praise, thanksgiving and anamnetic encounter of the mystery of faith' (Saliers, 1979, p. 187). If we focus instead on this essential character, and the web of embodied, human, spiritual actions that compose it, we can conceive of worship as allowing us to 'practise' being Christian in the world. It might help to remember that Saliers is an accomplished jazz musician as well as a theologian, so his notion of rehearsal, or practice, carries the double meaning of both 'actually performing something' and 'preparing for performance/learning to perform something'.

This makes sense to me. I have several times found myself, shortly after reacting to a new and unexpected situation, asking myself 'Where did I learn to do that?' or 'How did I know what to do there?' and, on reflection, wondering whether it might have been experiences in worship that had prepared me. It is rare ever to think of a 'direct' translation between liturgy and such life experiences. Worship is not 'role play', like in a corporate training programme. So to say, 'I was confronted with a request for money by a beggar on the street and knew what to do because it had happened to me in Mass' is neither the case nor the point. The point is that liturgy shapes us not as automata, stuck repeating a limited repertoire of given acts, but as free agents, artists really, trained to act in a whole heap of ways in response to a whole heap of situations. By engaging our whole selves, body and mind, over and over, through the arts, with words, inhabiting numerous stories, amid a cast of biblical and saintly characters, over time, we become accomplished improvisers.

However, this rehearsal is only effective if worship is both ethically performed (those words, those sounds, those actions have to be holistic, not abusive) and ethically engaged: the 'translation' of the gospel to real-world situations must have been modelled in the preaching, the music, the prayers and other aspects (such as gestures and symbol-usage) so that the work of figuring it out is never taken for granted.

One of the most effective ways of doing this is for worship leaders to admit when they get things wrong. You preach something that is challenged by further events in the world: go back and speak a new word. You choose a hymn that hurts some of those in the congregation that sing it: apologize, explain how it hurt, choose a different one and invite all to sing anew. This way, everyone sees that Christian ethics are not a counsel of perfection; that belongs to God alone. As human action, our worship, just like every other aspect of our lives, must be attuned to new circumstances, adapted to new cultures, reformed by encounter with cultural realities – the people, the earth and the causes that the gospel demands we care about most.

Much has been written in recent years on worship and culture, and it is, for reasons I hope the above paragraphs demonstrate, a really important development in our understanding of the relation of worship and ethics. However, the fallible nature of worship as an organism (just like any other form of human expression or art) must be emphasized. For example, through ten years' study of the worship of Protestant and Catholic churches in the Republic of Ireland and Northern Ireland, I came to see that worship, while following the rubrics to the letter, could play a significant role in supporting (at worst) or not challenging (at best) the sectarianism that still mars life on that island. Although peace was preached by the official representatives of the main churches, some congregations in those same churches were weekly habituated to ritualizations that were not peace-oriented, because their liturgies were immersed in, and reflective of, their cultures. So, people were vetted rather than greeted as they entered church, they referred to fellow Christians as their 'opposites' in faith, or as 'the other religion', and many churches did not pass the Peace, or even pray for peace (Garrigan, 2010).

Such a problem is not the unique possession of the Irish. Generally speaking, if you live in Europe or North America and your liturgy is reflective of or supportive of the political status quo, you probably have a problem on your hands. Liturgy, being dependent upon cultural forms, can perform the unethical as easily as the ethical; it takes constant turning of one's ear to the gospel, and the constant help of the Holy Spirit, to try to make sure its ethics are Christian ethics.

The reason that worship can preach or perform the unethical is because it is human. It may be a tried and tested place where mystery can be met; but that affords it no special exemption in the realm of the Incarnate. For all that God's Spirit has, mercifully, been known to show up in Christian worship down the years, our liturgies are nonetheless a material and an historical construct, led by human beings and, as such, they are as prone to flaw and failure (some may say sin) as every other aspect of the lives they desire to support. Worship is, ultimately, like any other relationship. It is a work of love, over a long haul. Boring on many days. Sometimes very annoying. But, over time, it can shape us in ways that are life-giving, allowing us to discern and put into practice how we ought to live – our ethics.

Further reading

Brunk, T. M. (2007), *Liturgy and Life: The Unity of Sacrament and Ethics in the Theology of Louis-Marie Chauvet* (New York: Peter Lang).

Garrigan, S. (2010), *The Real Peace Process: Worship, Politics, and the End of Sectarianism* (London: Equinox).

Lathrop, G. (2006), *Holy Things: A Liturgical Ecclesiology* (Minneapolis, MN: Fortress Press).

O'Meara, T. F. (2007), *God in the World: A Guide to Karl Rahner's Theology* (Collegeville, MN: Liturgical Press).

Saliers, D. (1979), 'Liturgy and Ethics: Some New Beginnings', *Journal of Religious Ethics* 7, pp. 179–89.

Tisdale, L. T. (2010), *Prophetic Preaching: A Pastoral Approach* (Louisville, KY: Westminster John Knox Press).

Walton, J. (2000), *Feminist Liturgy: A Matter of Justice* (Collegeville, MN: Liturgical Press).

Chapter 20

Mission

Ruth A. Meyers

In a treatise on worship and mission written half a century ago, J. G. Davies began with the observation that 'worship and mission are treated as two totally distinct objects of theological investigation', suggesting 'their complete dichotomy and even incompatibility' (Davies, 1966, pp. 9–10). Davies set out to remedy this disjuncture, proposing that worship, like mission, is a response to God's redemptive activity in Christ. In the decades since then, Christian understanding and practice of mission have changed significantly. Although it is still common to think of worship as a cultic activity within the Church, forming and strengthening Christians for mission outside the Church, some scholars and practitioners recognize a much more dynamic relationship between mission and worship.

MISSION AT THE BEGINNING OF THE TWENTY-FIRST CENTURY

Anglicans are coming to understand the Church as a community engaged in mission and recognizing that mission takes place locally as well as globally. Viewed in this way, mission is central to Christian faith and life. It is not primarily a programme or activity, perhaps one among several programmes of the Church. Rather, mission is rooted in God's identity and purpose, that is, God's love for the world and God's desire to restore all creation to wholeness and unity. From this perspective, the Church does not have a mission, but rather God's mission has a Church. The Church participates in the mission of God by proclaiming and enacting God's creating and reconciling love for the world.

This changing understanding of mission is emerging against the backdrop of enormous changes in the world. Scholars describe the UK and other Western countries today as post-Christian or post-Christendom, with an ever smaller percentage of the population participating in Church life or even knowing about Christian faith. As the report of a Church of England working group explained:

> The Christian story is no longer at the heart of the nation . . . Our multicultural and multifaith society reinforces a consumerist view that faiths and their differences are simply issues of personal choice, to be decided on the basis of what 'works' or makes you happy.   (*Mission-Shaped Church*, 2004, p. 11)

Thus, we can no longer assume, as we have for centuries, that everyone, or at least the vast majority of the population, is Christian and will be schooled in the basics of the Christian story and Christian practices. Today, the mission field is as close as one's own neighbourhood.

Mission certainly takes place in the world, outside the church's assembly for worship. But worship itself is an important locus of mission, a place and time where the people of God celebrate and participate in God's self-giving love for the sake of the world. Moreover, there is a dynamic relationship between worship and daily life. God's steadfast love and merciful judgement infuse both worship and the world outside worship. The experience of God in worship forms people for participation in God's mission in the world, and encounters with the God of Jesus Christ in daily life shape participation in worship.

WORSHIP AS MISSION

The mission of God is God's movement outward towards the world, a love for the world evident in creation and in covenant with Israel, a passion revealed in the life, death and resurrection of Jesus. Through the Spirit, God calls together a community to participate in this mission, to embody God's healing, reconciling and saving love for the world, and to proclaim the good news of God's reign. While worship is not all there is to mission, it is an essential dimension of it. Lutheran liturgical scholar Thomas Schattauer expresses it this way:

> The visible act of assembly (in Christ by the power of the Spirit) and the forms of this assembly – what we call liturgy – enact and signify this mission . . . The liturgical assembly of God's people in the midst of the world enacts and signifies the outward movement of God for the life of the world.
>
> (Schattauer, 1999, p. 3)

When worship is mission, the assembly embodies and inhabits worship in such a way that ritual texts and patterns come alive, for people today, through speaking and singing, in symbols and actions. Such worship turns outward, for the sake of the world.

In worship, the people of God come together – assemble – as a community. Far more than a collection of individuals, they gather as a local assembly, in a particular place and at a particular time. They also represent the whole people of God, throughout the world and over time. For example, in the Eucharistic Prayer, the assembly joins saints and angels and the whole company of heaven in proclaiming God's praise with the song 'Holy, holy, holy Lord'. The assembly's communion with one another manifests the communion we have with God in Jesus Christ and anticipates the fullness of communion that is God's promise, the new creation in which the world is reconciled to God (2 Corinthians 5.17–20).

The term 'assembly' can mean simply a gathering or coming together, but it can also describe a deliberative body empowered to make decisions. Understood in this way, the assembly has agency, that is, it can discern and act. A liturgical assembly is not a passive meeting of individuals concerned with their personal salvation, but a purposeful gathering of a community, called together by God for the sake of the world.

In the grassroots Liturgical Movement that swept through churches during the twentieth century, it became common to describe liturgy as the 'work of the people', since the Greek word *leitourgia* is formed from *leitos*, 'concerning the people', and *ergon*, 'work'. 'The work of the people' became a rallying cry as liturgical reformers fostered a move away from worship as the work of a few vested, ordained leaders on behalf of a largely passive congregation of laity. But *leitourgia* actually means 'work done on behalf of the people', that is, 'public work' or 'public service'. Understood in this way, liturgy is not just about the people who gather, who proclaim and respond to the Word, who offer intercession, who celebrate the sacrament. Rather, liturgy is about the common good, an offering 'for the life of the world' (John 6.51). Understood in this way, liturgy, or worship, is mission, work on behalf of the whole world.

While the assembly's action is important, the primary actor in worship is God, who calls the community together, as the Greek term *ekklesia* suggests. Often translated as 'church', in the New Testament *ekklesia* is used for gatherings of the Christian community. Literally translated, *ekklesia* means 'called out'; God calls and gathers the assembly.

Gathered by God, the assembly embodies and enacts its participation in the reign of God. Worship is an act of remembering, proclaiming in the community today the story of God's mighty acts in salvation history, particularly the Incarnation, life, death and resurrection of Jesus. Through remembering, the assembly also anticipates the fullness of the reign of God and receives a glimpse and a foretaste of that promised future. Worship is thus an encounter with the God of Jesus Christ, in which the assembly participates in God's reconciling love for the world. For example, in the exchange of the Peace, worshippers greet one another with the Peace of Christ, recalling the risen Jesus' greeting to his disciples who had gathered in fear behind locked doors (John 20.19–23). In so doing, they embody Christ for one another and thus enact a ministry of reconciliation.

Worship, including the exchange of the Peace, is a symbolic activity. Like the greeting that is far more than two individuals saying 'Hello', worship is always more than what appears on the surface. Yet worship uses very basic elements of everyday life – water, bread, wine, oil. In worship, through the purposeful action of the assembly in its encounter with God, these common things reveal the mystery of God. Water, with a power that is both life-giving and death-dealing, recalls the waters of creation over which the Spirit breathed, the waters of the Red Sea through which the Israelites escaped from slavery, the waters of Jordan in which Jesus was baptized. With symbolic language and symbolic acts, the assembly enters and enacts the truth of God's reign. 'The church in its assembly around word and sacrament enacts a ritual symbol of God's gracious purpose for the world and so participates in God's world-encompassing mission' (Schattauer, 1999, p. 13).

WORSHIP FORMING PEOPLE FOR MISSION

The symbolic activity of worship forms and deepens the assembly's identity as a people called and sent by God. Through active engagement in liturgy, Christians orient their lives to God.

Christian identity is rooted in baptism, which establishes a covenantal community: 'you are a chosen race, a royal priesthood, a holy nation, God's own people, in order that you may proclaim the mighty acts of him who called you out of darkness into his marvellous light' (1 Peter 2.9). After centuries of baptism celebrated as a private rite, of importance primarily for the infant candidate and immediate family, baptism today is normally celebrated within the course of public worship on Sunday. It is a communal act, calling for the assembly to witness the baptismal birth and to welcome and support those who are baptized, whether infant or adult.

The identity established in baptism shapes a Christian's entire life. Through baptism, Christians are brought by God into relationship with God and one another, and sent by God to bear God's compassion and mercy for the world. Baptism is thus not only a one-time rite but an animating force for the whole Christian community.

> One test of the liturgical celebration of baptism is whether, over time, it enables the whole Church to see itself as a baptized community, called to partake in the life of God and to share in the mission of God to the world.
>
> (*CWCI*, 2006, p. 10)

The identity formed in baptism is renewed in other acts of Christian worship, especially the Eucharist. In the great thanksgiving of the Eucharist, the baptismal community remembers Jesus' crucifixion and resurrection, his self-offering for the life of the world, and its members offer themselves, their souls and bodies, in union with his sacrifice. In the great thanksgiving, the assembly remembers God's mercy and liberating judgement of the world and so bears witness to God's involvement with the world. In the Eucharistic Prayer, thanksgiving yields to supplication, as the community gives voice to its hope for the fulfilment of God's promises. Then, through sacramental eating and drinking of the bread and wine, Christ's body and blood, the assembly feeds on Christ so that they may be Christ's body in the world.

Beyond the great sacraments of the gospel, baptism and Eucharist, every act of Christian worship shapes a people for mission. In acts of praise and thanksgiving, the assembly acknowledges God as the source of life, as one involved in the world, and most especially as the one who sends the Son and the Spirit. Worship thus turns hearts and minds, bodies and souls to God and acknowledges God's abiding love for the world and ultimate sovereignty over the world.

Proclamation of the word is also a key aspect of formation. Across a wide spectrum of Christian traditions, the reading of Scripture is ordinarily part of Christian worship. Scripture anchors the community in salvation history, enabling Christians to see how God has been at work in ages past and offering good news for the world today. Lutheran scholar Clayton Schmit explains, 'The mission of God in today's churches and local ministries is informed, inspired, and corrected by the mission established in Scripture' (Schmit, 2009, p. 175).

BRINGING THE WORLD TO WORSHIP

Worship not only forms the community for mission; it also engages the assembly in mission. In worship, the assembly brings the sufferings and hopes of the world to God, and in story and prayer sees its deepest yearnings as part of God's yearning for the world. The proclamation of the word is often followed by a sermon that explores the connections between Scripture and the contemporary needs, concerns and hopes of the world. But it is in the intercessions that the sufferings and yearnings of the world become the focus of the assembly's attention.

While in some traditions, especially Eastern Christian tradition, intercession is part of the Eucharistic Prayer, the recent worship books of most Western churches locate the intercessory prayers immediately after the gospel and homily. The inner logic of this sequence suggests that the assembly's prayers for the world and for the Church are a response to the proclamation of the word. Having heard anew the story of God's love for the world – or, more accurately, a portion of that story – the assembly then speaks its yearning for God's continuing action in the world today. The community remembers what God has done, the mission of God revealed especially in sending Jesus and sending the Spirit, and remembers God's promises of justice, peace, forgiveness, reconciliation, mercy. In light of this good news of salvation for the whole world, the assembly can see more clearly the broken and hurting places in the world, the sin that separates humankind from God and from one another, the evil powers that corrupt and destroy God's creation. And so worship moves from proclamation to intercession, speaking aloud before God the truth about the world and the assembly's hope for God's promised new creation.

Perhaps the clearest scriptural command for Christians to intercede is in 1 Timothy: 'I urge that supplications, prayers, intercessions, and thanksgivings should be made for everyone, for kings and all who are in high positions, so that we may lead a quiet and peaceable life in all godliness and dignity' (1 Timothy 2.1–2). Christians are to be concerned with the whole world, to pray 'for everyone', because, as the letter-writer explains, God 'desires everyone to be saved' (1 Timothy 2.4).

The assembly's ministry of intercession is rooted in Christ, particularly in Christ's priestly ministry. Hebrews depicts Christ as the great High Priest who mediates a new and eternal covenant. Because he is a high priest who sympathizes with our weaknesses, we can approach him and 'receive mercy and find grace to help in time of need' (Hebrews 4.16).

It is not just our own needs, though, that are presented at the throne of grace, as J. G. Davies has pointed out. In early Jewish tradition, while many types of individual might intercede with God, the work of intercession was entrusted to priests. The book of Exodus directs, 'Aaron shall bear the names of the sons of Israel in the breastpiece of judgement on his heart when he goes into the holy place, for a continual remembrance before the Lord' (Exodus 28.29). The high priest literally carried the names of the twelve patriarchs on his garments, symbolically representing the whole people of Israel, as a sign of his intercession for them.

For Christians, this work of intercession is taken up in perpetuity by Christ, who 'always lives to make intercession for them' (Hebrews 7.25). Christians thus came to understand that their prayers, intercessions as well as praise and thanksgiving, are offered through Christ and with Christ and in Christ.

While Christ's priesthood is unique, Christians through baptism are associated with that priesthood. Intercession is thus a baptismal ministry. In early Christian baptismal practice, the newly baptized participated in the assembly's intercessory prayers for the first time immediately after their baptism. Interceding for the needs of the world was both a privilege and a responsibility of the body of Christ, the priesthood constituted through baptism. While today participation in the prayers of intercession is not restricted to those who are baptized, it is nonetheless an essential element of worship. Through intercession, the assembly carries out its liturgy, its public work for the sake of the world.

The scope of intercession must therefore be wide. True worship draws us beyond ourselves, turning us outward, offering prayer not only for those we know and love but also for the local community, for the entire world, and even for our enemies (Matthew 5.44). Through such prayer, the assembly exercises its baptismal priesthood and so joins in God's mission, the movement of God's love towards the world.

ENGAGING THE CONTEXT

Intercession is one key place where worship attends to the world. But engaging the context requires more than bringing the needs of the world before God in worship. Understanding mission as God's movement towards the world means recognizing that God is at work in the world, even before we do anything. Worship that engages its context will draw upon the language and thought patterns of the local culture, acknowledging and celebrating where God is at work as well as those places desperately in need of God's healing mercy.

For example, in a congregation that regularly incorporated video clips and the culture's music, members of the congregation, including children and teens, became attentive to theological themes in contemporary film and music, regularly suggesting selections for use in worship. Worship planners and leaders wove these contemporary symbols with inherited texts, symbols and patterns of worship, creating a rich tapestry that drew worshippers deeply into the mystery of God. Formed by this worship, members of this community became more aware of God at work in their daily lives. They found their lives increasingly shaped by patterns of salvation history, caught up in the trajectories of God's grace.

Not every congregation, and perhaps not even most congregations, will incorporate contemporary film and music into its worship. But Christian worship itself is a richly symbolic world and a profoundly embodied experience which has the potential to resonate deeply with contemporary Western cultures. Water, bread, wine and oil, the primary symbols of worship, are the stuff of everyday life, and their use in worship not only can speak vividly in the assembly but also can enable members of the community to make connections between worship and everyday life. Receiving the bread of life in the assembly's Eucharist, for example, may enable worshippers to recognize Christ in ordinary meals. 'Give us this day our daily bread', we pray, recognizing God's providence in giving daily sustenance.

However, while worship may connect to daily life, it also challenges contemporary cultural patterns in some significant ways. The growth of electronic communication and the multiplication of electronic devices has created expectations of instant gratification. Flip a switch or open a tablet, and the world is at one's fingertips. Email arrives nearly instantaneously. A Twitter feed scrolls across a smartphone, and we are instantly connected to people around the world. But the horizon of worship extends beyond the immediacy of the present moment. Worship brings the assembly into God's time, where events of the past continue to bear meaning for the community today even as the congregation gives voice to its longing for the fullness of God's reign to come. Here worship contrasts with contemporary culture, resisting the incessant demand for immediate gratification and inviting the assembly to step into eternity.

Not only is the contemporary Western world bombarded with instantaneous communication and a constant stream of images; it also has a soundtrack playing underneath most of its activities and in public places such as elevators and airports. Some assemblies incorporate this into their worship. For example, a congregation might sustain the final note of its response to the prayers of intercession as the leader of the prayers sings the next petition. Or a musician might play underneath as the president recites the Eucharistic Prayer. The musical foundation enhances the texture of the prayer and draws the assembly more fully into worship. But become truly silent, and people wonder what has gone wrong, or who has made a mistake. Yet silence is an important part of the rhythm of worship, creating a space where the assembly can contemplate the mighty acts of God or reflect on the sin that ruptures relationship with God and with other people.

Worship also offers a powerful challenge to the individualism and consumerism so prevalent in contemporary Western culture. Advertisements and strategic product placement confront us in nearly every arena of life. The seduction of consumerism drives us to fulfil basic human needs with an array of wondrous items that promise to bring health, happiness and fulfilment. In contrast, Christian worship orients our lives to God. By praising the God of creation, the assembly recognizes God as the source and sustainer of life. By retelling the ancient stories of God's involvement in the world, the assembly remembers that God knows and responds to the desires of every human heart. By giving voice to its hopes for the life of the world, the assembly places itself in the hands of a just and merciful God.

RENEWING WORSHIP

Many contemporary worship practices and new liturgical books, including *Common Worship*, reflect the insights of the twentieth-century Liturgical Movement, which sought to renew worship by recovering ancient patterns and connecting worship to daily life. Today, in the early twenty-first century, churches in different parts of the world are experimenting with forms of worship that respond to the people's hungers and hopes. The Church of England has encouraged 'fresh expressions' of Church to engage secular culture in a variety of ways. While there is no comparable official endorsement at the church-wide level in the Episcopal Church in the USA, some congregations and some dioceses are engaging the phenomenon of 'emerging' or 'emergent' Church.

In an ethnographic study of worship in fresh expressions or emerging churches in the UK and the USA, Bishops Michael Perham and Mary Gray-Reeves sought to discover what emerging churches might learn from worship practices in the inherited church as well as what the inherited church might learn from emerging worship.

The church needs to begin a dialogue of sorts between itself as institution and its essence as the body of God's salvation, called to proclaim and include all who seek to be part of Jesus Christ, especially those who have no knowledge or understanding of this sacred story.   (Gray-Reeves and Perham, 2011, p. 4)

Gray-Reeves and Perham found vital communities whose worship draws upon ancient Christian traditions as well as contemporary cultural artefacts. Leaders of these communities tend to understand their work as bringing the wider culture and context into conversation with the institutional church. In this exchange, emergent churches are 'participating in the making of a new creation, a new church, born of a relationship between faith and the local context of the world in which we live' (Gray-Reeves and Perham, 2011, p. 8).

By connecting local life-experience with Christian tradition, emerging churches engage in God's mission. These communities understand themselves to be proclaiming the gospel in new ways to those who find themselves on the margins of society, to those who have never heard the good news of Jesus Christ, and to those who have not found a place in the inherited institutional church. While 'the heart for mission, the heart for reconciliation, the ability to listen and live in the wider culture and convey back to the institution, are central to our Anglican understanding of ministry and mission', Perham and Gray-Reeves suggest that emerging churches understand the call to every Christian to participate actively in God's mission 'perhaps more clearly than many in the inherited churches, who somehow imagine the *missio Dei* happens without them' (Gray-Reeves and Perham, 2011, pp. 122, 124).

However, participation in God's mission is not limited to emerging churches; inherited churches also engage in God's mission through their worship. They might learn from emerging churches a new appreciation for symbols and a care for worship that engages the entire assembly. Yet worship that is mission is embedded in patterns handed down through the ages: gathering as an assembly of God's people, proclaiming and responding to the Word, interceding as a priestly people for the needs of the world, giving thanks over the bread and cup and sharing in a holy meal, being sent forth to continue God's mission in the world.

CONCLUSION

The description of worship and mission sketched in this essay is as much aspirational as it is a lived experience. It is quite possible for worshippers to approach worship as a means of personal salvation, meeting their needs for connection with God and assuming that other members of the assembly likewise are there to have their needs met. It is quite possible for worship leaders and planners to perform worship as a dull routine, a duty to be observed that at best fills worshippers with divine grace and strengthens them for mission in the world.

It is quite possible, as Davies observed nearly half a century ago, to view worship and mission as entirely separate spheres of action.

Yet it is also possible to envision worship and mission as integrally related. In worship, the assembly engages in the mission of God by praising God, remembering God's mighty acts, enacting and signifying God's reconciling love for the world, proclaiming the good news announced by Jesus, engaging the context, praying for justice and peace, embodying justice and peace in interactions in the assembly, showing respect and care for Creation by the way we use material things in worship, and bearing witness and listening to those outside the assembly. Moreover, in worship, God is the primary actor, as Rowan Williams said in his address to the Fresh Expressions National Pilgrimage to Coventry Cathedral in 2008:

> Church is not primarily an event in which we do something, think something, feel something; it is being together in a situation where we trust God to do something and to change us – whether or not we notice it, let alone fully understand it. (Croft, Mobsby and Spellers, 2009, p. 7)

In the public service that is liturgy, the assembly responds to God's self-giving for the life of the world. Gathered by the Spirit, the assembly is drawn into Christ's liturgy, the Paschal Mystery of his dying and rising. In this public service, the assembly enacts and signifies God's reconciling love for all creation. Sent out from this worship, members of the assembly continue to participate in God's mission, living as the body of Christ in the world. They then return, again and again, bringing the hopes and hungers of the world into the encounter with God that is Christian worship.

Further reading

Croft, S., Mobsby, I., and Spellers, S. (2009), *Ancient Faith, Future Mission: Fresh Expressions in the Sacramental Tradition* (London: Canterbury Press).

Dally, J. A. (2007), *Choosing the Kingdom: Missional Preaching for the Household of God* (Herndon, VA: Alban Institute).

Davies, J. G. (1966), *Worship and Mission* (London: SCM Press).

Gray-Reeves, M., and Perham, M. (2011), *The Hospitality of God: Emerging Worship for a Missional Church* (London: SPCK).

Kreider, A., and Kreider, E. (2011), *Worship and Mission after Christendom* (Scottdale, PA: Herald Press).

Mission-Shaped Church: Church Planting and Fresh Expressions of Church in a Changing Context (2004) (London: Church House Publishing).

Schattauer, T. H. (ed.) (1999), *Inside Out: Worship in an Age of Mission* (Minneapolis, MN: Fortress Press).

Schmit, C. J. (2009), *Sent and Gathered: A Worship Manual for the Missional Church* (Grand Rapids, MI: Baker Academic).

Chapter 21

Culture

Phillip Tovey

For as long as the Church has existed, there have been questions about the relationship between worship and its cultural context. In the early Church, we can see the development of worship in a number of different contexts, partly language-based, for example, Greek, Latin and Syriac. With the expansion of the Church through missionary work after the Reformation and Counter-Reformation, questions of worship and culture became increasingly important. Perhaps more significant, in the last century, the issues began to be addressed systematically. They may seem to have arisen particularly with the Roman Catholic Church's Second Vatican Council (Flannery, 1981) but in fact many other churches have an interest (Farhadian, 2007). This chapter will look at the more modern contexts of the worship and culture debate, beginning with the official documents of the Roman Catholic Church, the Lutheran World Federation (LWF) and the Inter-Anglican Liturgical Consultation (IALC). In relation to these documents, consideration will be given to three specific examples of cultural context, and finally some theoretical approaches will be discussed.

THE ROMAN CATHOLIC CHURCH

The Second Vatican Council in its document *Sacrosanctum Concilium* looked particularly at the reform of the liturgy and the promotion of active participation by the laity (Flannery, 1981). The cultural nature of the Roman rite is set alongside the participation of the laity in cultural contexts that are not Western. How are non-Western people to participate in a liturgy that comes from a Western culture? Even in the West, the linguistic question of the use of Latin or the vernacular in the Mass and other services is a cultural one. Thus, a section of *Sacrosanctum Concilium* discusses adaptation of the liturgy for the temperament and traditions of different peoples. Positive statements are made in this section about other cultures:

> Anything in these peoples' way of life which is not indissolubly bound up with superstition and error she [i.e. the Church] studies with sympathy, and, if possible, preserves intact. She sometimes even admits such things into the liturgy itself, providing they harmonize with its true and authentic spirit . . .
>
> (*Sacrosanctum Concilium* §37)

Section 38 of the document goes further, saying: 'Provisions shall also be made . . . for legitimate variations and adaptations to different groups, regions, and peoples, especially in mission lands, provided that the substantial unity of the Roman rite is preserved.' Section 40, however, considers that in some places and circumstances 'an even more radical adaptation' of the liturgy is needed. No details are given of such an adaptation, but the process is outlined and provision made for experimentation and for experts to draft the necessary liturgical legislation.

This lack of definition of 'radical adaptation' has led to much discussion as to what exactly might be allowed. In the extended post-conciliar process, the instruction *Inculturation and the Roman Liturgy* (Roman Catholic Church, 1994) is of particular importance: possible adaptations, including in language, music, posture, dance and art, are considered, though limitations are set out in a section on 'Necessary Prudence'. The instruction also describes the procedural details by which an episcopal conference may submit a proposal for change to the Vatican.

There have been criticisms of the amount of progress that has been made since 1963, as there are few concrete examples of more radical adaptation (Tovey, 2003). One example that deserves our attention is *The Roman Missal for the Dioceses of Zaire* (1988); this incorporated various aspects of local culture, including music, movement and liturgical text, all of which are important dimensions of inculturation. According to Kabasele Lumbala (1998), the Zairian Mass goes back to experimentation in 1969. This was followed by pastoral material in 1974, with the final approval of the rite in 1988. From this we can see that it took 19 years for the development of a more radical adaptation. Features of the rite include the invocation of the ancestors at the beginning, the procession of the Gospel book, the penitential rite after the profession of Christian faith, and a particular preface for the situation in Zaire. On a more generic level, Lumbala sees the introduction of dance and the important place given to the natural environment as key features of African culture. One further aspect that he does not discuss as critical to an African understanding is the place of the ancestors, which is significant not only in the Zaire missal. There have been other proposals for changes in parts of Africa and a few have had some official sanction; the Zaire Mass, however, is perhaps the most significant (see Tovey, 2003).

In the area of marriage rites there has been much influence from contemporary culture (Stevenson, 1982). This can be seen in classical times in the use of crowns in the Eastern Church and veils in the Western Church, representing different cultural approaches. In the Anglo-Norman synthesis, the inclusion of vows in the service was another innovation, bringing important aspects of the local culture into the public worship of the church (Searle and Stevenson, 1992). The Roman Catholic marriage rite approved in the Philippines provides our second important example of inculturation. This rite relies particularly on the inclusion of culturally relevant aspects of popular religiosity. Thus, customs like the use of the *arras* (wedding coins or tokens, typically 13 in number, symbolizing Jesus and the Apostles) and the 'wedding cord' (symbolizing unity) are included in the rite (see Antonio, 2002). We find another cultural adaptation in India, with traditional customs such as the use of the *thali* (necklace) instead of a wedding ring. Marriage is an area where cultural change continues, for example, in more modern Western societies where the importance of the giving away of the bride by her father was minimized under the influence of feminism in the twentieth century.

The instruction on inculturation may have made the process in the Roman Catholic Church more bureaucratic and therefore more difficult for episcopal conferences to be able to bring about truly radical adaptation. This has been complicated by the recent directions on translation, notably *Liturgiam authenticam* (2001), which will be discussed later. However, the primary document *Sacrosanctum Concilium* puts liturgical inculturation high on the Roman Catholic agenda.

THE ANGLICAN COMMUNION

Anglicanism has produced two important and positive statements on inculturation: York 1989 (Holeton, 1990) and Kanamai 1993 (Gitari, 1994). As there is no central authority in Anglicanism comparable to the Vatican, there is a variety of sources of information on the Churches' attitude to worship and culture, and these two documents, along with various Lambeth Conference resolutions, are critical in understanding Anglican approaches.

The origins of Anglicanism are set within a discussion of provincial autonomy in the universal Church. Two features are held to have been inherited from the medieval period. First is diversity; liturgical texts were not uniform at this time, and there were many local variations. England had the rite of Sarum alongside that of York, Hereford and Bangor. Across the mainland of Europe there was also diversity, extant examples of which are the surviving rites in Milan and Toledo. Cranmer argued for the right of an individual church, by which he meant a national church, to order its liturgy in the way it saw fit. On the other hand, he brought greater uniformity to the worship of the Church of England, helped by the impact of the printing press. The tension between the two factors of provincial autonomy and uniformity has continued within the Anglican Communion. As some new provinces developed, they produced their own prayer books; this happened, for example, in the USA in 1795. Others translated the English liturgy into the vernacular, and thus unity in the past was seen by some as a unity around the 1662 Book of Common Prayer. The Lambeth Conferences have repeatedly reiterated the right of provinces to create their own liturgy. The encouragement to inculturation is one further step in the diversification of Anglican liturgy.

The 1989 York statement, 'Down to Earth Worship', begins by quoting the 1988 Lambeth Conference, which urged 'the Church everywhere to work at expressing the unchanging Gospel of Christ in words, actions, names, customs, liturgies, which communicate relevantly in each contemporary society' (Holeton, 1990, p. 8). The same conference affirmed: 'This conference resolves that each Province should be free, subject to essential universal Anglican norms of worship, to seek that expression of worship which is appropriate to the Christian people in their cultural context' (p. 8). This last statement of 'universal Anglican norms of worship' is as problematical as the Second Vatican Council phrase 'the unity of the Roman rite', indicating a tension between unity and diversity. The York statement roots inculturation in the Incarnation of Jesus Christ and says that the Church must relate to society incarnationally. It proceeds by asking a series of questions and giving some examples of diversity of practice within Anglicanism. These questions concern issues of language, music, architecture, ceremonial, political context and the sacramental elements. While it does not have any bureaucratic apparatus to monitor the progress of inculturation, the document is concerned to encourage its development.

The 1993 Kanamai statement, 'African Culture and Anglican Liturgy', was a particular African expression of the York statement. The Kanamai meeting worked in groups in various areas and tried to make suggestions as to where people and provinces might develop their liturgy. A wide-ranging set of issues is discussed, including Eucharist, birth and initiation, and burials, but the longest discussion is on the problematic issue of Christian marriage in Africa. There is a large variation in customs between different peoples, and a dissociation between models inherited from the missionary movement in which marriage is a single event, and local customs in which marriage is often a multi-stage process (see Hastings, 1973; Kisembo, Magesa and Shorter, 1977). It may seem that the Kanamai document provided more questions than answers; like many of the IALC documents, however, its importance lies in the way in which the gathering of liturgists around the Communion leads to developments in the ongoing process of liturgical renewal. It could well be argued that the Kanamai consultation particularly influenced the new liturgies for the Anglican Church in Kenya and in the Congo. This is explained further in the work of Kings and Morgan (2001) and Tarrant (2006).

Anglicans have also had much discussion over questions of language, particularly in relation to God and women, and this will be returned to later. There have also been issues around the eucharistic elements, particularly in contexts where wheat and vines do not grow. For further discussion on eucharistic elements see Uzukwu (1982), Tovey (2003), the IALC statement 'Eucharistic Food and Drink' (2005) and Tovey (2006).

THE LUTHERAN WORLD FEDERATION

Another important document on the relationship of worship and culture is the 1996 Nairobi statement on Worship and Culture (LWF, 1996). Worship is seen in four models:

1 Worship as transcultural;
2 Worship as contextual;
3 Worship as counter-cultural;
4 Worship as cross-cultural.

This document presents a stronger argument than that of Anglican common identity versus provincial autonomy. Within the contextual section of the document, a number of important processes of inculturation are identified. First is that of dynamic equivalence, which is described as going 'far beyond mere translation'. Second is that of creative assimilation which is seen as enriching the *ordo* rather than re-expressing it. In working on these two different trends the document states:

> An important criterion for dynamic equivalence and creative assimilation is that sound or accepted liturgical traditions are preserved in order to keep unity with the universal Church's tradition of worship, while progress inspired by pastoral needs is encouraged . . . It is understood that not everything can be integrated with Christian worship . . . Elements borrowed from local culture should always undergo critique and purification, which can be achieved through the use of biblical typology.   (LWF, 1996, 3.6)

In this we see a common issue of the tension between the Christian tradition and the new culture. The question is: who makes the judgement between the different possibilities? There is always a political element in decisions which is dependent on the polity of local churches and their relationship with international bodies.

The Nairobi statement is of particular importance as it discusses inculturation at a more theoretical level than we have seen previously. This is handled in different ways by different churches. As we have seen, the Second Vatican Council opened the possibility of more radical adaptation but did not identify exactly what this was, so further documentation, attempting to clarify the issues, has resulted (Roman Catholic Church, 1994). This documentation, on the whole, has provided only bureaucratic solutions to the problems. Anglicanism has looked at the issue more pragmatically and from specific examples, but so far it does not have a sustained agreement on the process. The great advantage of the Nairobi statement is that it puts inculturation in a network of theological statements about Christian worship, for example, baptism and Eucharist, and discusses particular possible processes of inculturation. Like Anglicanism, Lutheranism is not centralized but a federation and so can only commend this document to its constituent churches. This does not mean, however, that this statement should be ignored; indeed it is a significantly important document in understanding questions of inculturation because it attempts a definition and identifies a process.

Having looked at three churches and some official statements that have been made on inculturation, I want to consider some further issues that do not arise from the official workings of denominations but have occurred as movements or issues within particular churches. In this I focus on questions of language, the place of children, and the place of social liberation within the liturgy. Various approaches to inculturation examine it less from a 'worship and culture' position and more from a 'worship and justice' position. This is an important alternative way of looking at issues of liturgy and culture.

LITURGICAL LANGUAGE

Questions of inclusive language, in relation both to women and to God, are a significant issue within the contemporary Church. To take an example from the Church of England, it was unfortunate that at the production of *The Alternative Service Book* in 1980 the importance of inclusive language was not yet recognized, although it was in other parts of the Communion: for example, there was the jarring 'I confess I have sinned against you and against my fellow men' in the confession for the Eucharist. Awareness of this problem led to the formation of women's liturgical communities, like, for example, the Saint Hilda Community (1996) and the work of writers like Janet Morley (1988), who pioneered the use of inclusive language and inclusive collects. When the Church of England report, *Making Women Visible* (1989), was published, much of this was officially recognized. More problematic, however, was the question of addressing God with words such as Father, King and Lord, which some saw as patriarchal. This is a particular difficulty in relation to the doctrine of the Trinity and its application in the baptismal formula, where some people preferred to speak of God as Creator, Redeemer and Sanctifier. Many churches, however, regard this as an inadequate baptismal formula, e.g. the Roman Catholic Church (Congregation for the Doctrine of the Faith, 2008).

Questions of inclusive language go beyond the use of 'men' as a generic term, although the confession in the Church of England was much improved by changing 'we have sinned against our fellow men' to the more biblical 'we have sinned against our neighbour'. This is illustrative of the ways in which inclusive language can be enriching to the liturgy, and can correct bias against women. The issue is, however, one that is much deeper and the patriarchal nature of previous liturgical writing can be seen in a number of ways, including the exclusion of women in lectionary liturgical text, and in an overemphasis on masculine images for the deity to the suppression of alternatives. Let us take some examples of this. One issue is the inclusion of biblical characters in the liturgy where previously they have been excluded. In the gospel reading for Candlemas, does the reading stop with Simeon or include Anna? As another example, in Prayer 1 of the *Supplementary Eucharistic Prayers of the Anglican Church of Canada* (1998), we find 'Your Spirit speaks through Huldah and Micah, through prophets, sages, and saints in every age' (p. 15) and 'His head anointed for burial by an unknown woman, Jesus gathered together those who loved him' (p. 16). In this we see the recovery of histories; women from the Bible who previously were unmentioned in the liturgy are now brought to the fore.

An alternative approach is in the use of feminine imagery in prayer, which has been quite successfully employed in the collects of Janet Morley. To take an Advent example:

> God our deliverer,
> whose approaching birth
> still shakes the foundations of our world,
> may we so wait for your coming
> with eagerness and hope
> that we embrace without terror
> the labour pangs of the new age,
> through Jesus Christ, Amen.
> (Society of St Francis, 2009, p. 542)

Here, aspects of birthing pain and quaking might be seen as relating both to the process of giving birth and to the eschatological event. In using such imagery, Morley has diversified the images and metaphors used in contemporary prayer. This is a further enrichment of the liturgy with metaphors that have a scriptural basis (see Tovey, 1991).

Some issues within feminism go beyond what might be seen as enrichment, to challenging the tradition; not least, as we have seen, in the use of 'Creator, Redeemer, and Sanctifier' in relation to the Trinity. Liturgists in the West have adopted some of the theories of feminist theologians with regard to language, but a similar cultural movement can be seen in the requirements in contemporary society for the use of inclusive language for publication and broadcasting. The exception to this is the Roman Catholic Church, which, in its instruction on translations of liturgical texts, *Liturgiam authenticam* (2001), seems to reject feminist critique of contemporary language in preference for words such as 'men', 'Lord' and traditional formularies (see sections 29–31).

What language should we use in worship? This has been much debated. Clearly language changes and, where there are issues of translation, there are questions of the theory of translation. Debate today is still centred on language and gender, and the appropriateness of dynamic equivalence.

CHILDREN, THE EUCHARIST AND SUBCULTURES

The Roman Catholic Church has produced a number of resources for use with children, notably the *Directory for Masses with Children* (1974), *Eucharistic Prayers for Masses with Children* (1977), and the *Lectionary for Masses with Children* (1993). Claire Johnson (2001) has advocated that this is another example of liturgical inculturation, children's culture being something different from adult culture. Johnson sees a difference in the liturgical process of textual creation for the directory; that is, rather than starting with an *editio typica* which is then translated into other languages, the Masses with children started with texts composed in modern vernaculars, which were then translated into Latin for the purpose of approval. The work began with small groups of people in different cultures rather than coming from a centralized authority. Johnson identifies ten principles of the culture of children in order to show that they are a particular subculture. This is a problematic exercise as it assumes that children's culture is the same worldwide (Tovey, 2010). However, this is probably to be classified in Roman Catholic terms simply as an adaptation rather than a more radical adaptation.

A number of other churches have developed eucharistic prayers for use with children, notably the Church of Scotland, the United Reformed Church, and various provinces of the Anglican Communion. All these assume that children have a distinct subculture to which some liturgical adaptation is needed. Of particular interest is the prayer of the Anglican Church of Southern Africa (2008), which is highly responsive in its nature and includes specific questions for the children to ask, e.g. 'Why do we give thanks and praise at this table?' This has reminiscences of the Passover meal with the inclusion of questioning by the children. While many questions can be raised concerning these prayers, they are the development of the principle of active participation in the liturgy by the laity, in this case children.

Once the possibility of distinctive prayers and rites for a particular subculture is raised, then there arises another possibility: the potential diversity of liturgy even within one country. There has been much argument in the Church of England, through alternative worship, fresh expressions and *Mission-Shaped Church*, about the relationship between traditional church culture and emerging culture in society. Trevor Lloyd (1990) shows that the Service of the Word was an attempt to deal with liturgy in the cultural context of inner-city deprivation. Others argue for new approaches to postmodern culture. In this discussion, it is easy for certain groups to be ignored: for example, deaf church, with its problems of translating contemporary vernaculars into sign language. The Roman Catholic Church in England and Wales (1992) has approved a special eucharistic prayer suitable for signing, although it is required that the priest also say the words.

Thus what begins as a question of pastoral adaptation of liturgy for children becomes a question of inculturation for subcultures. If there are prayers for use with children, then why not have prayers for deaf church, or Goth church or any youth subculture? The boundaries at present are fluid.

LITURGY AND JUSTICE

Classical discussion of worship and culture has had two particular poles: one concerning inculturation, the other justice. This can be illustrated in India: Sundar Clarke's book, *Let the Indian Church Be Indian* (1980) focusing on inculturation, led to an experimental order for celebrating the Eucharist. In this liturgy, various Indian cultural aspects are included, such as the lighting of the lamp with the words:

> We take refuge in the Divine Light
> Flame of truth
> The Soul's Ray
> We take refuge in the Embodiment of Glory
> The Lamp of our Path
> The Essence of love.   (Clarke, 1980, p. 132)

This ritual expresses prayer in a more Indian mode. The inculturation approach to liturgy is also seen in the experimental Masses suggested in the Roman Catholic Church in South India (Thurian and Wainwright, 1983).

Alongside the questions of inculturation has developed the issue of social justice, not least in relationship to the dalits. Dalit liberation theology has grown in strength since the 1980s, as the numbers of dalits (converted in mass movements in the colonial period) attending church has greatly increased. Their position is particularly difficult in Indian culture and there is much violence and discrimination against them. Caste has been a problematical issue since the beginning of Christian work in India and Dalit liberation theologians have said that attempts at inculturation have come too much from the Brahmin tradition and have not listened enough to the voice of the dalits in their oppression. This is particularly helpfully developed and explained in the work of Paul Collins (2007). In the new liturgy of the Church of South India (2006) prayers that are crafted within the context of oppression have been worked into the liturgical text. This can be seen most clearly in some of the litanies:

In your comforting presence, we remember the poor and homeless, the widows and exploited women, the undernourished children and the victims of war . . .
In your comforting presence, we remember those who cannot and may not read and write, those who are denied the power of knowledge and skill, those who are rendered voiceless . . .
In your comforting presence, we remember those who work without getting their due, the landless labourers, child labourers . . .

(*Book of Common Worship*, 2006, pp. 17–18)

This simple extract shows how Dalit theology is directly influencing the text of the liturgy. Questions of social justice, however, are wider than this example; in other parts of the world, justice for the earth may well be in the context of global warming (Peters, 2002).

THEORETICAL PERSPECTIVES

In the discussion of worship and culture it would be impossible not to mention the work of H. Richard Niebuhr. His classic work, *Christ and Culture* (1951), provided a particularly helpful way of looking at the issue, with a number of different models of the relationship between Christ and culture: Christ against culture, Christ of culture, Christ above culture, Christ and culture in paradox, and Christ transforming culture. To some degree this has been supplemented by the work of Bevans (1992) in *Models of Contextual Theology*, where he postulates a taxonomy of models: translation, anthropological, praxis, synthetic, transcendental, and counter-cultural. Bevans's work is based on the missionary imperative of the Church and looks at alternative approaches that have been taken by Christian people. These models can be helpfully used in discussing worship and culture. There are those who believe that the issue is simply one of translation. This has been the approach of some Anglicans keen to translate the Book of Common Prayer into other languages and cultures. Others have wanted to look more deeply at humanity and the nature of culture from human beings as created in the image of God, which may perhaps be typified by the inculturation models discussed above. Questions of praxis and justice have developed in relation to feminists, or dalits, or liberation theology and their application to worship. Synthetic approaches may talk about the goodness of God working in his creation in ways that we have not appreciated before and this might be applied to Christian worship in controversial issues such as same-sex blessings. Transcendental approaches look to a more 'spiritual' approach, as might be seen in the liturgy of some Indian ashrams. Counter-cultural approaches are perhaps the antithesis of the synthetic and wish to resist elements of the world. This might be seen in some reactions of modern Roman Catholic worship.

Such typologies are of great help in that the Christian Church has not been inclined to respond to any one particular issue in any one particular way, nor has it taken consistently any one approach to the issue of worship and culture. Indeed Bevans is helpful in identifying six different approaches; approaches which are not necessarily always antithetical. Thus, in regard to some issues, people and churches may be very strict on the fact that we must translate the tradition into modern idiom, while in other areas being sympathetic to a more synthetic approach. This can be seen in the inherent contradiction of all the major documents discussed in the first half of this chapter, where there was on the one hand a desire to preserve the tradition and on the other hand the desire to incarnate the tradition into a particular culture.

CONCLUSION

The question of worship and culture is a complex one. Many other elements could have been brought into consideration: architecture, eucharistic elements and music, for example. What is perhaps helpful is the vision of Schillebeeckx (1985), who sees church history as being an unfolding of what has gone before, alongside a continual leading and revelation of the Holy Spirit. Christians will continue to debate what is appropriate in answer to the fundamental questions of the relationship of Church and culture. The mission imperative of the gospel means that we cannot ignore the nexus of issues relating to worship and culture.

Further reading

Bevans, S. B. (1992), *Models of Contextual Theology* (Maryknoll, NY: Orbis Books).

Chupungco, A. J. (1982), *Cultural Adaptation of the Liturgy* (New York: Paulist Press).

Collins, P. M. (2007), *Christian Inculturation in India* (Aldershot and Burlington, VT: Ashgate).

Farhadian, C. E. (2007), *Christian Worship Worldwide: Expanding Horizons, Deepening Practices* (Grand Rapids, MI: Eerdmans).

Kabasele Lumbala, F. (1998), *Celebrating Jesus Christ in Africa: Liturgy and Inculturation* (Maryknoll, NY: Orbis Books).

Tovey, P. (2003), *Inculturation of Christian Worship: Exploring the Eucharist* (Aldershot and Burlington, VT: Ashgate).

Chapter 22

Ecumenism

Myra N. Blyth

This chapter will argue that the relationship between ecumenism and worship is a dynamic one. On the one hand, the ecumenical movement has given rise to liturgical renewal, providing it with a theological rationale and a practical context. On the other hand, liturgy in ecumenical contexts has provided a vital impetus in the churches' search for unity. By uniting in common prayer, Christians experience and learn from the riches of different liturgical traditions. In the first part of the chapter, the meaning and roots of the ecumenical movement will be described in order to set contemporary liturgical renewal within an historical context. In the second part, four factors – theological, ritual, ecclesial and cultural – that have influenced liturgical renewal will be explored to illustrate its dynamic relationship with ecumenism. It will become clear that the challenges arising from the dynamic relationship between liturgical renewal and ecumenism are: to celebrate but not exaggerate the unity achieved in the area of eucharistic theology; to nurture common prayer in a manner in which all traditions can participate with integrity; to make liturgy universal and particular by integrating into the common *ordo* resources from the local culture and context.

In its long history, the World Council of Churches' Faith and Order Commission has brought together Roman Catholics, Orthodox, Anglicans and Protestants as equal participants in dialogue and common prayer. The work of this commission has enabled some of the most contentious historic divides in Christian history to begin to be bridged. It has also provided a unique context in which to explore and nurture the dynamic relationship between liturgy and the unity of the Church. The goal of unity in the modern ecumenical movement has gradually evolved. *Oikos* (house) and *oikumene* (whole inhabited earth) serve to highlight the root meanings of the term 'Œcumenical'. Unity in God's household means peace within and between God's children; the 'whole inhabited earth' points to the unity and integrity of all creation in harmony with its creator. This discussion emphasizes the first of these meanings but the two are interrelated. Unity between churches was conceived as organizational union in the early years of the World Council of Churches but this has gradually been replaced by the goal of unity in diversity (*koinonia*). Relational ecumenism emphasizes God's redeeming, reconciling activity in the Church and in the world, celebrated through common worship and witness. Recent statements on ecumenism stress that unity is both a spiritual gift and a calling which is rooted in the life of the triune God, so is expressed in terms of relationship. The shifting vision from institutional to relational ecumenism and the broadening of ecumenical concerns from unity among the churches to unity between faiths and within a divided and unjust world are reflected in words addressed to a meeting at the World Council of Churches in Geneva in February 2012 by Archbishop Rowan Williams: 'Unity is neither a means nor an end . . . Unity is what God has given us in the church . . . The responsibility of Christians who receive the gift of unity lies in seeking a life in which no one is without the other. This life, constantly moving us forward into a further truth, compels all who live within the love of God to ask the question: Who is not yet here?'

The special role played by the World Council of Churches' Faith and Order Commission was to provide a broad framework for multilateral dialogue and experimentation in which liturgical specialists and theologians could meet. Also undergirding and supporting this story of renewal in liturgy is the spirit of Vatican II (1962–5), which inspired a climate of ecumenical openness between all the churches. The documents on liturgy and ecumenism adopted at the closing session of the Council authorized Catholic ritual revision along the lines proposed by the Liturgical Movement, which had flourished during the nineteenth and early twentieth centuries and explicitly encouraged Catholic participation in the worldwide search for the visible unity of Christ's Church. Though unity between the churches remains a long way off, the achievements of the ecumenical movement in the last century have been remarkable.

THEOLOGICAL COALESCENCE ON THE MEANING AND PRACTICE OF THE EUCHARIST

Helped by the open ecumenical climate that Vatican II fostered, the World Council of Churches' Faith and Order Commission, at its fifth World Conference in Accra (1974), considered a draft text on *Baptism, Eucharist and Ministry* (*BEM*) written by Max Thurian. This document attempted to find a common understanding (rooted in Scripture and tradition) in these key areas of doctrine on which all churches could agree. The draft text was sent to selected churches and theologians for comment. In the light of their initial responses, a formal discussion document was sent to all the churches for detailed consideration, requesting a response at the highest level. It attracted unprecedented attention and to this day stands as the most comprehensive ecumenical discussion in modern times. At the next Faith and Order world meeting held in Lima, Peru (1982), a revised text was presented and adopted; it sought to create a convergence document on these three central doctrinal issues. The pastoral and liturgical success of these discussions was that churches looked back together to the early Church and rediscovered the roots of Christian life and practice. Everyone acknowledged that they had something to learn. In an appendix to the *BEM* document, a eucharistic rite (widely known as the Lima Liturgy) gave liturgical expression to the theological convergence achieved in the dialogue. *BEM* theologically underpinned the textual revision of eucharistic rites advocated by the liturgical renewal movement, such as the greater participation of the laity, the frequency of Communion and the rigorous exploration of early-Church sources for liturgical norms. But beyond this, and largely incidentally, the Lima Liturgy was adopted and adapted by many churches around the world as a model. Its attraction was the perception that it was a text, ancient and modern, through which the churches would be able to celebrate together a common faith.

The coalescence in eucharistic theology embodied in *BEM* moved the churches beyond the theological impasse of Reformation and Counter-Reformation arguments to a renewed understanding of the Eucharist. This coalescence is highlighted by Geoffrey Wainwright using a fivefold structure following the order of the creeds (Wainwright, 2007, pp. 54–62): Father, Son, Holy Spirit, Church and kingdom. In 'The Eucharist as thanksgiving to the Father' (Eucharist 3), prominence is given to the historical and sacramental dimension to the Eucharist, emphasizing God's creating and redeeming activities in all creation. In 'The memory of Christ's death or anamnesis', which is historically the most controversial part, Catholics and Protestants affirm that Christ's sacrifice on the cross is 'unique and can neither be repeated nor prolonged'. Concerning Christ's presence, there is also significant unanimity around the claim that 'the church confesses Christ's real, living and active presence in the Eucharist'. To help overcome difficulties historically around a special moment of consecration, the text under the heading 'The Eucharist as invocation of the Spirit' recalls the accent within the earliest eucharistic liturgies where 'the whole "prayer action" was thought of as bringing about the reality promised by Christ. The invocation of the Spirit is made both on the community and on the elements of bread and wine' (Eucharist 14). The emphasis on the Spirit maintains both an ecclesial and an eschatological perspective (Eucharist 17.18) and in 'The Eucharist as meal of the Kingdom' (Eucharist 4) the promise of the renewal of all creation is celebrated both as a future promise and as a present foretaste (Eucharist 4). In 'The Eucharist as communion' (Eucharist 20) the stress is on reconciled relationships both in the life of the Church and in the world.

In the Lima Liturgy, Wainwright also notes how the prayers of thanksgiving consist of both praise and beseeching (cf. Lathrop, 1998, pp. 25–8). The praise prayer remembers the events of God in creation and redemption. The beseeching prayer asks for the presence and power of the Holy Spirit to make God's promised future a present reality: transfiguring the assembly and the meal. In the Eastern tradition the words of institution are placed within the prayer of praise while in the Roman tradition they are within the beseeching prayer. For pastoral and missional reasons, the Lima Liturgy places the words of institution in the praise prayer: the majority of modern eucharistic prayers and rites followed this pattern and this meaning was considered more accessible to contemporary culture. By placing the words of institution within the praise prayer, the liturgy leaves the beseeching prayer to focus on the epiclesis, i.e. the invocation of the Holy Spirit to come and transform the meal. The Lima Liturgy explicitly does not choose between these two historic patterns but rather tries to build consensus by offering a shared pattern.

BEM represented a necessary but not sufficient step towards eucharistic fellowship between the churches. The continuing challenge that arose from this document was to make clear just how much more work was needed in the area of ecclesiology. Moreover, the effect of the Lima Liturgy was to raise false expectations among Christians that eucharistic fellowship was a possibility. The Lima text was originally intended to be only a liturgical expression of theological convergence, embodying the common convictions of the churches about the meaning and practice of the Lord's Supper. However, it became more than this; as Best and Heller note, it

> enabled Christians to experience, in a setting of shared prayer and praise, the fruits of a growing communion amongst the churches. Ecumenical progress became not just something to be written about; it could be prayed and sung together with others and this at the central moment of Christian worship.
>
> (Best and Heller, 1998, p. 3)

REVISION OF RITES AND AGREEMENT ON A COMMON *ORDO*

In parallel to the theological discussions on the Eucharist in the 1980s and based on the study of early texts, a new ecumenical consensus emerged on the shape or pattern of worship. This led to the development of a common *ordo* for worship by Catholic, Orthodox and Protestant liturgists. This *ordo*, based on scholarly research, has gradually influenced the thinking, practice and ongoing revision of liturgical texts in many churches. At a meeting convened by the Faith and Order Commission to explore the relationship between worship and the unity of the Church, the question was: how might ecumenical worship in a still divided Church help people to glimpse the fuller koinonia God desires for his people? The report of this consultation (Ditchingham, 1995) recognizes that parallel to theological convergence there was positive growth and development in church unity because of liturgical renewal facilitated by the experience of worship in ecumenical contexts. However, it also identified a significant gap between liturgy and theology. In the words of Gordon Lathrop: 'Liturgical scholars . . . are frequently surprised when they discover theologians still struggling over issues which belong to other pastoral times and seem appropriate only to radically different forms of the liturgy than those celebrated' (Lathrop, 1998, p. 48, n. 8). In short, the consultation report concluded that the *lex orandi–lex credendi* dialectic, i.e. what we pray is what we believe, '[has] tended to become separated in ecumenical discussions not to mention in the lives of the churches' (Ditchingham, 1995).

Partly in response to this problem, the Ditchingham conference called for agreement on a 'common *ordo*' that is a 'common ordering and scheduling of the most primary elements of Christian worship'. The recommendation argues that, by building on convergence already reached on fundamental patterns of Christian worship, agreement on a common *ordo* can be a powerful inspiration for unity. The appeal for a common *ordo* was subsequently developed by a group of participants at a consultation on ecumenical eucharistic practice (1996) who proposed a simple ecumenical *ordo* based on *BEM* and the Lima text. Their proposal, which was not part of the consultation report but is an appendix to it, reads:

> We have found in the pattern of Eucharistic worship . . . and in the varied celebrations of this pattern, a witness to the historic catholic faith. We have also encountered therein a simple form of celebration which may be carried out in a rich variety of ways, which responds to the needs of the world in the present time and which is capable of inculturation in many places. This pattern (*ordo*) . . . is consistent with that listed in *BEM* but the proposed *ordo* . . . seeks to show the inherent simplicity and clarity of the Eucharistic service as a whole, and the dynamic relationships among its parts.
>
> (Best and Heller, 1998, p. 29)

The *ordo* set out in their proposal conceived the liturgy as an event, shaped by a word-service and a table-service. Throughout the liturgy, words and sign-actions are juxtaposed. The word-service includes reading and preaching and leads to the community interceding in prayer for the world; the table-service includes thanksgiving, followed by eating and drinking together and leads to mission in the world. While this common *ordo* helped churches to come closer to one another, recognizing in each other marks of the true Church, full eucharistic fellowship could not be realized because of unresolved ecclesial questions relating to baptism and ministry.

ECCLESIAL INTEGRITY, TRADITION AND ECUMENICAL WORSHIP

Worship at ecumenical meetings globally and locally has brought renewal to the worship life of many churches. In confessional prayer there is opportunity to experience together the prayers and rites of a particular tradition; and in inter-confessional prayer new texts following the common *ordo* have been created for ecumenical gatherings. Since reaching the point of consensus around a common *ordo*, however, new concerns have been raised over the legitimacy of ecumenical worship which has resulted in a new framework for common prayer in ecumenical meetings.

Ecumenical worship texts have flourished at local, regional and global gatherings over recent decades. The seventh assembly of the World Council of Churches (WCC) in Vancouver (1982), where the Lima Liturgy was celebrated, is remembered as 'the worshipping assembly'. Here, ecumenical worship moved from being a rather bland Protestant hymn–prayer sandwich to a global multicultural feast. As Eden Grace recalls, 'no longer was worship a *problem* to be addressed by the assembly; it was now a vital and vibrant *experience* to be celebrated *at* the assembly' (Grace, 2002, pp. 3–27). Key to the success of the worship in this event was the attention paid to the outward form of the worship. Grace writes: 'It was a rare quantum leap in truth and joy' because of the 'degree of care that had gone into the outer "frame" of the worship' (Grace, 2002, p. 4). The feeling generated in Vancouver was that worship has more power to unite and reconcile than do documents and negotiations.

A prolific sharing of resources from Christian worship brought new songs and chants and symbolic actions into the churches across the globe. Songs of struggle and resistance against oppression, which originated in Latin America and Africa, were received as a living testimony to the struggles of the churches in the South in the face of oppression. They were also a source of inspiration and challenge to the churches in the North to connect liturgy with life. Michael Hawn writes:

> The liturgical relationship of the Euro-American church with the world church is no longer one way – north to south or east to west – but reciprocal. Shared sung prayer within an environment characterized by liturgical plurality may be one of the most powerful symbols of our common future in mission and worship.
> (Hawn, 2003, p. 31)

In ecumenical gatherings the themes of the meetings, and the context in which the meetings occurred, increasingly influenced the style and the texts used in the worship. Immense creativity and rigorous editorial work went into these occasions. Compilers of these texts sought to embrace cultural diversity while recognizing the importance of being faithful to tradition and respecting theological differences. Increasingly, however, inclusive language and inculturation became problematic for some member churches. Some would say that just when ecumenical worship was getting really exciting, when the liturgical spring was bursting with promise, threatening signs of an ecumenical winter started to loom upon the horizon. Others would say that the point came when critical reflection was urgently needed to appraise the status of worship in ecumenical meetings. It was the second view which was expressed strongly by the Orthodox members of the WCC but it was a view that found some support from European and North American church leaders. Reflecting this wider concern of the churches, Mary Tanner writes:

> There is no such thing as an ecumenical liturgy, but rather the liturgy of a particular ecclesial tradition to which others are invited . . . the experience of the richness of other traditions is an important element in the ecumenical movement and it may well be that the tendency in the past has been to move too quickly away from offering the worship of authentic ecclesial traditions in favour of a mixed and impoverished experience.   (Tanner, 2005)

The Special Commission on Orthodox Participation in the WCC, set up by the WCC assembly in 1998, to address concerns of the Orthodox member churches, sought to find ways forward which 'will allow all to pray together with integrity' (World Council of Churches, 2003, para. 41). Their work was complex and the result controversial. The difficulties experienced in common worship, especially but not only by Orthodox churches, included ecclesiological, theological, liturgical and cultural concerns. The recommendations are a mixture of doctrinal and practical considerations. First, the report clarifies the status of worship in ecumenical settings. It makes clear that the WCC is not and cannot function as a supra-church and therefore inter-confessional common prayer in ecumenical meetings is not the worship of an ecclesial body. The commission furthermore rejected the term 'ecumenical worship' as confusing and unhelpful and recommended instead the language of confessional and inter-confessional common prayer for all ecumenical gatherings hosted by the WCC. This shift in language meets the sensitivities of those for whom worship is always eucharistic, but it by no means resolves to the satisfaction of all the question of the ecclesial character of ecumenical common prayer. Second, the report makes 'practical recommendations for common prayer . . . on how to use language, symbol, imagery and rites, in ways which would not cause theological ecclesiological and spiritual offence'. Building on the principle of the interconnectedness of praying and believing, *lex orandi–lex credendi*, the report states that 'many of our divisions become apparent precisely in our common prayer' and, hence, 'the pain of division is felt most acutely in common prayer'. The report carefully distinguishes between confessional prayer as that which has an ecclesial identity emerging out of a single ecclesial tradition and inter-confessional prayer as representing patterns that churches have in common (service of the word, daily office, and so on) but not being the established liturgy of any one confession and therefore having no ecclesial standing. The framework for ecumenical common prayer, presented as an appendix to the commission report, was adopted by the WCC member churches in 2003 and has consequently changed the tone and direction of worship in ecumenical meetings globally and locally in the early twenty-first century. For Margot Kässmann, former Bishop of Berlin-Brandenburg, however, the report, and especially the framework for common prayer, represents a backward step on the ecumenical journey. It is 'a document of fear which takes great care to establish the boundaries that divide us. It builds fences rather than tearing them down' (Kässmann, 2003, p. 67).

WORSHIP, CULTURE AND THE MISSION OF THE CHURCH

Particularly significant for current and future developments in worship is the relationship between worship and mission and especially the place of inculturation. This missional dimension to worship renewal was given prominence by Vatican II's *Sacrosanctum Concilium* (1962) where a new attitude to the language of the liturgy is justified on the grounds of inculturation:

> Even in the liturgy, the church has no wish to impose a rigid uniformity in matters which do not implicate the faith or the good of the whole community; rather does she respect and foster the genius and talents of the various races and peoples.   (*Sacrosanctum Concilium*, 1996, §37)

The related but narrower focus at this time of the WCC assembly in Uppsala (1968) was on worship in a secular age. This secular Western approach to the discussion of religious cultural relevance was swiftly broadened and deepened by mission studies that focus on ways of making worship culturally relevant and appropriate. The challenge today for the churches worldwide in discerning how a transcultural faith can be practised in a contextually appropriate way is succinctly put in the Lutheran World Federation Nairobi statement on worship (LWF, 1996). It urges local churches everywhere to worship and witness in a way that is transcultural, contextual, counter-cultural and cross-cultural. The fourfold test – elaborated in the statement – encourages churches to pay equal attention to these four dimensions of the gospel. There is, as John Witvliet notes, a challenge here for everyone:

> To those of us who have pursued cultural relevance with just about all our attention and energy it calls us to dwell with the transcultural dimensions of our faith and determine which parts of our culture we should resist. To

those of us inclined to make universal pronouncements the document calls for us to see the contextual nature of our own formulations and to learn from formulations of other cultural contexts that may challenge, complement or enrich our understanding. To those of us with few contacts with people unlike ourselves it invites us to risky and rewarding prospects of forming cross-cultural friendships. (Witvliet, 2007, p. 274)

In short the document challenges congregations, using this model of worship and culture, to celebrate the strengths and correct the weaknesses in their worship. The challenges presented by inculturation need with the help of this fourfold test outlined in the Nairobi statement to be creatively and critically embraced.

New worship renewal movements responding to the demands of a changing global culture, such as neo-Pentecostalism in the southern hemisphere and 'fresh expressions of church' emerging particularly in Europe and North America, are often marginal to the ecumenical discussions and dialogues between the churches in membership of the Faith and Order Commission. Nevertheless, it seems that some of the key principles of worship established through the ecumenical movement have continuing and widening appeal. Robert Webber (2009) highlights, for example, how in evangelical churches formerly influenced by the charismatic movement there is a renewed interest in the place of Scripture in worship, in the use of ancient texts and sources, in the sacraments and mystery, and in the narrative structure of worship. Similar observations are made by Mary Gray-Reeves and Michael Perham (2011) who ask the question: what might emergent churches learn from the Church's liturgical tradition? They explore this question by visiting 14 emerging churches within two Anglican provinces, seven in the USA and seven in England. Of the 20 principles identified by the authors as characterizing Anglican worship, they found emerging churches remarkably compliant but in three respects they noted divergence: first, few emergent churches feel bound by texts but many were very conventional in their shaping of worship. Second, on the Eucharist, emergent churches seem universally to be at odds with the tradition and, third, most do not observe liturgical vestments. But emergent churches are avid borrowers, better than most at recovering lost texts and practices deep in the tradition. These examples suggest that, while untouched by formal ecumenism and under-represented in WCC discussions, many traditional evangelical and newly emerging churches have been and are indirectly influenced, in their worship, by the theological and liturgical consensus reached through the modern ecumenical movement.

CONCLUSION

The relationship between worship and ecumenism which has been mapped in this chapter has shown that renewal in worship has been positively enabled by the ecumenical openness of churches towards one another and critically shaped by a mixture of theological, ritual, ecclesial and cultural factors. Foundational to the liturgical developments has been the return to the roots of Christian worship in Scripture and the early Church. The agreement of theologians and liturgists on a common eucharistic *ordo* has been crucial. As the Nairobi statement acknowledges:

> The shared core liturgical structure and the shared liturgical elements in local congregational worship are expressions of Christian unity across time, space, culture, and confession. The recovery in each congregation of the clear centrality of these transcultural and ecumenical elements renews the sense of this Christian unity and gives all churches a solid basis for authentic contextualization. (LWF, 1996, para. 2.3)

It has also been evident in this account of the relationship between liturgy and ecumenism that, while the open relationship between churches has positively enabled liturgical renewal, the reverse is also true, that renewal in worship has been constrained by the continuing divisions between the churches. The emphasis, for example, in the report of the special commission on the integral relationship between worship and the ecclesial tradition within which it is ordered has raised questions in a new and disturbing way about the status and integrity of worship in ecumenical settings. The continuing challenges arising from this dynamic relationship between worship and ecumenism can be summed up in pastoral, ecclesial and missiological terms: the pastoral challenge, to celebrate but not exaggerate the unity achieved in the area of eucharistic theology; the ecclesial challenge, to nurture common prayer in a manner in which all traditions can participate with integrity; the missiological challenge, to make worship universal and particular by integrating into the common *ordo* resources appropriate to the local culture and context.

Further reading

Best, T. F., and Heller, D. (eds) (1998), *Eucharistic Worship in Ecumenical Contexts: The Lima Liturgy – and Beyond* (Geneva: WCC).

Ditchingham Report (1995) (Geneva: WCC, Faith and Order).

Grace, E. (2002), 'The Tradition of "Ecumenical Worship" in Light of the Recent Orthodox Critique', *Ecumenical Review* 54.1, pp. 3–27.

Gray-Reeves, M., and Perham, M. (2011), *The Hospitality of God: Emerging Worship for a Missional Church* (London: SPCK).

Hawn, C. M. (2003), *Gather into One: Praying and Singing Globally* (Grand Rapids, MI: Eerdmans).

Kässmann, M. (2003), 'A Voice of Dissent: Questioning the Conclusions of the Report of the Special Commission on Orthodox Participation in the WCC', *Ecumenical Review*, 55.1, pp. 67–71.

Lathrop, G. W. (1998), 'The Lima Liturgy and Beyond: Moving Forward Ecumenically', in T. F. Best and D. Heller (eds), *Eucharistic Worship in Ecumenical Contexts* (Geneva: WCC).

Lutheran World Federation (1996), *Nairobi Statement on Worship and Culture: Contemporary Challenges and Opportunities* [Online]. Retrieved from: <http://www.worship.ca/docs/lwf_ns.html>.

Sacrosanctum Concilium (1996), Constitution on the Sacred Liturgy, 4th December 1963, in A. Flannery (ed.), *Vatican Council II: The Basic Sixteen Documents* (Dublin: Costello Publishing).

Tanner, M. (2005), *The Significance of the Special Commission on Orthodox Participation in the WCC, in Grace in Abundance: Orthodox Reflections on the Way to Porto Alegre* (ed. Gennadios, Metropolitan of Sassima) (Geneva: WCC).

Wainwright, G. (2007), 'The Eucharistic Dynamic of BEM', in T. F. Best and T. Grdzelidze (eds), *BEM at 25: Critical Insights into a Continuing Legacy* (Geneva: WCC).

Webber, R. (2008), *Ancient-Future Worship: Proclaiming and Enacting God's Narrative* (Grand Rapids, MI: Baker Books).

Witvliet, J. (2007), 'Inculturation, Worship and Dispositions for Ministry', in C. E. Farhadian (ed.), *Christian Worship Worldwide: Expanding Horizons, Deepening Practices* (Grand Rapids, MI: Eerdmans).

World Council of Churches (2003), 'Final Report of the Special Commission on Orthodox Participation in the WCC', *Ecumenical Review* 55.1.

Bibliography

Liturgical texts

Book of Common Prayer and Administration of the Sacraments and Other Rites and Ceremonies of the Church (1979), The Episcopal Church (New York: Church Hymnal Corporation and Seabury Press).

Book of Common Worship (2006), Church of South India (Chennai: Church of South India).

Common Worship: Christian Initiation (2006) (London: Church House Publishing).

Common Worship: Pastoral Services (2000, 2005) (London: Church House Publishing).

Common Worship: Services and Prayers for the Church of England (2000) (London: Church House Publishing).

Enriching Our Worship 2 (2005), The Episcopal Church (New York: Church Publishing).

The Methodist Worship Book (1999) (Peterborough: Methodist Publishing House).

New Patterns for Worship (2002) (London: Church House Publishing).

Pastoral Care of the Sick: Rites of Anointing and Viaticum (1972, 1982) (International Commission on English in the Liturgy).

Rite of Penance (1974, 1975) (International Commission on English in the Liturgy).

Three Supplementary Eucharistic Prayers for The Book of Alternative Services and Two Services of the Word (1998), Anglican Church of Canada (Toronto: Anglican Book Centre).

Other works

Adam, A. (1992), 'Liturgical Time (The Liturgical Year)', in A. Adam, *Foundations of Liturgy: An Introduction to Its History and Practice* (Collegeville, MN: Liturgical Press).

Addleshaw, G. W. O., and Etchells, F. (1948), *The Architectural Setting of Anglican Worship* (London: Faber).

Anglican Church of Southern Africa (2008), *Worship Resource Manual* (Marshall-town: Anglican Church of Southern Africa).

Antonio, D. W. (2002), *An Inculturation Model of the Catholic Marriage Ritual* (Collegeville, MN: Liturgical Press).

ARCIC Agreed Statement on Eucharistic Doctrine, and Elucidation, *The Final Report* (1982). [Online]. Retreived from: <http://www.anglicancommunion.org/ministry/ecumenical/dialogues/catholic/arcic/docs/arcic1_final_report.cfm>.

Asad, T. (1993), *Genealogies of Religion: Discipline and Reasons of Power in Christianity and Islam* (Baltimore, MD: Johns Hopkins University Press).

Atkinson, D. (2011), *The Church's Healing Ministry: Practical and Pastoral Reflections* (Norwich: Canterbury Press).

Atwell, R. (1998), *Celebrating the Saints* (Norwich: Canterbury Press, 1998).

Augustine (2008), *Confessions*, tr. H. Chadwick (Oxford: Oxford Paperbacks).

Bachelard, G. (1969), *The Poetics of Space*, tr. M. Jolas (Boston, MA: Beacon Press).

Baldovin, J. F. (1991), *City, Church and Renewal* (Washington, DC: Pastoral Press).

Balthasar, H.U. von (1975), *Elucidations* (London: SPCK).

Barker, M. (2003), *The Great High Priest: The Temple Roots of Christian Liturgy* (London and New York: T&T Clark).

Baumstark, A. (1958), *Comparative Liturgy* (London: Mowbray).

Becker, E. (1973), *The Denial of Death* (New York: Free Press).

Bell, C. (1989), 'Ritual, Change, and Changing Rituals', *Worship* 63, pp. 31–41.

Bell, C. (1992), *Ritual Theory, Ritual Practice* (New York: Oxford University Press).

Bell, C. (1997), *Ritual: Perspectives and Dimensions* (New York: Oxford University Press).

Bell, C. (2005), 'Ritual Reification', in G. Harvey (ed.), *Ritual and Religious Belief: A Reader* (New York: Routledge), pp. 265–85.

Best, T. F., and Heller, D. (eds) (1995), *So We Believe, So We Pray* (Geneva: WCC).

Best, T. F., and Heller, D. (eds) (1998), *Eucharistic Worship in Ecumenical Contexts: The Lima Liturgy – and Beyond* (Geneva: WCC).

Best, T. F., and Heller, D. (eds) (2004), *Worship Today* (Geneva: WCC).

Bevans, S. B. (1992), *Models of Contextual Theology* (Maryknoll, NY: Orbis Books).

Bishop, E. (1909), 'Fear and Awe Attaching to the Eucharistic Service', in *The Liturgical Homilies of Narsai*, tr. R. H. Connolly (Cambridge: Cambridge University Press).

Bradshaw, P. (2001), *A Companion to Common Worship*, vol. 1, Alcuin Club Collections 78 (London: SPCK).

Bradshaw, P. (ed.) (2006), *A Companion to Common Worship*, vol. 2, Alcuin Club Collections 81 (London: SPCK).

Bradshaw, P. F. (1981), *Daily Prayer in the Early Church: Study of the Origin and Early Development of the Divine Office* (London: SPCK/Alcuin Club).

Bradshaw, P. F. (1995), *Two Ways of Praying: Introducing Liturgical Spirituality* (London: SPCK).

Bradshaw, P. F. (2nd edn, 2002b), *The Search for the Origins of Christian Worship: Sources and Methods for the Study of Early Liturgy* (London: SPCK).

Bradshaw, P. F. (ed.) (2002a), *The New SCM Dictionary of Liturgy and Worship* (London: SCM Press).

Bradshaw, P. F., and Johnson, M. E. (2011), *The Origins of Feasts, Fasts and Seasons in Early Christianity*, Alcuin Club Collections 86 (London: SPCK).

Bradshaw, P., and Johnson, M. E. (2012), *The Eucharistic Liturgies: Their Evolution and Interpretation* (London: SPCK/Collegeville, MN: Liturgical Press).

Bradshaw, P., and Melloh, J. (eds) (2007), *Foundations in Ritual Studies: A Reader for Students of Christian Worship* (London: SPCK/Grand Rapids, MI: Baker Academic).

Brand, E. L., and Kühn, U. (2003), 'Ministry, Ministerial Offices', in E. Fahlbusch et al. (eds), *The Encyclopedia of Christianity* 3 (Grand Rapids, MI: Eerdmans/Leiden: Brill), pp. 539–44.

Breward, I. (1980), *The Westminster Directory: Being a Directory for the Publique Worship of God in the Three Kingdomes* (Bramcote: Grove Books).

Brown, D. (2004), *God and Enchantment of Place: Reclaiming Human Experience* (Oxford and New York: Oxford University Press).

Brown, R. (2009), *Can Words Express Our Wonder? Preaching in the Church Today* (London: Canterbury Press).

Brunk, T. M. (2007), *Liturgy and Life: The Unity of Sacrament and Ethics in the Theology of Louis-Marie Chauvet* (New York: Peter Lang).

Burke, P. (1987), *The Historical Anthropology of Early Modern Italy: Essays on Perception and Communication* (Cambridge: Cambridge University Press).

Burns, S. (2006), *Worship in Context: Liturgical Theology, Children and the City* (Peterborough: Epworth).

Buttrick, D. (1987), *Homiletic Moves and Structures* (Philadelphia, PA: Fortress Press).

Byock, I. (2012), *The Best Care Possible: A Physician's Quest to Transform Care through the End of Life* (New York: Avery).

Casel, O. (1962), *The Mystery of Christian Worship* (London: Darton, Longman and Todd).

Chaplin, D. (2009), *Leading Common Worship Intercessions: A Simple Guide* (London: Church House Publishing).

Chauvet, L.-M. (1992), 'What Makes the Liturgy Biblical? – Texts', *Studia Liturgica* 22.2, pp. 121–33.

Chauvet, L.-M. (1995), *Symbol and Sacrament: A Sacramental Reinterpretation of Christian Existence* (Collegeville, MN: Liturgical Press).

Chauvet, L.-M. (2001), *The Sacraments: The Word of God at the Mercy of the Body* (Collegeville, MN: Liturgical Press).

Chupungco, A. (2010), *What, Then, Is Liturgy? Musings and Memoir* (Collegeville, MN: Liturgical Press).

Chupungco, A. J. (1982), *Cultural Adaptation of the Liturgy* (New York: Paulist Press).

Church of England Liturgical Commission (1989), *Making Women Visible: The Use of Inclusive Language with the ASB* (London: Church House Publishing).

Clarke, S. (1980), *Let the Indian Church Be Indian* (Madras: Christian Literature Society).

Cocksworth, C. J. (1993), *Evangelical Eucharistic Thought in the Church of England* (Cambridge: Cambridge University Press).

Collins, P. M. (2007), *Christian Inculturation in India* (Aldershot and Burlington, VT: Ashgate).

Comme le Prévoit: On the Translation of Liturgical Texts for Celebrations with a Congregation (1969), Consilium for Implementing the Constitution on the Sacred Liturgy (Vatican City).

Congregation for the Doctrine of the Faith (2008), *Responses to Questions Proposed on the Validity of Baptism Conferred with the Formulas* (Rome). [Online]. Retrieved from: <http://www.vatican.va/roman_curia/congregations/cfaith/documents/rc_con_cfaith_doc_20080201_validity-baptism_en.html>.

Cooke, B. (1980), *Ministry to Word and Sacraments: History and Theology* (Philadelphia, PA: Fortress Press).

Couturier, M.-A. (1989), *Sacred Art* (Austin: University of Texas Press).

Cowley, P. (1960), *Advent: Its Liturgical Significance* (London: Faith Press).

Craddock, F. (1971), *As One Without Authority* (Nashville, TN: Abingdon Press).

Craddock, F. (1985), *Preaching* (Nashville, TN: Abingdon Press).

Crichton, J. D. (rev. edn, 1992), 'The Theology of Worship', in C. Jones, G. Wainwright, E. Yarnold and P. Bradshaw (eds), *The Study of Liturgy* (London: SPCK/New York: Oxford University Press).

Croft, S., Mobsby, I., and Spellers, S. (2009), *Ancient Faith, Future Mission: Fresh Expressions in the Sacramental Tradition* (London: Canterbury Press).

Dallen, J. (1986), *The Reconciling Community: The Rite of Penance* (New York: Pueblo).

Dally, J. A. (2007), *Choosing the Kingdom: Missional Preaching for the Household of God* (Herndon, VA: Alban Institute).

Davies, J. D. (1990), *Cremation Today and Tomorrow* (Bramcote: Grove Books).

Davies, J. G. (1966), *Worship and Mission* (London: SCM Press).

Davies, J. G. (1971/2), 'The Introduction of the Numinous into the Liturgy: An Historical Note', *Studia Liturgica* 8.4.

Day, D. (1998), *A Preaching Workbook* (London: SPCK).

Day, D. (2005), *Embodying the Word: A Preacher's Guide* (London: SPCK).

Day, J. (forthcoming, 2014), *Reading the Liturgy* (London: T&T Clark).

De Zan, R. (1997), 'Bible and Liturgy', in A. J. Chupungco (ed.), *Handbook for Liturgical Studies 1: Introduction to the Liturgy* (Collegeville, MN: Liturgical Press), pp. 33–51.

Denis-Boulet, N. M. (1960), *The Christian Calendar* (London: Burns & Oates).

Dillistone, F. W. (1986), *The Power of Symbols* (London: SCM Press).

Ditchingham Report (1995) (Geneva: WCC, Faith and Order).

Dix, G. (1946), *The Theology of Confirmation in Relation to Baptism* (London: Dacre Press).

Dix, G. (3rd edn, 2005 (1945)), *The Shape of the Liturgy* (London and New York: Continuum).

Doig, A. (2008), *Liturgy and Architecture: From the Early Church to the Middle Ages* (Aldershot and Burlington, VT: Ashgate).

Doll, P. (1997), *After the Primitive Christians: The Eighteenth-Century Anglican Eucharist in its Architectural Setting*, Alcuin/GROW Joint Liturgical Studies 37 (Cambridge: Grove Books).

Doll, P. (2005), *Liturgy and Architecture for a Pilgrim People* (London: Affirming Catholicism).

Donne, J. (1971), *The Complete English Poems*, ed. A. J. Smith (London: Penguin).

Douglas, M. (1970), *Natural Symbols* (London: Barrie & Rockliff).

Duchesneau, C., and Veuthey, M. (eds.) (1992), *Music and Liturgy: The Universa Laus Document and Commentary*, tr. P. Inwood (Washington, DC: Pastoral Press).

Dudley, M., and Rowell, G. (eds) (1990), *Confession and Absolution* (London: SPCK).

Dudley, M., and Rowell, G. (eds) (1993), *The Oil of Gladness: Anointing in the Christian Tradition* (London: SPCK).

Dunstan, A. (rev. edn, 1992), 'Hymnody in Christian Worship', in C. Jones, G. Wainwright, E. Yarnold and P. Bradshaw (eds), *The Study of Liturgy* (London: SPCK/New York: Oxford University Press), pp. 509–19.

Dupré, L. (2000), *Symbols of the Sacred* (Grand Rapids, MI: Eerdmans).

Durber, S. (2007), *Preaching Like a Woman* (London: SPCK).

Earey, M. (2002), *Liturgical Worship* (London: Church House Publishing).

Erikson, E. (1966), 'Ontology of Ritualization in Man', *Philosophical Transactions of the Royal Society of London*, series B, 251.772, pp. 337–49.

Fagerberg. D. (2004), *Theologia Prima: What Is Liturgical Theology?* (Chicago, IL: Hillenbrand).

Farhadian, C. E. (ed.) (2007), *Christian Worship Worldwide: Expanding Horizons, Deepening Practices* (Grand Rapids, MI: Eerdmans).

Ferguson, E. (1993), 'Toward a Patristic Theology of Music', *Studia Patristica* 24, pp. 266–83.

Fisher, J. D. C. (1965), *Christian Initiation: Baptism in the Medieval West* (London: SPCK).

Fisher, J. D. C. (1970), *Christian Initiation: The Reformation Period* (London: SPCK).

Flannery, A. (1981), *Vatican Council II* (Leominster: Fowler Wright).

Foley, E. (1990), 'Music, Liturgical', in P. E. Fink (ed.), *The New Dictionary of Sacramental Worship* (Dublin: Gill and Macmillan), pp. 854–70.

Foley, E. (1995), *Ritual Music: Studies in Liturgical Musicology* (Beltsville, MD: Pastoral Press).

Gaillardetz, R. (1994), 'North American Culture and the Liturgical Life of the Church: The Separation of the Quests for Transcendence and Community', *Worship* 68, pp. 403–16.

Garrigan, S. (2010), *The Real Peace Process: Worship, Politics, and the End of Sectarianism* (London: Equinox).

Gelston, A. (2008), *The Psalms in Christian Worship: Patristic Precedent and Anglican Practice* (Norwich: Canterbury Press).

General Instruction on the Roman Missal (1969), in A. Flannery (ed.), *Vatican Council II: The Conciliar and Post Conciliar Documents* (Dublin: Dominican Publications, 1992), pp. 154–205.

General Introduction to the Lectionary for Mass (1969; expanded 2nd edn, 1981) (Vatican City: Sacred Congregation for the Sacraments and Divine Worship).

Gennep, A. van (1960), *The Rites of Passage* (Chicago, IL: University of Chicago Press).

Gerrish, B. A. (1993), *Grace and Gratitude: The Eucharistic Theology of John Calvin* (Edinburgh: T&T Clark).

Gitari, D. M. (1994), *Anglican Liturgical Inculturation in Africa: The Kanamai Statement* (Bramcote: Grove Books).

Grace, E. (2002), 'The Tradition of "Ecumenical Worship" in Light of the Recent Orthodox Critique', *Ecumenical Review* 54.1, pp. 3–27.

Gray-Reeves, M., and Perham, M. (2011), *The Hospitality of God: Emerging Worship for a Missional Church* (London: SPCK).

Grillo, A. (2008), *Grazia visibile, grazia vivibile: Teologia dei sacramenti 'in genere ritus'* (Padua: EMP-Abbazia S. Giustina).

Grimes, R. L. (1990), 'Emerging Ritual', *Proceedings of the North American Academy of Liturgy*, pp. 15–31.

Grimes, R. L. (1992), 'Reinventing Ritual', *Soundings* 75.1, pp. 21–41.

Grimes, R. L. (rev. edn, 1995), *Beginnings in Ritual Studies* (Columbia, SC: University of South Carolina Press).

Guardini, R. (1937), *The Spirit of the Liturgy*, tr. A. Lane (London: Sheed & Ward).

Guiver, G. (1996), *Pursuing the Mystery: Worship and Daily Life as Presences of God* (London: SPCK).

Guiver, G. (2000), *Company of Voices: Daily Prayer and the People of God* (Norwich: Canterbury Press).

Guiver, G. (2002), 'Prayer', in P. F. Bradshaw (ed.), *The New SCM Dictionary of Liturgy and Worship* (London: SCM Press), pp. 380–2.

Guiver, G. (2009), *Vision upon Vision: Processes of Change and Renewal in Christian Worship* (Norwich: Canterbury Press).

Guiver, G. (rev. edn, 2011), *Company of Voices*, (Norwich: Canterbury Press).

Halgren Kilde, J. (2008), *Sacred Space: An Introduction to Christian Architecture and Worship* (Oxford and New York: Oxford University Press).

Haselock, J. (2002a), 'Gesture', in P. F. Bradshaw (ed.), *The New SCM Dictionary of Liturgy and Worship* (London: SCM Press), pp. 227–30.

Haselock, J. (2002b), 'Posture', in P. F. Bradshaw (ed.), *The New SCM Dictionary of Liturgy and Worship* (London: SCM Press), pp. 377–9.

Hastings, A. (1973), *Christian Marriage in Africa* (London: SPCK).

Hawn, C. M. (2003), *Gather into One: Praying and Singing Globally* (Grand Rapids, MI: Eerdmans).

Headley, C., and Nichols, B. (2006a), 'Wholeness and Healing', in P. Bradshaw (ed.), *A Companion to Common Worship*, vol. 2, Alcuin Club Collections 81 (London: SPCK), pp. 142–67.

Headley, C., and Nichols, B. (2006b), 'Reconciliation and Restoration', in P. Bradshaw (ed.), *A Companion to Common Worship*, vol. 2, Alcuin Club Collections 81 (London: SPCK), pp. 168–79.

Heathcote, E., and Spens, I. (1997), *Church Builders* (Chichester: Academy Editions).

Hoffman, L. A. (1993), 'How Ritual Means: Ritual Circumcision in Rabbinic Culture and Today', *Studia Liturgica* 23, pp. 78–97.

Holeton, D. (1990), *Liturgical Inculturation in the Anglican Communion: Including the York Statement 'Down to Earth Worship'*, Alcuin/GROW Joint Liturgical Studies 15 (Bramcote: Grove Books).

House of Bishops of the Church of England (2000), *A Time to Heal* (London: Church House).

Hughes, G. (2003), *Worship as Meaning: A Liturgical Theology for Late Modernity* (Cambridge: Cambridge University Press).

Huizinga, J. (1949), *Homo Ludens* (London: Routledge & Kegan Paul).

Inge, J. (2003), *A Christian Theology of Place* (Aldershot and Burlington, VT: Ashgate).

International Anglican Liturgical Consultation (2005), *Eucharistic Food and Drink*. [Online]. Retrieved from: <http://www.anglicancommunion.org/resources/liturgy/docs/ialcreport.cfm>.

International Committee on English in the Liturgy (ICEL) (1997), *Opening Prayers: Scripture-Related Collects for Years A, B & C of The Sacramentary* (Norwich: Canterbury Press).

Irvine, C. (1993), *Worship, Church and Society: An Exposition of the Work of Arthur Gabriel Hebert* (Norwich: Canterbury Press).

Irvine, C. (ed.) (2007), *The Use of Symbols in Worship*, Alcuin Liturgy Guides 4 (London: SPCK).

Irvine, C., and Bergquist, A. (2011), 'Thinking about Liturgy', *Anaphora* 5.2, pp. 45–56.

Irwin, K. (1991), *Liturgical Theology: A Primer* (Collegeville, MN: Liturgical Press).

Irwin, K. (2002), '*Lex Orandi, Lex Credendi* – Origins and Meaning: State of the Question', *Liturgical Ministry* 11, pp. 57–69.

James, W. (1902), *Varieties of Religious Experience* (London: Longmans, Green and Co.).

Jasper, D., and Jasper, R. C. D. (1990), *Language and the Worship of the Church* (New York: St Martin's Press).

Jensen, R. (1995), *Thinking in Story: Preaching in a Post-Literate Age* (Lima, OH: CSS).

John Chrysostom (1982), *On the Incomprehensible Nature of God*, tr. P. W. Harkins (Washington, DC: Catholic University of America Press).

John Chrysostom (1999), *The Treatise on the Priesthood*, tr. and notes W. R. W. Stephens (Peabody, MA: Hendrickson Publishers), pp. 27–86.

Johnson, C. (2001), 'The Children's Eucharistic Prayers: A Model of Liturgical Inculturation', *Worship* 75.3, pp. 209–77.

Johnson, M. (1993), 'Liturgy and Theology', in P. Bradshaw and B. Spinks (eds), *Liturgy in Dialogue: Essays in Memory of Ronald Jasper* (London: SPCK), pp. 202–25.

Johnson, M. E. (2001), *Images of Baptism* (Chicago, IL: Liturgy Training Publications).

Johnson, M. E. (ed.) (1995), *Living Water, Sealing Spirit: Readings on Christian Initiation* (Collegeville, MN: Liturgical Press).

Johnson, M. E. (ed.) (2000), *Between Memory and Hope: Readings on the Liturgical Year* (Collegeville, MN: Liturgical Press).

Johnson, M. E. (rev. edn, 2007), *The Rites of Christian Initiation: Their Evolution and Interpretation* (Collegeville, MN: Liturgical Press).

Joncas, J. M. (1997), 'Liturgy and Music', in A. J. Chupungco (ed.), *Handbook for Liturgical Studies 2: Fundamental Liturgy* (Collegeville, MN: Liturgical Press), pp. 281–321.

Joncas, J. M. (2002), 'Music as Worship', in P. F. Bradshaw (ed.), *The New SCM Dictionary of Liturgy and Worship* (London: SCM Press), pp. 326–9.

Jungmann, J. (1975), 'Liturgy', in K. Rahner (ed.), *Encyclopaedia of Theology: A Concise Sacramentum Mundi* (London: Burns & Oates), pp. 851–64.

Jungmann, J. A. (1959), *The Early Liturgy to the Time of Gregory the Great* (London: Darton, Longman and Todd).

Jungmann, J. A. (2007), *Christian Prayer through the Centuries*, tr. J. Coyne, ed. C. Irvine (London, SPCK/Alcuin Club).

Kabasele Lumbala, F. (1998), *Celebrating Jesus Christ in Africa: Liturgy and Inculturation* (Maryknoll, NY: Orbis Books).

Kasper, W. (1993), *The Theology of Marriage* (New York: Crossroad).

Kässmann, M. (2003), 'A Voice of Dissent: Questioning the Conclusions of the Report of the Special Commission on Orthodox Participation in the WCC', *Ecumenical Review* 55.1, pp. 67–71.

Kavanagh, A. (1973), 'The Role of Ritual in Personal Development', in J. Shaugnessy (ed.), *The Roots of Ritual* (Grand Rapids, MI: Eerdmans), pp. 145–60.

Kavanagh, A. (1978), *The Shape of Baptism* (New York: Pueblo).

Kavanagh, A. (1992), *On Liturgical Theology* (Collegeville, MN: Liturgical Press).

Kereszty, R. A. (ed.) (2003), *Rediscovering the Eucharist: Ecumenical Conversations* (New York: Paulist Press).

Kertzer, D. (1989), 'The Future of Ritual in Modern Society', *The Family Therapy Networker* 13.4 (July), pp. 20–9.

Kieckhefer, R. (2004), *Theology in Stone: Church Architecture from Byzantium to Berkeley* (Oxford and New York: Oxford University Press).

Killinger, J. (1985), *Fundamentals of Preaching* (London: SCM Press).

Kings, G., and Morgan, G. (2001), *Offerings from Kenya to Anglicanism: Liturgical Texts and Contexts Including 'A Kenyan Service of Holy Communion'* (Cambridge: Grove Books).

Kisembo, B., Magesa, L., and Shorter, A. (1977), *African Christian Marriage* (London: G. Chapman).

Kitchen, M. (1991), 'The Bible in Worship', in K. Stevenson and B. Spinks (eds), *The Identity of Anglican Worship* (London: Mowbray).

Kreider, A., and Kreider, E. (2011), *Worship and Mission after Christendom* (Scottdale, PA: Herald Press).

Kubicki, J. M. (1999), *Liturgical Music as Ritual Symbol: A Case Study of Jacques Berthier's Taizé Music* (Leuven: Peeters).

Ladrière, J. (1973), 'The Performativity of Liturgical Language', *Concilium* 9, pp. 50–62.

Lampard, J. S. (2005), *Go Forth, Christian Soul: The Biography of a Prayer* (Peterborough: Epworth).

Lampe, G. W. H. (2nd edn, 1967), *The Seal of the Spirit: A Study in the Doctrine of Baptism and Confirmation in the New Testament and the Fathers* (London: SPCK).

Lathrop, G. (2006), *Holy Things: A Liturgical Ecclesiology* (Minneapolis, MN: Fortress Press).

Lathrop, G. W. (1998), 'The Lima Liturgy and Beyond: Moving Forward Ecumenically', in T. F. Best and D. Heller (eds), *Eucharistic Worship in Ecumenical Contexts* (Geneva: WCC).

Lathrop, G. W. (1999), *Holy People: A Liturgical Ecclesiology* (Minneapolis, MN: Fortress Press).

Lawler, M. (1993), *Marriage and Sacrament: A Theology of Christian Marriage* (Collegeville, MN: Liturgical Press).

Liturgiam authenticam: On the Use of the Vernacular Languages in the Publication of the Books of the Roman Liturgy (2001), Congregation for Divine Worship and the Discipline of the Sacraments (London: Catholic Truth Society).

Liturgy Office England and Wales (1992), *Eucharistic Prayer for the Deaf*. [Online]. Retrieved from: <http://www.liturgyoffice.org.uk/Resources/Rites/DeafEP.html>.

Lloyd, T. (1990), 'Liturgy for the Urban Deprived', *Studia Liturgica* 20.1, pp. 81–94.

Lloyd, T. (1999), *A Service of the Word* (Cambridge: Grove Books).

Lloyd, T. (2000), *Dying and Death Step by Step: A Funerals Flowchart* (Cambridge: Grove Books).

Lloyd, T., and Tovey, P. (2004), *Celebrating Forgiveness: An Original Text Drafted by Michael Vasey*, Alcuin/GROW Joint Liturgical Studies 58 (Cambridge: Grove Books).

Long, T. (1989), *The Witness of Preaching* (Louisville, KY: Westminster John Knox Press).

Lowry, E. (1989), *How to Preach a Parable: Design for Narrative Sermons* (Nashville, TN: Abingdon Press).

Lutheran World Federation (1996), *Nairobi Statement on Worship and Culture: Contemporary Challenges and Opportunities* (Lutheran World Federation). [Online]. Retrieved from: <http://www.worship.ca/docs/lwf_ns.html>.

Maly, E. (1981), 'Still a Case for Infant Baptism?', in M. Taylor (ed.), *The Sacraments: Readings in Contemporary Sacramental Theology* (New York: Alba House), pp. 95-103.

Massey, J. E. (2006), *Stewards of the Story: The Task of Preaching* (Louisville, KY: Westminster John Knox Press).

Mayne, M. (2010), *To Trust and to Love*, ed. J. W. Huffstetler (London: Darton, Longman and Todd).

McKenna, E. J. (1990), 'Music Ministries', in P. E. Fink (ed.), *The New Dictionary of Sacramental Worship* (Dublin: Gill and Macmillan), pp. 852–4.

Mead, M. (1973), 'Ritual and Social Crisis', in J. Shaugnessy (ed.), *The Roots of Ritual* (Grand Rapids, MI: Eerdmans), pp. 87–101.

Merton, T. (1976), *Meditations on Liturgy* (London: Mowbray).

Mission-Shaped Church: Church Planting and Fresh Expressions of Church in a Changing Context (2004) (London: Church House Publishing).

Mitchell, N. D. (1995), 'Emerging Rituals in Contemporary Culture', in L.-M. Chauvet and F. Kabasele Lumbala (eds), *Liturgy and the Body* (London: SCM Press/Maryknoll, NY: Orbis Books), pp. 121–9.

Mitchell, N. D. (1999), *Liturgy and the Social Sciences* (Collegeville, MN: Liturgical Press).

Monshau, M., (ed.) (2006), *The Grace and Task of Preaching* (Dublin: Dominican Publications).

Morley, J. (new edn, 2005 (1988)), *All Desires Known* (London: SPCK).

Moryadas, A. (2002), 'Ritual', in A. Moryadas and A. Morris (eds), *John Pawson: Themes and Projects* (London and New York: Phaidon Press).

Mosebach, M. (2006), *The Heresy of Formlessness: The Roman Liturgy and Its Enemy* (San Francisco, CA: Ignatius Press).

Myers, R. A. (1997), *Continuing the Reformation: Re-Visioning Baptism in the Episcopal Church* (New York: Church Publishing).

National Conference of Catholic Bishops (1977), *Eucharistic Prayers for Masses with Children* (Washington, DC).

National Conference of Catholic Bishops (1993), *Lectionary for Masses with Children* (Collegeville, MN: Liturgical Press).

Nichols, A. (1996), *Looking at the Liturgy: A Critical View of Its Contemporary Form* (San Francisco, CA: Ignatius Press).

Nichols, B. (ed.) (2010), *The Collect in the Churches of the Reformation* (London, SCM Press).

Niebuhr, H. R. (1951), *Christ and Culture* (New York: Harper).

O'Loughlin, T. (2010), *The Didache: A Window on the Earliest Christians* (London and Grand Rapids, MI: Baker Academic), pp. 85–128.

O'Loughlin, T. (2012), 'Divisions in Christianity: The Contribution of "Appeals to Antiquity"', in S. Oliver, K. Kilby and T. O'Loughlin (eds), *Faithful Reading: New Essays in Theology and Philosophy in Honour of Fergus Kerr OP* (London: T&T Clark), pp. 221–41.

O'Meara, T. F. (2007), *God in the World: A Guide to Karl Rahner's Theology* (Collegeville, MN: Liturgical Press).

Otto, R. (1923), *The Idea of the Holy: An Inquiry into the Non-Rational Factor in the Idea of the Divine and Its Relation to the Rational*, tr. J. W. Harvey (London: Oxford University Press).

Pecklers, K. (ed.) (2006), *Liturgy in a Postmodern World* (London: Continuum).

Peters, G. (2002), *Earth Day Eucharist*. [Online]. Retrieved from: <http://earthministry.org/resources/worship-aids/sample-worship-services/earth-day-eucharist>.

Pontifical Biblical Commission (1993), 'The Interpretation of the Bible in the Church', in D. P. Béchard (ed.), *The Scripture Documents: An Anthology of Official Catholic Teachings* (Collegeville, MN: Liturgical Press 2002), pp. 244–317.

Power, D. (1984), *Unsearchable Riches: The Symbolic Nature of Liturgy* (New York: Pueblo).

Prétot, P. (2006), 'La Liturgie: Une Expérience corporelle', *La Maison-Dieu* 247, pp. 7–36.

Preus, J. S. (1987), *Explaining Religion: Criticism and Theory from Bodin to Freud* (New Haven, CT: Yale University Press).

Pritchard, J. (2005), *Leading Intercessions: Creative Ideas for Public and Private Prayer* (Collegeville, MN: Liturgical Press).

Ramshaw, G. (2001), 'The Pit, or the Gates of Zion? A Report on Contemporary Western Liturgical Language', *Worship* 75.1, pp. 12–19.

Ramshaw, G. (2009), *Christian Worship: 100,000 Sundays of Symbols and Rituals* (Minneapolis, MN: Fortress Press).

Richter, K. (1990), *The Meaning of Sacramental Symbols* (Collegeville, MN: Liturgical Press).

Robinson, M. (2006), *Gilead* (London: Virago).

Robinson, M. (2009), *Home* (London: Virago).

Rodger, P. C., and Vischer, L. (eds) (1964), *The Fourth World Conference on Faith and Order: The Report from Montreal 1963* (London: SCM Press).

Roman Catholic Church (1994), *Inculturation and the Roman Liturgy* (Rome: Vatican Press).

Rordorf, W. (1968), *Sunday: The History of the Day of Rest and Worship in the Earliest Centuries of the Christian Church* (London: SCM Press).

Rutherford, R. (2001), *Honoring the Dead: Catholics and Cremation Today* (Collegeville, MN: Liturgical Press).

Sacred Congregation for Divine Worship (1974), *Directory for Masses with Children* (Washington, DC: United States Catholic Conference).

Sacrosanctum Concilium (1996), Constitution on the Sacred Liturgy, 4th December 1963, in A. Flannery (ed.), *Vatican Council II: The Basic Sixteen Documents* (Dublin: Costello Publishing).

Sagovsky, N. (1978), *Liturgy and Symbolism* (Bramcote: Grove Books).

Saliers, D. (1979), 'Liturgy and Ethics: Some New Beginnings', *Journal of Religious Ethics* 7, pp. 179–89.

Saliers, D. E. (1994), *Worship as Theology: Foretaste of Glory Divine* (Nashville, TN: Abingdon Press).

Saliers, D. E., and Saliers, E. (2004), *A Song to Sing, A Life to Live: Reflections on Music as Spiritual Practice* (San Francisco, CA: Jossey-Bass).

Schattauer, T. H. (ed.) (1999), *Inside Out: Worship in an Age of Mission* (Minneapolis, MN: Fortress Press).

Schillebeeckx, E. (1985), *The Church with a Human Face: A New and Expanded Theology of Ministry* (New York: Crossroad).

Schlafer, D. (1995), *Your Way with God's Word* (Cambridge, MA: Cowley Publications).

Schlafer, D. (1998), *What Makes This Day Different? Preaching Grace on Special Occasions* (Cambridge, MA: Cowley Publications).

Schmemann, A. (1966), *Introduction to Liturgical Theology* (Leighton Buzzard: Faith Press/New York: St Vladimir's Seminary Press).

Schmemann, A. (1972), 'Liturgy and Theology', *The Greek Orthodox Theological Review* 17, pp. 86–100.

Schmit, C. J. (2009), *Sent and Gathered: A Worship Manual for the Missional Church* (Grand Rapids, MI: Baker Academic).

Searle, M. (1987), 'Infant Baptism Reconsidered', in M. Searle (ed.), *Alternative Futures for Worship*, vol. 2: *Baptism and Confirmation* (Collegeville, MN: Liturgical Press), pp. 15–54.

Searle, M. (1991), 'Fons Vitae: A Case Study in the Use of Liturgy as a Theological Source', in G. Austin (ed.), *Fountain of Life* (Washington, DC: Pastoral Press), pp. 217–41.

Searle, M. (rev. edn, 1992), 'Ritual', in C. Jones, G. Wainwright, E. Yarnold and P. Bradshaw (eds), *The Study of Liturgy* (London: SPCK/New York: Oxford University Press), pp. 51–8.

Searle, M., and Stevenson, K. (1992), *Documents of the Marriage Liturgy* (Collegeville, MN: Liturgical Press).

Seasolz, K. R. (2005), *A Sense of the Sacred: Theological Foundations of Christian Architecture and Art* (New York and London: Continuum).

Second Vatican Council (1965), *Dogmatic Constitution on Divine Revelation* (*Dei Verbum*). [Online]. Retrieved from: <www.vatican.va/archive/hist_councils/ii_vatican_council/documents/vat-ii_const_19651118_dei-verbum_en.html>.

Shakespeare, S. (2008), *Prayers for an Inclusive Church* (Norwich: Canterbury Press).

Sheehy, J. (2007), 'Sacred Space and the Incarnation', in P. North and J. North (eds), *Sacred Space: House of God, Gate of Heaven* (London and New York: Continuum).

Skelley, M. (1991), *The Liturgy of the World: Karl Rahner's Theology of Worship* (Collegeville, MN: Liturgical Press).

Society of St Francis (2009), *The Daily Office SSF* (London: Mowbray).

Spinks, B. D. (1991), 'Worship and Evangelism', in M. Perham (ed.), *Liturgy for a New Century* (London: SPCK), pp. 101–5.

Spinks, B. D. (2006a), *Early and Medieval Rituals and Theologies of Baptism: From the New Testament to the Council of Trent* (Aldershot and Burlington, VT: Ashgate).

Spinks, B. D. (2006b), *Reformation and Modern Rituals and Theologies of Baptism: From Luther to Contemporary Practices* (Aldershot and Burlington, VT: Ashgate).

Spinks, B. D. (2010), *The Worship Mall: Contemporary Responses to Contemporary Culture*, Alcuin Club Collections 85 (London: SPCK).

Spinks, B. (ed.) (2008), *The Place of Christ in Liturgical Prayer: Trinity, Christology, and Liturgical Theology* (Collegeville, MN: Liturgical Press).

Spinks, B., and Berger, T. (2009), *The Spirit in Worship – Worship in the Spirit* (Collegeville, MN: Liturgical Press).

St Hilda Community (1996), *The New Women Included: A Book of Services and Prayers* (London: SPCK).

Staal, F. (1979), 'The Meaninglessness of Ritual', *Numen* 26.1, pp. 2–22.

Stancliffe, D. (2003), *God's Pattern: Shaping our Worship, Ministry and Life* (London: SPCK).

Stancliffe, D. (2008), *The Lion Companion to Church Architecture* (Oxford: Lion Hudson).

Stevenson, K. (1981) (ed.), *Symbolism and the Liturgy*, vols. 1 and 2 (Bramcote: Grove Books).

Stevenson, K. (1982), *Nuptial Blessing: A Study of Christian Marriage Rites*, Alcuin Club Collections 64 (London: SPCK).

Stevenson, K. (1987), *To Join Together: The Rite of Marriage* (New York: Pueblo).

Stevenson, K. (2002), *Do This: The Shape, Style and Meaning of the Eucharist* (Norwich: Canterbury Press).

Stevenson, K. (ed.) (2011), *Anglican Marriage Rites: A Symposium*, Alcuin/GROW Joint Liturgical Studies 71 (Norwich: SCM-Canterbury Press).

Stott, J. (1982), *I Believe in Preaching* (London: Hodder and Stoughton).

Stratford, T. (2002), *Using Common Worship: A Service of the Word* (London: Church House Publishing).

Studia Liturgica 28 (1998), entire volume.

Tabouret-Keller, A. (1998), 'Language and Identity', in F. Coulmas (ed.), *The Handbook of Sociolinguistics* (Oxford: Blackwell).

Taft, R. (1986), *The Liturgy of the Hours in East and West* (Collegeville, MN: Liturgical Press).

Talley, T. (2nd edn, 1991), *The Origins of the Liturgical Year* (Collegeville, MN: Liturgical Press).

Tanner, M. (2005), *The Significance of the Special Commission on Orthodox Participation in the WCC, in Grace in Abundance: Orthodox Reflections on the Way to Porto Alegre* (ed. Gennadios, Metropolitan of Sassima) (Geneva: WCC).

Tarrant, I. (2006), *Anglican Swahili Prayer Books: Tanzania 1995 and Congo 1998* (Norwich: SCM-Canterbury Press).

Taylor, B. B. (1993), *The Preaching Life* (Cambridge, MA: Cowley Publications).

Taylor, J. (1839), *The Whole Works of the Right Rev Jeremy Taylor D.D., Lord Bishop of Down, Connor and Dromore: Volume VII – Containing Episcopacy Asserted, an Apology for Authorised and Set forms of Liturgy and a Discourse on the Liberty of Prophesying* (London: Longman, Orme, Brown, Green and Longmans, et al.).

Thurian, M. (1983), *Priesthood and Ministry: Ecumenical Research* (London: Mowbray).

Thurian, M., and Wainwright, G. (eds) (1983), *Baptism and Eucharist: Ecumenical Convergence in Celebration* (Geneva: WCC).

Tisdale, L. T. (1997), *Preaching as Local Theology and Folk Art* (Minneapolis, MN: Fortress Press).

Tisdale, L. T. (2010), *Prophetic Preaching: A Pastoral Approach* (Louisville, KY: Westminster John Knox Press).

Torevell, D. (2000), *Losing the Sacred: Ritual, Modernity and Liturgical Reform* (Edinburgh: T&T Clark).

Tovey, P. (1991), *Praying to God as Mother* (Bramcote: Grove Books).

Tovey, P. (2003), *Inculturation of Christian Worship: Exploring the Eucharist* (Aldershot and Burlington, VT: Ashgate).

Tovey, P. (2006), 'Inculturation: Bread and Wine at the Eucharist', in B. D. Spinks and M. E. Fassler (eds), *Colloquium: Music, Worship, Arts*, vol. 3 (New Haven, CT: Yale Institute of Sacred Music).

Tovey, P. (2010), 'Two Models of Inculturation and Eucharistic Prayers with Children', in M. C. Ross and S. Jones (eds), *The Serious Business of Worship: Essays in Honour of Bryan D. Spinks* (London: T&T Clark).

Troeger, T. (1996), *Ten Strategies for Preaching in a Multimedia Culture* (Nashville, TN: Abingdon Press).

Turner, V. (1969), *The Ritual Process: Structure and Anti-Structure* (Chicago, IL: Aldine).

Underhill, E. (repr. 2010 of 3rd edn, 1936), *Worship* (Cambridge: James Clarke).

United States Conference of Catholic Bishops (2007), *Sing to the Lord: Music in Divine Worship* (2007), (Washington DC: USCCB Publishing).

Universa Laus (1980), 'Music in Christian Celebration', document 1. [Online]. Retrieved from: <www.universalaus.org/images/pdffiles/1-document-ul-uk.pdf>.

Uzukwu, E. (1982), *Liturgy: Truly Christian, Truly African* (Eldoret: Gaba Publications).

Vogel, D. W. (ed.) (2000), *Primary Sources of Liturgical Theology: A Reader* (Collegeville, MN: Liturgical Press).

Vorgrimler, H. (1992), *Sacramental Theology* (Collegeville, MN: Liturgical Press).

Wainwright, G. (1980), *Doxology: The Praise of God in Worship, Doctrine and Life – A Systematic Theology* (New York: Oxford University Press).

Wainwright, G. (1997), *With One Accord: Where Worship and Ecumenism Embrace* (New York and Oxford: Oxford University Press).

Wainwright, G. (2007), 'The Eucharistic Dynamic of BEM', in T. F. Best and T. Grdzelidze (eds), *BEM at 25: Critical Insights into a Continuing Legacy* (Geneva: WCC).

Walsh, C. J. (2000), 'Minding Our Language: Issues of Liturgical Language Arising in Revision', *Worship* 74.4, pp. 482–503.

Walter, T. (1994), *The Revival of Death* (London and New York: Routledge).

Walton, J. (2000), *Feminist Liturgy: A Matter of Justice* (Collegeville, MN: Liturgical Press).

Ward, P. (2005), *Selling Worship: How What We Sing Has Changed the Church* (Carlisle: Paternoster Press).

Webber, R. (2008), *Ancient-Future Worship: Proclaiming and Enacting God's Narrative* (Grand Rapids, MI: Baker Books).

Westermeyer, P. (1998), *Te Deum: The Church and Music – A Textbook, a Reference, a History, an Essay* (Minneapolis, MN: Fortress Press).

Whitaker, E. C., and Johnson, M. E. (eds) (rev. edn, 2003), *Documents of the Baptismal Liturgy*, Alcuin Club Collections 79 (London: SPCK).

White, J. F. (2006), 'The Spatial Setting', in G. Wainwright and K. B. Westerfield Tucker (eds), *The Oxford History of Christian Worship* (Oxford and New York: Oxford University Press).

Williams, R. (1982), *Resurrection* (London: Darton, Longman and Todd).

Witvliet, J. (2007), 'Inculturation, Worship and Dispositions for Ministry', in C. E. Farhadian (ed.), *Christian Worship Worldwide: Expanding Horizons, Deepening Practices* (Grand Rapids, MI: Eerdmans).

Woods, T. E., Jr (2008), *Sacred Then and Sacred Now: The Return of the Old Latin Mass* (Fort Collins, CO: Roman Catholic Books).

World Council of Churches (1982), *Baptism, Eucharist and Ministry*, Faith and Order Paper no. 111 (Geneva: World Council of Churches).

World Council of Churches (2003), 'Final Report of the Special Commission on Orthodox Participation in the WCC', *Ecumenical Review* 55.1.

Wybrew, H. (2013, reissue of 1st edn), *The Orthodox Liturgy* (London: SPCK).

Yates, N. (2008), *Liturgical Space: Christian Worship and Church Buildings in Western Europe 1500–2000* (Aldershot: Ashgate).

Index